Real People, Regular Lives:

Autism,

Communication,

& Quality of Life

Sally R. Young, Ph.D.

Cover artwork by Roy Bedward www.roybedwardenterprises.com

Cover design by Sarah Pollpeter.

ISBN 978-0-615-40079-2

Dedication

To the brave individuals whose lives are depicted here.
You keep the light alive.

To Sandra - Poet in Waiting
and to all whose voices have been stilled.

Praise for *Real People*

"I opened this book and didn't put it down until I had read it from cover to cover. In the tradition of Oliver Sacks, Robert Coles, and Douglas Biken, Sally Young shares compelling stories of the silenced and the misunderstood.

Real People, Regular Lives not only shines a light on how access to communication transforms the lives of those with autism but actually challenges current understandings of autism itself. This is a work that will be studied and shared for decades to come."

Paula Kluth, Ph.D.
Author of *"You're Going to Love This Kid":
Teaching Students with Autism in the Inclusive Classroom*

"*Real People* gives us a look at what has become of some of that first group of non-verbal autistics who learned to use FC. Varying degrees of independence, including full independence, in the actual typing process has been gained over time. Most remarkable is that FC afforded these 'real people' the actualization of living real lives.

Renewed hope and a future of possibility for all our nonverbal children with autism exist in these pages. *Real People* is a 'must read' for parents of every nonverbal autistic child and the professionals who serve them."

Judy Endow, MSW
Self-advocate, author, consultant, international speaker
Winner of Autism Society Media Excellence of 2010 Award for
The Power of Words: How We Talk about People with Autism Spectrum Disorders Matters!
Winner of 2010 International Book Awards Autobiography/Memoirs Finalist for
Paper Words: Discovering and Living with My Autism.

"Valuable and thorough documentation of a range of individual case histories, from which much can be learned."

Phil Schwarz
Member, Board of Directors, Autism National Committee
Vice-chair, Board of Directors, Asperger's Association of New England
Parent and self-advocate

"*Real People, Regular Lives* is so long overdue! Dr. Young invites us to bear witness to stories of ten remarkable autistic adults who through the use of FC, have found their expressive voice, and are able to impart details of their inner world and everyday lives. She helps us to replace outdated limiting assumptions about non-verbal people with a broader perspective on human diversity. I cannot wait to recommend this book to parents and professional colleagues."

Lisa A Lieberman, MSW, LCSW
Parent of a young adult with ASD, counselor, national speaker and author of
A Stranger Among Us: Hiring In-home Support for Children and Young Adult with Disabilities

"Many do not accord full personhood to people with the most apparently severe disabilities. *Real People, Regular Lives* strongly challenges this diminution of personhood. It begins with cutting–edge thinking on what autism really is and how we can best support each person with autism to have a regular life, shaped according to personal preference. Individuals' stories follow. This is an important addition to the literature that helps us better understand people with autism. It is a 'must read' for parents, other family members and friends of people with autism, for professionals, and for scientists who are striving to learn more about autism."

Sandra McClennen, Ph.D.
Licensed Psychologist
Professor Emerita of Special Education
Eastern Michigan University

"*Real People,Regular Lives* tells stories that must be told, of individuals with much to say - and much to teach the world. Given a voice, these remarkable 'real people' challenge our previous thinking about the true nature of autism and related conditions. In addition to the moving stories, the author presents a well-documented discussion of what might be happening in the dyadic process known as Facilitated Communication."

Charlene Brandl, M.S.
Author of *Facilitated Communication Case Studies: SEE US SMART!*

About the Author

Sally Young has been working with nonverbal autistic adults and their families since 1983. She has worked in both residential agencies and day programs in a variety of roles including teaching adaptive physical education and expressive arts. Today she works as an independent consultant helping people find ways to communicate and improve the quality of their day-to-day lives. Sally holds a Masters degree in clinical psychology and a Ph.D. in special education and is a co-author of *Listening with the Whole Body: Clinical Concepts and Treatment Guidelines for Therapeutic Listening*.

Preface

When Facilitated Communication (FC) swept into Marin County, California in 1991, I was operating an expressive arts program. The program was provided through an agency that served 30 adults who were categorized in the "severe and profound" range of developmental disability. Most did not speak. Many were autistic. Several had grown up in state institutions.

Most of the people did not have the basic work skills required to hold jobs in the community or in a sheltered workshop setting. At that time, working in the visual arts – painting, drawing, ceramics, weaving and woodworking – was their only sanctioned expressive outlet. They loved these activities and routinely functioned at higher levels in the art studio than in other environments.

I had worked with these individuals since 1984; initially as an adaptive physical education aide, then as a middle manager in their group homes and later as the day program coordinator. In these roles, I had become intimately familiar with their histories, capabilities, idiosyncrasies and daily routines. I knew their parents, families, staff and roommates. Suffice it to say, I thought I knew them well.

My colleagues began to undergo FC training. I was one of the last holdouts. Although I considered myself an advocate for the right to communicate and a supporter of self-expression, I was deeply skeptical of this new method. I did not understand why the facilitator needed to look at the letters or why the FC speakers needed touch to be able to point to the letters.

Eventually, I decided to try FC, if only to understand it for myself. After attending training sessions, I brought a letterboard into the art studio. With my assistance, the artists began making choices by pointing to "Yes" or "No" on the letterboard. Once I experienced the arm and hand movement and the intention behind the movement, I could no longer deny that something was happening.

Soon, people were typing whole words and eventually communicating full thoughts and feelings. I began to witness unexpected and uncharacteristic positive behavior. I saw people sit and type for extended periods when previously they rarely achieved the calm-alert state necessary for focusing on a task. I saw people with extreme sensitivity to touch tolerate hand-to-hand touch. I saw people who rarely stopped pacing sit at a worktable to type. Even though FC on its face seemed preposterous, experientially it could not be denied.

Before FC, I had always given people the opportunity to make simple choices such as selecting an activity or choosing the colors they wanted to use. Some did not give responses that were clear or easy to interpret. As a result, I was often forced to guess what they wanted by observing their behavior.

FC became a useful tool for the artists to express their choices. They also often surprised me by their answers. A woman who never wanted to touch anything wet or messy asked to work with clay. A man who would never do anything except work with wood asked to try weaving. These contradictions were mildly puzzling, but I was pleased they were expanding their artistic repertoires.

Although I was excited about the changes in their routines, the process was not straightforward. Sometimes a person's behavior would deteriorate as soon as we approached a new activity. This resistance could take many forms: bolting out of the room, pushing or throwing the materials or steadfastly retreating to the old, familiar activity. In all cases, the behavior seemed to communicate a message that was the exact opposite of the earlier typed message.

I assumed I had inadvertently influenced the typing, so I became more vigilant. I also started to question the FC speakers about the incongruity between their typed messages and their behavior. I referred to it as "contrary behavior." Although they could not explain why this contrary behavior was happening, they often typed requests such as, "Be more firm." or "Help me do it."

Although it ran very much against the grain of my personality and my belief system, I responded by pushing a little harder when they tried to resist or flee. Often, these responses were amazingly effective. Befuddled by this contrary behavior, I searched for possible explanations. Soon, I began to hear about movement disorders and the pieces started to fall into place.

In addition to improving my methods for offering choices, FC opened up new worlds of interaction. As the typing became more fluid, our conversations began to expand. We discussed their artworks, feelings and internal states. The contrary behavior began to diminish.

These astounding conversations piqued my curiosity. I began to see things I had never noticed before. For example, one man always started to clean up his art materials shortly before I announced it was time to do so. I had always assumed he was anxious and restless and therefore had a short attention span. Once we started using FC, I saw him in a new way. FC gave me a window to glimpse his intelligence and his extremely ordered internal world. Only then, when I began to "presume competence," did it occur to me that perhaps he knew when to start cleaning up because he could tell time! From then on, he served as my timekeeper in the studio.

In 1995, I moved to the Midwest to attend graduate school and study under Anne Donnellan, Professor of special education at the University of Wisconsin. Anne was one of a handful of professors worldwide willing to view FC with an open mind. She and Martha Leary, a Speech and Language Pathologist, were studying movement disorders in autism and other developmental disabilities. In 2001, Anne, Don Cardinal, a Professor of special education at Chapman University, and I were named co-principal investigators on a grant funded by The Nancy Lurie Marks Family Foundation.

The grant's purpose was to study the impact of FC on quality of life. Don was to conduct a nationwide survey of Augmentative and Alternative Communication (AAC) users and I was to conduct two or three case studies for a journal article to accompany the survey results. Through a mailing fluke, I ended up with 13 volunteers and did not have the heart to turn anyone away. Nine of hese respondents eventually became the people profiled in this book.

I mailed out interview questions, set up phone interviews and invited people to send whatever they would like to share about their FC journeys. Before long, I received packages in the mail and a steady stream of faxes and emails; among them, a binder of 214 single-spaced pages, complete with table of contents, a 40-page portfolio documenting every instance of important typed messages and hundreds of Canon Communicator paper strips meticulously pasted onto standard computer paper.

I had scarcely imagined that I would receive this kind of response. Clearly, their communications were precious to them. I began to feel as if I were the keeper of sacred texts from a hidden civilization.

Before I could adequately assess the mountain of data that I had received, our grant funding ran out and in 2005, I abandoned the project to take a full-time job. As I packed up the files and put them into storage, I promised myself that I would someday return to these stories, these voices and these people.

In early 2009, I was laid off from my job and I knew it was time to make good on my promise. I decided to transform the material into a book describing how FC helped this group of autistic individuals as they struggled to show the world that they are real people determined to live regular lives.

Here are their stories.

Foreword

In 1990 when the phenomenon of Facilitated Communication (FC) came to the US, I was - in turn - skeptical, curious, convinced and devastated. I watched students I had known for 10 or more years sit and work hard at pointing to letters for an hour or more – far surpassing their assessed abilities. And at times I saw them typing things that the support person could not know. I was very excited but I was also devastated by the fact that though I'd been an "expert" in autism for 20+ years I could not begin to explain what I was seeing. I knew that I had to understand their experience in a way that I had not contemplated. That is, until FC, I assumed (along with most of the rest of the field) that my experience of people with the autism label was the same as their own experience: not interested in relationships, little or no imagination and "they can't talk because they have nothing much to say", etc. My first words when I saw someone successfully typing were: "Omigod, what have we done?"

Some were in turmoil like me; others were concentrating on the single question of authorship. Much of that research was useful in reminding us that as long as one person is supporting the other's typing, a certain caution was and is appropriate. Still, since it is the nature of human communication that we are always co-constructing our conversations, even the authorship question is not as simple as some researchers would suggest. Too often the researchers also ignored or dismissed the considerable evidence that these nonverbal, severely challenged people were showing evidence of concentration, cooperation, and creativity that had rarely been seen or acknowledged by we who thought ourselves so knowledgeable.

So, what held these autistic individuals back to this point? What was delaying the presentation of these abilities and often causing us to miss them entirely? I had the good fortune to be friends with Martha Leary and David Hill who, equally befuddled, found their way to the notion that perhaps people with autism had "movement disorders" or movement differences.[1] With that information, two wonderful doctoral students helped me put these questions and many more in a journal article [2] that came to the attention of Sally Young.

Into our world of confusion, excitement and curiosity in Madison came this woman who had been working with severely challenged clients via the visual arts for many years. As an expressive arts instructor, Sally never had been burdened by the canon of autism that stressed what these people could not do. Indeed, she assumed that since communication is part of being human, all people have something to communicate and the desire to do so.

What is required is a modality, medium or method that works for them along with personalized supports. Sally's perspective enlivened our discussion and enhanced our awareness that it is not possible to be an expert in autism. Each human being is unique.

As with the patients in Oliver Sacks' *Awakenings,*[3] each autistic individual has developed his/her own version of autism – perhaps as a function of their movement differences. Their similarities, individual personalities, abilities and challenges are as diverse as those of the general population. What our professional definitions and categories and notions of "spectrums" reveal is our experience of them; we label people as autistic because they tend to disturb us in similar ways. But our experience is not necessarily theirs. When a person pushes away from hugs because they cause pain, for example, we assume it is because they are uninterested in human contact. In fact, they tell us they do want contact but they may need it to happen under idiosyncratic conditions. Therefore, what we must strive for is not so much expertise in the abstract concept called autism, but a more "local," more contextualized knowledge and a deeper understanding of the personal experience of the individuals.

Real People, Regular Lives offers such insight into the lived experience of the individuals who were willing to share their stories with us via this research project. They and their families offer us the local knowledge that is rarely available except in works by other self-advocates who generally do not need augmentative systems to communicate.

In this remarkable book, Sally Young has provided the sensitivity and commitment to the individual and the scholarship that offers us another critical lens with which to view these lives and relationships. Through her efforts, we can learn more about how autism is experienced – at least by the people portrayed here who had a chance to communicate about their lives.

Here we can see their uniqueness. And, through her analysis we can come to understand that the people we "accuse of having autism"[4] have thoughts, hopes, dreams and emotions that are often indistinguishable from our own. This book expands the simple but powerful idea that all human beings are real people no matter how extraordinary their support needs. And each person has the right to and capacity for a real life with the dignity and respect we expect for ourselves.

Anne M. Donnellan, Ph.D.
Director, USD Autism Institute
University of San Diego
Professor Emerita
University of Wisconsin-Madison

References

1.Hill, D. A., & Leary, M. R. (1993). *Movement disturbance: A clue to hidden competencies in persons diagnosed with autism and other developmental disabilities*. Madison, WI: DRI.

2. Donnellan, A. M., Sabin, L. A., & Majure, L. A. (1992). Facilitated communication: Beyond the quandry to the questions. *Topics in Language Disorders, 12*(4), 69-82.

3. Sacks, O. (1990). *Awakenings*. New York: HarperCollins.

4. Lovett, H. Personal Communication, March 1996.

Notes

All proceeds from the sale of this book will go to the Conference Scholarship Fund of the Autism National Committee (Autcom). This fund provides financial support for individuals with autism who wish to attend Autcom conferences.

The participants signed release forms saying they did not want to have their confidentiality protected. Instead, they wished to have their real names used in association with their stories and writing. The personal stories were approved by the FC speakers, their family members and other participants.

In most cases, the essays in the "In their Own Words" sections were pieced together from different transcripts, many of which were several years old. As a result, the stories present an historical rather than a current picture of the FC speakers, their thinking and their lives.

The views in this book are entirely my own and do not necessarily reflect the policies or beliefs of the Nancy Lurie Marks Family Foundation or other donors.

Throughout the book I have made a clear distinction between receptive language and expressive language. Receptive language is the ability to understand the meaning of words and sentences. Expressive language refers to the ability to use words to describe thoughts, feelings and ideas and form them into coherent sentences. For the most people, receptive and expressive language develop concurrently. In the case of FC however, it seems important to make the distinction because these skills may not have developed together.

Some FC speakers submitted transcripts with typos and punctuation errors intact while other transcripts had been cleaned up for readability. In order to achieve similarity across all material, I changed the FC transcripts to adhere to common standards for spelling and punctuation. Grammar and sentence structure were never changed.

In accord with common usage, people who do not speak are referred to as "nonverbal." Individuals who type to speak are referred to throughout the book as "FC speakers" or "typers." "Facilitated communication" or "typing" means transcripts written with the assistance of a facilitator using physical touch as a means of support. "Independent typing" means the facilitator was present while the message was typed, but did not physically touch the FC speaker.

Daniel McConnell was not part of the original study group. His story was added in 2009. Having started using FC in 2007, Daniel is part of a new generation of typers.

Acknowledgements

Over the past 20 years, it has been an honor to play a small part in the FC story. I have known many FC speakers who have shared their words and their worlds with me. I have had the privilege of watching them as they grew, took on new challenges and changed in unimaginable ways. Time and again, I have been overwhelmed by their wise and powerful, yet gentle words. They have changed me for the better in so many ways and I am thankful.

Even though I do not know the FC speakers, families and care providers on a face-to-face basis, they opened their lives to me. They entrusted me with their stories; their triumphs as well as their heartaches. All were willing to take a courageous stand for FC.

In 2001, the original funding for this work was provided by a generous grant from the Nancy Lurie Marks Family Foundation. Grant funding does not come readily for controversial projects such as this one. I thank the Foundation for its willingness to fund the initial stages of this project.

The Autism National Committee agreed to provide financial oversight for the donations. Anne and Paul Bakeman graciously and fastidiously did the necessary bookkeeping and maintained correspondence with the donors.

Ann Berhnardt and Betsy Carpenter, each in her own way, has given me something so fundamental. They both have permanent places in the list of acknowledgements for anything I ever write. Their gifts go beyond words.

My graduate school professor Anne Donnellan has been a source of inspiration. Her loyalty has always remained with the autistic individuals, even when that stance has taken her down unpopular paths.

My parents, Mabel and Ed Young, were determined that their only daughter be launched into adult life with a college degree in her pocket. While I did not appreciate their efforts then, I do now and wish I could tell them.

When the enormity of this task threatened to overwhelm me, Madeline Hafner propped me up and spurred me on, always reminding me why I do this work.

Robert Martin worked tirelessly in the initial stages of this book, wading through mountains of data. His excitement for the people and their stories was contagious and confirming.

Marilyn Campbell, editor and friend, provided compassionate editing along with questions and commentary that improved this book in many ways. With a quick hand and a quick wit, she made possible that which seemed impossible. It was magic.

Char Brandl and Sandra McClennen graciously and bravely volunteered to do last minute copy editing after the bank account had run dry.

Roy Bedward has been my teacher and constant companion on this FC journey for the past decade. His painting hung over my desk throughout the days of writing and now adorns the cover this book.

My nephew Tim Young rallied the troops so our entire family made donations to this book as the centerpiece of our 2009 Christmas gift exchange.

Several graduate students from the University of Wisconsin helped with the initial coding of data, especially Nathan Black, Jennifer Wheeler and Cornelia Gordon-Hempe.

Many additional friends, colleagues and family members have supported my efforts with patience, care and concern.

In 2009, monetary donations were given by the following individuals. These donations enabled me to purchase software along with editing and data management services. The contributions also provided much-needed emotional and psychological support.

Judy Bailey
Eric Bakeman
Paul, Anne, and Jen Bakeman
Judi Barta
June Bascom
Charlene Brandl
Gwen Cohnehour
Jeff Coy
Joyce Crews
Rebecca Goldman
Madeline Hafner
Becca and Ken Koscik
Kosik Construction
Sandra and Doug McClennen
Amanda McConnell
Kathleen McGinnity
Scott Opsahl
Walter and Joanna Page
Barb Rentenbach
Bob and Rita Rubin

Kendall and James Seybert
Sean Sokler and Barbara Cunningham
Lee Stanley
Judy and Darryl Stup
Mary and Tom Ulrich
Cheryl Van Lear
Gay and Wallace Wojtowicz
Jean Wood
Theresa Wood
Andrew Young
Ed and Nancy Young
Greg and Donna Young
Ian Young
Jim Young and Kathy Steinberger
Mike Young and Angie Mack
Sally Young II
Tim Young and Bea Palomino-Young
Todd and Kate Young
Virginia Young and Jane Lowe
Toni and Chhem Young-Pen

It does take a village to write a book. This is my village. I thank you all.

Table of Contents

Introduction

"Psychology needs to concern itself with the life as it is lived."

Gordon Allport[1]

For some individuals, FC has been the key to full-fledged membership in their families and communities and an avenue to pursue sophisticated forms of self-advocacy and self-expression. For others, it is little more than a promise broken; a hope unfulfilled.

For those of us who support FC speakers, the process has been an intense journey of seeing autistic individuals in a fresh light, getting to know them in a new way and watching them change in ways that go far beyond anything we could have imagined. At the same time, it has been a journey of swimming against the tide of public opinion.

The primary goal of this book is to provide descriptive, historical documentation of FC; a legacy or a map of the territory, if you will. It is now nearly two decades after FC first came to the United States. Who are the people who continue using it despite enormous controversy? What changes have come about for individual FC speakers and their families? What impact has FC had on the quality of their lives?

FC appears to be an agent of change. Change does not come readily for children with autism, and for adults, even less so. In fact, autism often has been seen as a condition in which change is almost non-existent. For some participants in this study, FC has allowed a new measure of control over their lives. For others, FC did not flourish and their lives were changed in different ways. Nevertheless, all of the FC speakers in the book have enjoyed the experience of being seen by others as competent, whole and real.

This book leans on a long history of qualitative research. It brings together a body of descriptive and anecdotal evidence from real life. In doing so, it allows participants to tell their own stories about their own lives.

The field of psychology and especially the realms of autism and developmental disability have a long history of taking the person out of their research methods. In 1970, Amedeo Giorgi published a book calling for bringing the whole human person back into the equation.[2] Giorgi criticizes the singular use of the natural sciences as a model for the study of psychology.

It is not difficult to understand that the information that is meaningful to humans as they live their lives might be categorically different from the information one might gain from the study of, say geology or physics. Giorgi's call is particularly important where the individuals being studied have no means to speak or refute the official scientific narrative that is constructed around them.

FC has intensified the natural science versus human science debate. Most of the FC studies to date have been proof-oriented, where the FC users are relegated to the background and the correctness of their answers is the pivot point that serves to validate or invalidate the method. In their book on the validation controversy, *Contested Words, Contested Science*, editors Doug Biklen and Don Cardinal looked critically at the validation process and actively worked to bring the research participants into the research conversation.[3]

FC is shifting sand under our feet. It defies reducing the questions to ones that can be answered with controlled variables in laboratory settings. Bringing the person into the foreground means asking questions that have complex answers. It means looking beyond behavior and acknowledging the existence and the importance of the inner life.

In contrast to the proof-oriented model of research, a process-oriented model would ask questions about how FC works, why it works with some dyads and not others, what it might mean to the people involved, and how it can be utilized in the most beneficial ways. In his book *Reasonable People*, Ralph Savarese addresses these issues when he asks if FC was so vehemently rejected because (a) it brought the person back into full view and (b) its adherents could not explain how or why it worked.[4]

What might it mean to gain access to expressive language well beyond the toddler years? What might it mean to acquire expressive language for the first time at age 40, 20 or even 10? What might it mean to have receptive language, so you could hear and perhaps understand everyone around you, yet be unable to speak? What might it mean to be unable to accurately convey in gesture or body language that which you are thinking, feeling, needing or wanting? What might it mean if most of your idiosyncratic body expressions were misjudged and misinterpreted?

All of the FC speakers in this book had some degree of receptive language, but virtually no expressive, word-based language until they were well past the typical developmental window for language learning. They apparently possessed healthy, active, observant minds locked in bodies that thwarted personal expression. How would this impact development? This is uncharted territory. There are no books or articles written on this topic. There is no history, no reference manual or explanatory framework.

Today, laboratory studies with large sample sizes and tightly controlled variables are highly revered in the human sciences. However, real life matters at least as much as laboratory findings. Broad descriptive studies can pave the way for more narrowly focused study designs.[5] In arguing for the importance of detailed study of individual lives, Gordon W. Allport noted, "Acquaintance with particulars is the beginning of all knowledge – scientific and otherwise…. Psychology needs to concern itself with the life as it is lived."[6]

In a similar vein, nearly thirty years ago Robert B. Edgerton argued for detailed study of the individual lives of persons with "mental retardation." He wrote:

> First we try to study the lives of mentally retarded persons in their entirety. Everything that forms a part of their lives – dreams, fears, communication, jobs, recreation, friends, and family—is important to us, as it is to the mentally retarded persons themselves….The method is not intended to provide simple answers; instead it is intended to provide the grounds for rejecting simple answers in favor of more full and accurate understanding.[7]

This book has been an effort to address the issues of which Allport and Edgerton speak. How can we gain a more accurate understanding of the lives of nonverbal individuals with autism? What are the particulars of their lives?

Ultimately too it is a clarion call for change. In the book *Naming Silenced Lives,* editor William Tierney noted, "We collect life histories as a way to document how we live now so that we might change how we live now."[8] In the current political and economic climate, there is good reason to believe that public funding for vulnerable people will to be cut as it has been over the past three decades.

There is hope that students and researchers begin studying the myriad of fascinating questions surrounding FC that have yet to be asked. How does having access to expressive language enhance personhood and self-esteem? How does the content of an individual's typed messages change over time and what can we infer from these changes? What makes a good facilitator? Why do some people have difficulty learning to become facilitators while others pick it up easily? What is the role of touch in FC? Why is validation elusive? How does having receptive language but no expressive language impact development? How does gaining access to expressive language change the brain, the personality or the self? What is the role of the facilitator in independent typing? What can be learned from FC speakers' idiosyncratic and poetic use of language?

The FC users and proponents featured on these pages have done their part in keeping the method alive. By providing a glimpse of what is possible, I hope this book will stimulate interest and encourage researchers from a variety of disciplines to take the next step and address these and many other unasked questions.

Organization of Book

Every effort has been made to let the people speak for themselves. By providing a container with minimized structure and abstraction and maximized transparency to the data, I have tried to put the participants front and center thereby giving the reader a direct experience of each individual. Through their words, perhaps we can begin to comprehend what FC has meant to them.

This book need not be read cover to cover. Although in reality everything is related to everything else, each chapter was written to be a somewhat self-contained unit. As a result there may be some redundancy from chapter to chapter.

Part I: Background
The three areas most relevant to this study are autism, communication and quality of life. This section provides the reader with a very brief introduction to each of these complex topics.

Part II: Personal Stories
Part II includes a chapter devoted to each of the ten FC speakers. Each chapter contains a brief portrait of the individual and a narrative account of

his or her FC journey. The final section in each of these chapters features the FC speaker's own words. These essays have been pieced together from numerous transcripts. A few words have been added to connect thoughts or sentences. Nothing substantive has been added that would alter the meaning of the original texts. The FC speakers have approved all changes to their writing and all of the participants have approved their narrative accounts for accuracy.

Part III: Prominent Themes

This section contains ten themes from daily life that have been impacted by FC. The original data set was coded into 43 distinct nodes. The prominent themes evolved by collapsing, combining and distilling the nodes into families or groupings. The themes reflect some of the the categories that are used for quality of life assessment in other populations, but they also include areas that are specific to these individuals.

In real life, the prominent themes are closely intertwined and constantly influence each other. They are not easily separated into distinct categories. However, dividing them makes the writing and reading more manageable. In some cases, information from the research literature that pertains to the theme is interspersed with the data and direct quotes. This section includes a large number of quotes to provide the reader with a direct experience of participants' voices as well as the similarities and differences between participants.

Part IV: Endings

In this section, I go beyond the data and present my thoughts and questions about the impact FC has had on individual lives. As a result of living with these issues for the past 20 years and living with these data for the past 18 months, I have come to believe that FC has a far-reaching impact on the inner lives of those who use it. The changes that people have experienced have been both internal and external, Both types play a role in a positive spiral of change that often accompanies the use of FC.

Appendices

Appendix A: Works by or about the participants.
Appendix B: Works by others who type to talk.
Appendix C: Interview questionnaire.
Appendix D: Code book.

References

1. Allport, G. W. (@1942). *The use of personal documents in psychological science.* New York: Social Science Research Council. (p. 56).
2. Giorgi, A. (1970). *Psychology as a human science: A phenomenologically based approach.* New York: Harper & Row.
3. Biklen, D., & Cardinal, D. N. (Eds.). (1997). *Contested words, contested science: Unraveling the facilitated communication controversy.* New York: Teachers College.
4. Savarese, R. J. (2007). *Reasonable people: A memoir of autism and adoption.* New York: Other Press.
5. Pedhazur, E. J., & Schmelkin, L. P. (1991). *Measurement, design and analysis: An integrated approach.* Hillsdale, NJ: Lawrence Erlbaum Associates.
6. Allport (@1942)
7. Edgerton, R. B. (1984). Introduction. In R. B. Edgerton (Ed.), *Lives in process: Mildly retarded adults in a large city.* Washington D.C.: AAMD. (pp. 1 & 3).
8. Tierney, W. G. (1993). Introduction: Developing archives of resistance. In W. G. Tierney & D. McLaughlin (Eds.), *Naming silenced lives: Personal narratives and the process of educational change.* New York: Routledge.

Part I:
Background

Background

"The more you put your mind to autism, the less clear the picture becomes."

Birger Sellin[1]

Autism, communication, and quality of life are all complex topics. Thrown together, complexity increases. This section presents a basic background on these topics and the ways in which they intersect.

Autism

From professional peer-reviewed journals to the popular media, autism is portrayed at best as a complex and puzzling disorder. At worst, it is seen as a thief that steals children from their parents and a plague that has cast its shadow in every corner of the globe.

The diagnostic label Autism Spectrum Disorder (ASD) conveys the wide range of functioning within the diagnosis. Historically there have been two informal subcategories—"high-functioning" and "low-functioning."

Generally, the label of high-functioning is assigned to those who can speak while the label of low-functioning is assigned to individuals who are nonverbal. Other attributes commonly associated with the low-functioning label are scoring very low on standardized IQ tests, having high levels of maladaptive behavior, and generally needing 24-hour support in daily life. By these criteria, the adults portrayed in this book would be considered to be in the low-functioning category.

Classical or "low-functioning" autism is almost universally regarded as the most tragic and devastating end of the spectrum. In these cases, most people think there is little reason for hope or quality of life. As Sacks notes,

> The picture of 'classical infantile autism' is a formidable one....A majority of Kanner-type children are retarded, often severely; a significant proportion have seizures and may have soft neurological signs and symptoms—a whole range of repetitive or automatic movements such as spasms, ticks, rocking, spinning, finger play, or flapping of the hands; problems of coordination and balance; peculiar difficulties sometimes in initiating movements akin to what is seen as in Parkinson.....Most people (and, indeed, most physicians), if asked about autism, summon up a picture of a profoundly disabled child, with stereotyped movements, perhaps head-banging; rudimentary language; almost inaccessible: a creature for whom very little future lies in store.[2]

It is difficult to predict outcome for individuals on the autism spectrum. The predictors most commonly used for a good outcome are IQ scores and language. The worst prognosis has always been attributed to those who have reached adulthood and who do not speak.[3]

Knowledge and research about adults with autism is scarce and this is especially true for "low-functioning" adults.[4] As Sacks has noted, "Indeed, in a strange way most people speak only of autistic children and never of autistic adults as if the children somehow just vanished from the earth."[5]

There are several plausible reasons for this. Changing behavior or teaching new skills to autistic individuals of any age is an arduous process and improvements are small and difficult to measure. In addition, as children with autism grow into adulthood, they become bigger and stronger and challenging or ritualistic behaviors can become more deeply ingrained. These behavioral issues make it difficult to be assured they will be able to follow a pre-designed research protocol.

Although we know that the plasticity of the brain continues through the lifespan, there is an unspoken assumption that change is not likely to occur once "low-functioning" individuals reach adulthood. Paired with this assumption comes a lack of funding for high quality services and therapeutic programs after the school years have ended. These things taken together can create a sense of futility for practitioners and researchers alike.

Diagnostic Criteria

The diagnostic criteria for autism found in the most recent edition of the Diagnostic and Statistical Manual of the American Psychiatric Association (DSM-IV) are based on a triad of impairment—social interaction, communication, and repetitive patterns of behavior. Mental retardation is not part of the official diagnosis. However, for many years it has been assumed to be present in as many as 75% of autistic individuals.[6] S o m e examples of behaviors that make up the diagnostic criteria listed in the DSM-IV include:

Social interaction
- Impairment of eye contact, facial expression, posture, gestures
- Lack of joint attention (sharing, showing, pointing)
- Lack of social reciprocity (uses others as tools, prefers solitary play)

Communication
- Delay or lack of speech and without compensating via body language
- Impairment in ability to initiate or sustain conversation
- Repetitive or idiosyncratic use of language
- Impaired imitative play or spontaneous pretend play

Repetitive or stereotyped patterns of behavior
- Preoccupation with restrictive patterns of interest
- Inflexible adherence to specific nonfunctional routines
- Stereotyped repetitive motor mannerisms
- Preoccupation with parts of objects

Each item on this list depends on observable behavior as well as the clinician's interpretation of that behavior. In other words, there are no biological markers or physical tests to confirm or deny the presence of autism. Using observable behavior as the sole diagnostic criteria has a serious drawback; it is coupled with an underlying assumption of congruence between inner state and outer, observable behavior.

Our perceptions and judgments of others are generally based on an assumption that there is congruence between inner state and outer behavior.[7] However, when this congruence is lacking, all forms of self-expression are subject to misinterpretation and all covert traits that are inferred from outer behavior, such as intelligence or emotion, can appear to be absent.[8] In fact, the assumption of congruence is so entrenched in the professions that when an individual cannot comply with standardized testing procedures, adaptive behavior can be scored and taken as a viable substitute for IQ.

The assumption of congruence has been seriously challenged by autistic individuals themselves. These individuals have repeatedly told us of their predicament; they are unable to act and behave in ways that accurately reflect their intentions, desires, or inner states. Dawn Prince-Hughes, a professor and individual with autism has noted, "The characteristics described in DSM-IV are just that: they are descriptions of coping behaviors and not descriptions, necessarily, of innate orientation.[9]

A New Lens for Autism

Historically, the professional autism literature has focused on short term outcomes while ignoring the inner, subjective perspective.[10] Prolific autistic author Donna Williams has noted that the label of autism describes only outer behavior and ignores inner reality.[11] Today we have easy access to the inner reality of many autistic individuals through the numerous autobiographical accounts that have been published since the 1980s.

These accounts provide countless examples of the lack of congruence between inner state and outer behavior. They also help us understand the reasons behind many types of behavior and allow us to see a person who is very different from the hopelessly unreachable being portrayed in traditional venues. In these autobiographical accounts, it is clear these individuals are sensitive, intelligent, multi-dimensional, and fully human. Through this lens, a more positive, hopeful and accurate picture emerges.

Using both subjective and objective information, Donnellan, Hill, and Leary provide an alternative to the traditional view of autism. These authors see the behavioral symptoms of autism as reflecting vast and pervasive sensory and movement differences.[12] Sensory and movement difference is an umbrella term for the neurological condition that prevents congruence between inner state and outer behavior.

The lens of sensory and movement differences provides a way to reconcile the information from both the inner and outer perspectives. For example, from the outer perspective, individuals with autism often have a flat affect and stiff, repetitive movements. These two traits make the individual seem almost robotic.

A very different picture emerges when these observations are incorporated with the inner vantage point that is described in the autobiographical literature. For example, Eugene Marcus does have a flat affect and repetitive movements. Using facilitated communication he described himself as a wooden Pinocchio but then went on to say he also had the soft beating heart of a real boy.[13] In a similar vein, Sue Rubin noted that her face was like concrete, never showing sadness or anger even though she might be experiencing those emotions.[14] In each of these cases, the speaker describes a lack of congruence between inner state and outer behavior.

Sensory and movement differences provide an explanatory framework for the rupture in professional knowledge that was created by the autobiographical accounts. Difficulties with sensory and motor functioning enjoy wide consensus in these accounts; recently they have also begun to gain acceptance in the mainstream autism literature.[15]

The lens of sensory and movement differences allows the observer to avoid taking behavior at face value or interpreting body language in the usual ways. This reorientation, in turn, opens the door to observing behavior with a powerful new set of assumptions about the individual with autism. We can "presume competence"[16] and see things in a fresh light. This stance is widely accepted for individuals with Tourette's Syndrome, Parkinson's Disorder, and other movement disorders.

Communication

Communication is a two-way street that involves both receiving and transmitting information. In other words, being able to communicate effectively implies having access to both receptive and expressive language.

A powerful connection exists between language and behavior. In typically developing toddlers, enormous behavioral changes are tied to expressive language development. Oliver Sacks recognized the importance of expressive language in describing the transformation when Temple Grandin began speaking at age six. He wrote:

> [H]er new powers of language and communication now gave her an anchor, some ability to master what had been total chaos before, her sensory system, with its violent oscillations of oversensitivity and undersensitivity, started to stabilize a little. There were many periods of backsliding and regression, but it is clear that by the age of six she had achieved fair language and, with this, had crossed the Rubicon that divides high-functioning people like her from low-functioning ones, who never achieve proper language or autonomy. With the access of language, the terrible triad of impairments— social, communicative, and imaginative—began to yield somewhat.[17]

Temple always had receptive language. Therefore, it appears that Sacks believes these important internal changes are tied to the acquisition of expressive language although he does not explicitly make that distinction. In other words, gaining access to *expressive* language was the catalyst for change.

A link between expressive language and behavior has been found in research in disabilities and other populations.[18] In 1988, in the Editor's Column of the Autism Research Institute (ARI) newsletter, Bernard Rimland discussed the sudden and unexpected changes that can occur when a child or adult gains access to expressive language. Rimland was so impressed with these changes that he referred to them as quantum behavioral improvement.[19]

Facilitated Communication

In the early 1990s, facilitated communication (FC) opened the doors of language-based communication for many nonverbal people with autism. From the perspective of those involved, this was a profound and life-changing event. Individuals who historically could not express a single need, other than possibly through one-word answers, crude gestures, or other non-valued means, began to communicate complex thoughts and emotions. Parents began to know their children in ways that went beyond their wildest dreams. Teachers, therapists and caregivers gained valuable information about autism from the inside perspective which helped them be more effective in their roles.

The texts produced through FC strongly support the notion of sensory and movement differences and provide example after example of the enormous gap between the outer behavior and the inner experience. When bodily self-expression is inaccurate and inadequate, FC provides an avenue for the outside observer to begin to know and understand the person. The transcripts portray people who are articulate, sensitive, and creative thinkers who have social and emotional needs that are not unlike the social and emotional needs of non-autistic individuals.[20]

FC is a viable technique for people who have severe communication impairment and the inability to point independently. The individual gains access to a keyboard with the assistance of a partner who offers both emotional and physical support. The physical support provides both touch and backwards resistance. The resistance pushes the typer's hand, wrist, or elbow back towards his or her chest.[21]

With training, some individuals have gained enough skill to type with only light touch on the shoulder or even with no touch at all. Others have begun to speak or read aloud what they have typed. The movement towards independent typing is usually achieved as the facilitator fades support from the wrist or lower arm by gradually moving the point of contact up from the wrist towards the elbow, then upper arm, and eventually the shoulder.

Learning and development often occur within the context of a dyadic (two-person) relationship. In FC as in other teaching methods, the facilitator provides support, or scaffolding, so that the child or less-able partner can function at a higher level than he or she could achieve alone. This allows the learner to experience higher levels of functioning.

Shortly after FC began to be used in the United States, it became mired in a firestorm of controversy in the professional literature and in the popular press. At best, this controversy stirred us to re-think our assumptions about intelligence, disability, communication, research methods, and the nature of reality. At worst, it marginalized a communication option that could have been helpful to a large number of individuals.[22]

The validation or authorship issue is perhaps the most volatile element in the debate. Since an assistant is supporting the arm or hand of the FC speaker, there is a very real and obvious danger of the assistant moving the person's hand to the letters. In effect, this would be tantamount to putting words into the speaker's mouth. Admittedly, all communication is a mutually created enterprise, but if the assistant is in fact moving the hand of the FC speaker, this makes the assistant responsible for the content of the message.

The evidence from some controlled experiments suggests that the FC messages were in fact influenced by the facilitators. The results are disturbing to opponents and proponents alike. Opponents maintain that these results provide conclusive evidence that the practice of facilitated communication should be abandoned. Proponents have responded by conducting controlled studies that take into account some of the variables that might be confounding the picture. To date, the findings from these studies reveal unexpected competencies and literacy in some nonverbal individuals with autism. Today, the balance is equal, with approximately half of studies confirming and half rejecting the validity of the typed messages.[23]

It is not uncommon for the results of research studies to directly contradict each other. When this occurs, a dialogue in professional journals between the two opposing viewpoints often ensues. Sometimes these conversations take place over a period of years as investigators on both sides of the argument attempt to obtain a stronger picture of their findings.

In the case of FC, however, the opponents effectively shut down the conversation in many peer-reviewed journals. As a result of the validation controversy and attacks from opponents, a number of people stopped using the technique. Others continued typing and practicing their skills. The stories in this book exemplify both of these trajectories.

In light of the early negative studies and loud condemnation from the opponents of FC, the interested and curious person might ask, "Why have so many seemingly sensible people, both parents and professionals, continued the practice?

Parents have been accused of being delusional out of desperation to find some means of helping their children. Professionals have been called charlatans. Funding for FC has been limited. Agencies, schools, and other funding sources avoid FC. Professional organizations have written formal policy statements against it. Why then would anyone continue to stand behind it?

The stories in this book describe immediate and long-term changes in which negative or difficult behavior decreased and positive behavior increased. Many nonverbal autistic individuals begin with few if any of the skills necessary to use FC. They lack the ability to sit at a table in a calm-alert state or focus their attention on a shared task. Many cannot tolerate touch. After starting to use FC, they began to acquire these abilities for the first time.

Even if for only brief periods, witnessing this uncharacteristically positive behavior is very compelling. Soon other changes may enter the picture. For example, some individuals have been successful in overcoming compulsions and increasing eye contact, joint attention and time on task. Disruptive behaviors sometimes decrease in frequency or intensity. These changes may be subtle at first, but become more clear over time.

In light of these positive steps, the genuine question to ask is not, "Why would people continue to use FC?" but rather, "How could anyone in good conscience stop using it?"

Instead of focusing on the controversy, this book presents the stories of ten individuals and describes the impact that FC has had on the quality of their day-to-day lives.

Quality of Life

Thinking about the quality of life for individuals with disabilities, especially those with profound levels of disability, is a recent phenomenon. In the 1960s, as society's paternalistic attitudes began to melt away, the focus of autism research began to shift from looking at the group as a whole to looking at the individual.[24] By the 1980s, the construct of quality of life provided an expanded vision for what might be possible for people who were given adequate supports.[25] At the same time, the notion of quality of life provided an impetus to study individual lives.[26]

Having a sense of control over one's daily life and destiny is a strong value in our society and the concept of self-determination has close ties to quality of life.[27] Most researchers agree that any systematic study of quality of life should include the subjective perspective of the individual as well as objective measures.[28]

Taylor and Bogdan have noted that the individual's subjective experience is central to a quality-of-life assessment.[29] They caution that individuals with disabilities often have very low expectations and can report high levels of satisfaction when their quality of life is, in fact, quite low by most people's standards. In a similar vein, Cummins has warned that definitions of quality of life are often downgraded for marginalized groups and fall far short of levels that would be considered adequate for the general population.[30]

Traditionally, outcome measures in the autism literature have been the ability to live independently and to enjoy a "normal" social life.[31] These narrow measures can render other positive outcomes invisible. A broader definition, such as focusing on the interaction between the individual and the environment would provide a more accurate and comprehensive measure of quality of life.[32]

According to Schalock, there are over 100 different definitions of quality of life, but he and others agree that five to eight key domains should be considered.[33]The effect of having access to expressive language on any of these domains is immediately apparent. Schalock suggests the following domains:

- Emotional well-being
- Interpersonal relations

- Material well-being
- Personal development
- Physical well-being
- Self-determination
- Rights.

The effectiveness of any intervention depends upon its ability to serve as a catalyst for change. For individuals who use FC, especially those in adulthood, change does not come readily. The behavioral changes that spontaneously arise from gaining access to expressive language can enhance every domain of quality of life.

References

1. Sellin, B. (1995). *I don't want to be inside me anymore*. New York: Basic Books.
2. Sacks, O. (1995). *An anthropologist on mars: Seven paradoxical tales*. New York: Vintagr. (pp. 245-6).
3. Seltzer, M. M., Shattuck, P. T., Abbeduto, L., & Greenberg, J. S. (2004). Trajectory of development in adolescents and adults with autism. *Mental Retardation and Developmental Diasbilities Research REviews, 10*, 234-247.
4. Seltzer, M. M., Krauss, M. W., Shattuck, P. T., Orsmond, G. I., Swe, A., & Lord, C. (2003). The symptoms of autism spectrum disorders in adolescence and adulthood. *Journal of Autism & Developmental Disorders, 33*(6), 565-581. Seltzer, M. M., Shattuck, P. T., Abbeduto, L., & Greenberg, J. S. (2004).
5. Sacks, O. (1995). (p. 246).
6. Rapin, I. (1997). Current Concepts. *The New England Journal of Medicine, 337*(2), 97-104.
 Dempsey, I., & Foreman, P. (2001). A review of educational approaches for individuals with autism. *International Journal of Disability, Development & Education, 48*(1), 103-116.
7. Jacobson, J. W., Mulick, J. A., & Schwartz, A. A. (1994). A history of facilitated communication: Science, pseudoscience, and antiscience. *American Psychologist, 50*, 750-765.
8. Donnellan, A. M., & Leary, M. R. (1995). *Movement differences and diversity in autism/mental retardation: Appreciating and accomodating people with communication and behavior challenges*. Madison, WI: DRI.
Leary, M. R., & Hill, D. A. (1996). Moving on: Autism and movment disturbance. *Mental Retardation, 34*, 39-53.

9. Prince-Hughes, D. (2004). *Songs of the gorilla nation: My journey through autism*. New York: Harmony. (p. 175).

10. Peter, D. (1997). A focus on the individual, theory and reality: making the connection through the lives of individuals. In R. I. Brown (Ed.), *Quality of Life for People With Disabilities -Models, Research and Practice* (pp. 27-55). Cheltenham, UK: Stanley Thornes, UK.

11. Williams, D. (1998). *Autism and sensing: The unlost instinct*. London: Jessica Kingsley.

12. Donnellan, A. M., Hill, D. A., & Leary, M. R. (2010). Rethinking autism: Implications of sensory and movement differences for understanding and support. *Disability Studies Quarterly, 30*(1).

13. Marcus, E. (May 5, 1998). *Keynote Speech: On almost becoming a person.* Paper presented at the No Time for Silence conference, Syracuse, NY.

14. Rubin, S. (1998). *Castigating assumptions about low-functioning autism & mental retardation.* Paper presented at the conference entitled Autism Through the Lifespan: Many Paths, One Destination, San Diego, CA.

15. Dawson, G., & Watling, R. (2000). Interventions to facilitate auditory, visual, and motor integration in autism: A review of the evidence. *Journal of Autism & Developmental Disorders, 30*(5), 415-421.

Leekam, S. R., Nieto, C., Libby, S. J., Wing, L., & Gould, J. (2007). Describing the sensory abnormalities of children and adults with aum. *Journal of Autism & Developmental Disorders, 37*, 894-910.

Wing, L., & Shah, A. (2000). Catatonia in autistic spectrum disorders. *British Journal of Psychiatry, 176*, 357-362.

16. Biklen, D. (2005). *Autism and the myth of the person alone*. New York: New York University.

17. Sacks, O. (1995). (p. 271).

18. Caufield, M. B., Fischel, J. E., DeBaryshe, B. D., & Whitehurst, G. J. (1989). Behavioral correlates of developmental expressive language disorder. *Journal of Abnormal Child Psychology, 17*(2), 187-201.

Ripley, K., & Yuill, N. (2005). Patterns of language impairment and behaviour in boys excluded from school. [Article]. *British Journal of Educational Psychology, 75*(1), 37-50.

19. Rimland, B. (1988). Language and quantum behavioral improvement. *Autism Research Review International, 2,* 3.

20. See Appendix - First-hand Accounts of FC Users.

21. Crossley, R. (1994). *Facilitated communication training*. New York: Teachers College.

22. See Appendix - FC Validation Studies

23. Biklen (2005).

24. Brown, R. I. (1997). Quality of life: The development of an idea. In R. I. Brown (Ed.), *Quality of Life for People With Disabilities -Models, Research and Practice* (pp. 1-11). Cheltenham, UK: Stanley Thornes Ltd.

Schalock, R. L. (2000). Three decades of quality of life. *Focus on Autism and Other Developmental Disabilities, 15*(2), 116-135.

25. Schalock (2000).

26. Edgerton (1984).

27. Salkever, D. S. (2000). Activity status, life satisfaction and perceived disability for young adults with developmental disabilities. *Journal of Rehabilitation, 66*(3), 4-13.

28. Brown (1997).

Cummins, R. A. (1997). Assessing Quality of Life. In R. I. Brown (Ed.), *Quality of Life for People With Disabilities -Models, Research and Practice* (pp. 116-150). Cheltenham, UK: Stanley Thornes Ltd.

Goode, D. (1997). Assessing the quality of life of adults with profound disabilities. In R. I. Brown (Ed.), *Quality of life for people with disabilities: Models, research and practice* (pp. 72-90). Cheltenham, UK: Stanley Thornes Ltd.

Schalock (2000).

29. Taylor, S. J., & Bogdan, R. (1990). Quality of life and the individual's perspective. In R. L. Schalock (Ed.), *Quality of life: Perspectives and issues*. Washington DC: American Association on Mental Retardation.

30. Cummins ((1997).

31. Lotter, V. (1978). Follow-up studies. In M. Rutter & E. Schopler (Eds.), *Autism: A reappraisal of concepts and treatment* (pp. 475 - ??). New York: Plenum.

32. Ruble, L. A., & Dalrymple, N. J. (1996). An alternative view of outcome in autism. *Focus on Autism and Other Developmental Disorders, 11*(1), 3-14.

33. Schalock (2000).

Part II:

Personal Stories

"I, with my many written words reach out to tell the untold story for there is a story every where to be told."

Wally Wojtowicz, Jr.

Things are Decidedly Better Now

Katherine Grace Dale

Snapshot

Kathy was born in 1964 and started using FC at age 28. She was a precocious child, but began losing skills when she was three years old. Kathy had an older brother who also had autism and the two of them were close. Rick's death, in 1997, was very hard on Kathy, but having access to language helped her get through that difficult time. Sensory sensitivity and anxiety determined much of Kathy's behavior when she was young, but today when she becomes anxious, Kathy can type with her staff or parents and discuss the issue. In addition, she has control over many aspects of her daily life from choosing food and clothing to deciding where to live and hiring staff.

About Kathy

Born: 1964.   **Started FC:** 1992 at age 28.

Current Facilitators: Heather (mother), Kent (step-father), Wendy (Support Coordinator), other support staff.

Access to FC: Most of the time at home with support staff.

Living Situation: Rented home with two roommates.

Day Program: Paid work shredding papers (3 hours/week), shopping, movies, TV, reading newspapers, exercise program.

Highest level of Independence: Forearm with pointer device (Kent and Wendy).

Secondary Participants: Heather and Kent.

Quote

"Living with autism is like being in a house without doors and without windows. FC allows me to go out of the house."

Kathy's Criteria for Quality of Life

Having Mom in my life to talk to, to be listened to, and to go places with.

Living in a big house with congenial roommates.

Six Things Kathy Wants You to Know

I go out of my way to help people understand and appreciate FC.

I am a proud FC speaker.

I like to be included in conversations.

I like to be part of the solution instead of part of the problem.

I am a woman and I have feelings like any other woman.

My only other thought is that I might be able to make a difference in someone else's life.

Six Things Kathy's Parents and Staff Want You to Know About Her

Kathy does not lose sight of her goals.

FC has opened up her life like a beautiful flower or jewel beyond description.

She is greatly energized by how much FC has improved her quality of life.

I can hardly conceive of what her life would be like now without FC!

We even arranged a change in service providers and a physical move to get regular support for her to use FC.

We have high respect for her and are proud of her as a person.

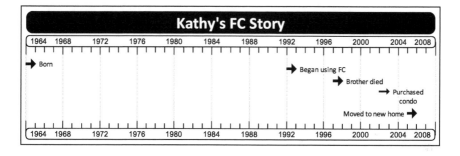

Kathy's Story

Katherine (Kathy) Grace Dale was born in 1964, 17 months after the birth of her brother, Rick. Both children were diagnosed with autism at an early age. Although they were different in many ways, they were always close.

Before Kathy's condition became obvious, the children's parents, Heather and Donald, were concerned about Rick's development. They sought help at The Child Study and Treatment Center, 60 miles from their home in Washington. Although little was known about autism at the time, Rick was eventually given the diagnosis.

Unlike Rick, who never talked, toddler Kathy was precocious in many respects, especially verbally. She talked a lot and used adjective, adverbs, and prepositions correctly. When she was about three and one-half years old, she began to lose her language as well as functional skills such as toileting. Before long, she, too, was diagnosed with autism. Heather remembers, "The diagnosis was devastating because we knew what her life ahead could be like."

Kathy and Rick lived at home until Rick was nine, when he moved to a group home. Later, both siblings lived in a residential center for children with autism. After they entered the adult service system, Kathy and Rick did not see each other frequently, but their bond continued when they were together for holidays and family vacations.

Kathy exhibited many sensory-related traits. She was quite sensitive to loud noises and could become very anxious in noisy environments. She loved soft, velvety fabrics. When stressed, she would occasionally exhibit pica behavior (eating inedible objects) and ingest blankets, sheets and clothing. If she did not like the feel of apparel on her body, she would become excessively anxious; sometimes hiding it or unraveling the fabric. Kathy loved scented items and would occasionally eat perfumed things such as deodorant. When anxious, she would obsessively pick up and toss tiny bits of lint, paper or dirt.

As a small child, Kathy would climb up high on the furniture. She had a good sense of balance, but no sense of danger. She once clambered to the top of a pump organ and shimmied back down. When she was five, she put on her bathing suit and escaped from the house by standing on a chair and removing the chain lock. She walked a few blocks to a motel where there was a swimming pool. The police eventually found her there.

Looking back, Heather says, "It was hard to know whether we were communicating with her. Kathy seemed self-focused much of the time. There was rarely, if ever, a sense of happiness about her."

In school, Kathy was introduced to various communication technologies. In high school, she used a picture system and also utilized basic sign language.

Although she used the signs for eat, drink, and toilet in a way that indicated she understood their meanings, she did so only intermittently.

In 1992, a support worker in her post-school work program wanted to try FC with Kathy. Heather thought, "Why not give it a shot?"

Kathy began, as most people do, making simple choices in daily life. Before long, the floodgates opened and she said things some people did not want to hear and asked questions she had never been able to ask. She started with deep questions about life, justice and power. Fortunately, she had a facilitator who spent many hours discussing these questions with her.

At one point, the staff at her work program tried to introduce a small communication device that could speak pre-programmed phrases, but by that time, Kathy had already learned FC and she wanted people to use it instead.

Heather and Donald divorced in 1974. In 1975, Heather married Kent Hamilton. Kathy had many questions for her mother about her parents' divorce. It did not take long for Heather and Kent to recognize how important it was for Kathy to participate in dialogue and to ascertain the answers to her questions. Heather recalls, "Kathy asked so many questions that it overtook her life and was overwhelming. She was puzzled about many things, some of which she had obviously thought about for a long time."

In 1997, Rick died of pneumonia after a brief illness. It was only after someone recognized his distress that he was rushed to the hospital. Heather wonders whether things might have ended differently if he had a means to communicate. Years earlier, Heather and Kent had unsuccessfully tried FC with Rick. It remains a source of sadness for Kathy that her brother never learned to use FC and that she was not able to help him communicate.

Kathy was deeply affected by Rick's death. A friend tried to comfort her by saying that at least Rick did not have autism anymore. This set in motion a line of thinking in which Kathy began wondering if death might be the way to get rid of her autism. Once she was able to articulate this thinking, she had many discussions with her parents about it. They repeatedly told Kathy that they wanted her here with them and she should not think about joining Rick. The possibility of that outcome still haunts Heather. She recalls, "We had no way of knowing where she was going with her thinking. We wonder what if we hadn't had FC?"

Having spent many years listening to but not participating in conversations, it is not surprising that Kathy sometimes misinterpreted meanings. One day, she showed a lack of enthusiasm for an activity she had said she wanted to do. Her staff told her that she was just "dabbling" and really needed to be "committed" to the activity. Suddenly, Kathy became very agitated and frightened. She typed that the word "committed" meant they were going to put her in an institution. She calmed down immediately once she understood what the staff meant.

Despite Kathy's success with FC, service providers, speech therapists and others tried to get Kathy to use other communication methods and devices. None appeared to be a successful substitute. Kathy was always very clear that she could express herself more fully with FC than with picture boards or pre-programmed devices.

In 2003, Kathy's service provider refused to train her staff in FC. Kathy began reporting ongoing difficulties with certain staff, but state investigators would not accept her claims since her accusations came through FC. With no resolution in sight, Heather and Kent began looking for a service provider that supported FC. The long process took its toll on Kathy and during that time she became distressed and depressed and experienced increased seizure activity.

In 2005, an opening with a new agency occurred, but Kathy would have to move to a new city, give up the condo she loved and lose her longtime roommate. However, she would be able to use FC with her staff. Heather says, "That was crucial, from our point of view, and worth the wait."

Heather reported that Kathy made none of her health decisions in childhood and early adult life. If she did not feel well, it was difficult to discover what was wrong. The usual medications were tried to help her feel less anxious, or for specific ailments, but results were less than satisfactory and often included negative side effects., The only way to judge a treatment's efficacy was to observe her behavior, bodily functions, mood and general health. Recently, Kathy was able to describe her digestive issues to her health professional, who thereupon suggested a gluten/casein-free diet. She has accepted the limitations of that diet and feels much better.

Kent quickly became a fluent FC facilitator, but for Heather it has been more of a struggle. It is not uncommon for one or both parents to have difficulty typing with their adult children. In some cases, emotional sensitivity and the inability to regulate emotions might explain this. Often, especially in the beginning, "neutral" relationships can sometimes be more successful. Heather wanted very much to be able to type with Kathy, but it took a long time and a lot of persistence and patience to achieve fluent conversation. Although this long and difficult process was hurtful for Heather, she wants to encourage others to keep trying, especially parents who might be having difficulty.

Kathy loves to champion FC and was incensed when "Frontline" presented a negative program. On two occasions, Kathy has been asked to give conference presentations on FC. She was proud to tell parents, service providers and direct care staff about her life with FC and the decisions she makes. Heather and Kent have worked to change the perception of FC as well as Washington state's neutral or negative stance.

Today, Kathy's bouts of anxiety occur less often. Sometimes she isn't aware of what is causing her distress. FC provides a means to dialogue and ferret out the problem. As a result, her pica and sensory difficulties are far fewer. She makes choices about many aspects of her life, from clothing to home ownership. She has been able to participate in choosing staff for her home and always poses insightful interview questions.

Kathy's parents say it is not easy for Kathy to confront difficult situations involving her own needs, but that FC enables her to discuss these incidents. When something appears to bother her, they get out the letter-board and ask her about it. They feel grateful to have an effective method that provides "a real relationship with her, with adult-to-adult interaction."

They wish Kathy had more people in her life who would be willing or able to use FC with her, because they understand its wide-ranging benefits. Heather believes, "Katherine continues to grow and change as she expresses herself and her desires. After FC, she carried herself differently. She acted as though she had more status. She would use the term, 'have more realness' and I think it meant that she was able to interact with the world and be more a part of it."

In Kathy's Own Words

"I am a lovely lady that has autism. I don't let the autism rule my life, but try to tone its effect on me by using facilitated communication to communicate. Autism is like living in a house without windows. FC helps me to make choices about what I want.

"Before I learned to use FC, I felt I was an idiot because I couldn't understand what was going on. I didn't have any idea what people around me were doing and I couldn't understand why nobody was like me.

"I didn't know that a total idiot was a malatroth. I knew that words had power before using FC, but I didn't know much about what that power was. Words were a kind of idiosyncratic noise, and I thought that the noises were quintessential in that they were familiar to me.

"I was very excited about people deciding to teach me FC although I thought that it wouldn't make much of a difference one way or another. I just decided that I was going to give it my best effort. I just thought that it might work. Well, nothing else had worked; why not give it a shot? I'll just give it one more try and see what happens and it worked for me. I just remember that I felt a sense of omnipotence when I was able to communicate with FC.

"Things are decidedly better now. People treat me much better since I learned FC. They listen to me more, and they are more open to my suggestions. Like I might suggest that I would like to go shopping. I have many more choices than I had before FC. I can decide when I want to go to bed. I can order my own meals at a restaurant. I can decide when I want to go home (on a trip or visit). And I have a couple of other things that I can do. I can decide when I want to have a friend over.

"My only disappointments were I just wanted people to have all the good things I was experiencing with FC. I had my brother in mind. Also, I hoped that I would be able to get a house. I had a condo but I hoped for a bigger yard. Now I do have a house and can knock around in the yard. I still would like you [Mom and Dad] to live there with me. Also, it is more difficult to get people to use FC. I don't mean that I don't have many disappointments. Disappointments are a fact of life and I have more than my share of them.

"I handle things much better knowing FC. I think in pictures and I can think in some words now. I decided very early on that I needed to become more fluent with words because I had to have a label for things. I still think mostly in pictures. I usually do see the picture and then find the words. I just have a good memory for words.

I like to dream about what it would be like to join the normal society and have a family of my own to raise and take care of. I need someone to take care of me, so that is a dream and not real. That makes me sad and I hope it helps others to understand that I who have a disability have the same desires as anyone else.

"I am very good at thinking and wanting to know about my world. I talk [using FC] with my roommate about the news in the paper several times a week. I have strong opinions but I like to talk with others so that I hear their side of the story. Sometimes I keep my opinion and sometimes I decide to change it. Changing my opinion is pretty rare, though.

"I find I am challenged by my initial hesitancy to reach out to others. I keep pushing and I ask others to help me, too, so that I have a broader number of people in my life. I find having friends hard and I am lonely. I feel sad because I think I miss out and people miss out in knowing me! I am an interesting person to know.

"I just want to say that I feel I am okay now. I feel that I have a purpose in life and I intend to make the most of it before I die. It is to show people that all disabled people are not stupid. "

They Couldn't Believe
I was so Smart

Doug Hahn

Snapshot

Doug was born in 1945 and started to use FC at age 48. He lived in a state residential facility for 30 years. In 1987, he moved into a community living home. When the agencies that supported Doug refused to use FC, Doug filed a lawsuit requesting communication services. Although he lost the lawsuit, FC has continued to play an important role in his family life with his two sisters, Judi and Barb. When their mother entered Hospice care, Doug was able to express his desire to be fully included in the process. Over the years, he has also been able to type information about his health and other medical concerns that has been helpful to his doctor. Doug continues to have a say in how he spends his money and where he goes on vacation.

About Doug

Born: 1945.   **Started FC:** 1993 at age 48.

Current Facilitators: Judi Barta (sister), Nicki Siemens (niece).

Access to FC: Four hours/week – only types for 10-15 minutes.

Living Situation: Group home with two other men.

Day Program: Adult Day Care Center.

Highest level of Independence: Forearm.

Secondary Participants: Judi Barta.

Doug's Criteria for Quality of Life

I like people.

I like to go places.

I like going on vacation.

Seven Things Doug Wants You to Know

I like vacations.

I like crafts.

I like Milestones (Day Program).

I like my sense of humor.

I like feeding birds.

I like my love of family.

I like my house.

Five Things Judi Wants You to Know About Doug

Family is very important to Doug.

He likes to be respected and doesn't like being put down or being talked down to.

He loves doing hobbies such as scrapbooking and painting crafts.

Doug has had swallowing problems develop in the past year and handles them fairly well.

Doug's ability to speak is not always accurate of everything he wants or needs to say. He verbalizes things that he doesn't mean, but it's like a tape playing in his head that he can't stop.

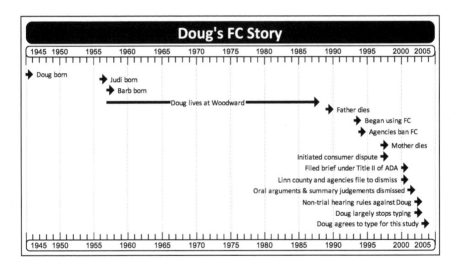

Doug's Story

Doug Hahn was born in 1945 and was 11 years old when his sister, Judi, was born. Today Judi is Doug's primary facilitator and co-guardian along with their youngest sister, Barb.

A family photo shows Judi and Barb, at 18 and nine months, respectively, sitting in Doug's lap. That peaceful scene was probably a rare moment. For autistic individuals, adolescence can be a particularly difficult time and Doug had a history of aggressive behavior, including hitting and head-butting. Judi says the only story she remembers hearing about Doug when they were children was that he threw his bed across the room.

With two small babies in the house, it would have been hard for the Hahns to manage a teen-age boy who was prone to aggression and growing bigger and stronger every day. In the 1950s, there were no community services or public school options for children with disabilities. As a result, Doug was placed in Woodward State Hospital-School where he lived for 30 years.

Conditions at the school must have been rough. Judi remembers that her father was always fighting with the school administrators about something and Doug's ear was permanently damaged from a beating he received while living there. To this day Doug will cry when a particular song triggers memories of Woodward.

In 1987, Doug moved into an eight-person group home in the community and later to a smaller home. Today, he shares a home with two other men.

Doug's parents were instrumental in starting the East Central Iowa ARC, which provides advocacy and services to individuals with development disabilities.

In 1993, after seeing an FC demonstration, Judi wondered if the process might benefit Doug. She had worked with individuals with disabilities and been aware of the tendency to underestimate their potential. She says, "It wasn't a big stretch for me to see Doug as facilitating and being able to type out his thoughts."

When given the opportunity to try FC, Doug was successful with several of the staff at his day program and his residential program. Judi attended a two-day workshop to learn the technique. Less than three months after she and Doug started to use FC with success, the day program and residential agencies banned it for all of their staff. Judi has been Doug's primary facilitator ever since.

FC quickly became a vital part of Doug's relationship with his family members, who began to see sides of Doug that they had never known. He expressed his affection for them and made choices about a variety of things, including his involvement in family gatherings. Everyone was surprised to learn these events were very important to him. He told them what he wanted for his birthday. When the siblings joined together to buy a gift for Mother's Day, Doug typed that he would like to make a contribution, too. When Judi asked him how much, he typed, "One dollar." (His unwillingness to spend his money has been consistent over the years.) Family members always teased each other about their quirks, so at last Doug became a full-fledged Hahn. They now could tease him for being a tightwad.

Soon after starting to use FC, Doug began to display uncharacteristic behavior. Historically, he had never initiated any activities except searching for food or gifts. Within a few months of using FC, Doug occasionally initiated a typing session with Judi. Over the years, he has used various methods to request FC. These include reaching for the word processor or carrying it to Judi, keeping his hand and pointer finger in typing position after Judi thought they were finished, and verbally asking to type by saying, "Do the computer" or "Alpha Smart, please."

By 1994, Doug typed information unknown to his facilitator that was verified as being correct. Once, he typed the exact date he was going to camp; another time, the name of the person who had just moved into his house.

Doug's typing has been a valuable asset in dealing with medical issues. In 1995, while visiting his sisters, he typed that he was feeling bad and that his chest hurt. In response, Judi and Barb took him to the emergency room, where physicians treated but did not admit him. On the following day, he continued to report that he did not feel well and was hospitalized after being diagnosed with a severe asthma attack.

In 1997, Doug's mother became very ill. After meeting with a hospice nurse to discuss their mother's condition, Doug typed, "I want to see her as much as I can." Without this information, the family might have tried to shield Doug from the day-to-day reality of the dying process. After visiting her in the nursing home, Doug would express to Judi what was on his mind. He was very sad about their mother's death, and also grappling with his fears thinking about Judi's and even his own death.

After his mother died, Doug was often agitated and experienced aggressive incidents. He started to verbalize that he wanted to go to heaven. Via FC, Judi asked pointed questions. In response he typed, "I am wanting to die. I would kill myself by taking medicine." As a result of this conversation, Doug was put on suicide precautions and provided a prescription for antidepressants along with counseling. When he did not improve and continued to type sentiments such as, "I feel sad all the time," the psychiatrist changed his medications and soon his mood and behavior improved. Without

FC, Judi and the professionals would not have fathomed the serious issues underlying his behavior.

FC had become central in Doug's interactions with his family and the evidence was mounting that his typing was not only reliable, but helpful in monitoring his health issues and understanding his behavior. It seemed clear that Doug should be able to communicate on a daily basis with the staff in his residence and day programs, not just when he visited Judi.

The agencies that operated Doug's programs would not allow the staff to use FC with him until he proved that he could read. Judi knew that many people who use FC disliked the idea of tests and were sometimes angry about being required to pass them. Despite this obstacle, she wanted to work with Doug on his test-taking skills. She set up index cards with written answers and so he could practice pointing independently to the correct card. Judi recalls, "Doug refused to practice and wouldn't do the test."

In 1997, during a family discussion, Doug typed, "I want you to tell them to stop keeping my mouth closed." Doug, Judi and Barb filed for a dispute resolution process with Linn County and two non-county agencies. The process was unsuccessful. In 2000, they filed a lawsuit against the agencies, contending that their failure to provide an adequate form of communication violated Doug's rights to participate in their services. The case rested on Section 504 of the Rehabilitation Act and Titles II and III of the Americans with Disabilities Act. In 2001, the county and the two agencies filed summary judgments to have the lawsuit dismissed. After hearing the evidence, the judge refused to dismiss.

The case went to court and the day of the final hearing coincided with a Halloween party given by Doug's day program. He has always loved Halloween and was looking forward to the party, but when Judi gave him a choice of going to court or attending the party, he chose to be in the courtroom. He sat quietly throughout the two-hour event. Judi saw this as a form of behavioral validation for his typing; he was exactly where he wanted to be.

In preparation for the trial, Judi assembled a meticulous portfolio documenting instances in which Doug's ability to type with her had been validated and/or helpful in daily life. The portfolio covered the years 1994-2001 and comprises 39 pages of supporting evidence including:

20 instances where Doug initiated FC.
18 instances when Doug typed information unknown to Judi but later confirmed to be correct.
88 instances where his typing helped resolve medical issues.

16 instances where the sisters were able to prevent or deal with
problematic behavior.
20 instances where Doug's behavior and typed messages matched.
25 instances where Doug's speech and typing matched.
10 instances where Doug's emotional response matched his typed
words.

The case went to trial in 2002. Doug's speech and language pathologist testified on his behalf, saying his typed communication had been shown to be more reliable than his verbal communication. Testimony was heard by other expert witnesses, a staff member (who testified at the risk of losing her job) and an individual with autism who types without physical support. The latter described the ways FC had changed her life and explained that her outer appearance did not reflect her real intelligence.

The trial judge did not rule in the Hahn family's favor. (In fact, his remarks created a Catch-22 situation in which he suggested that only people who can validate their FC can request the public funding they need to learn to use the method.)

FC was banned in all of Linn County and Doug's staff were told they could be fired for using it. Doug did not want to move to another county even though they might have been able to find a program where he would be allowed to use FC. He also declined to attempt another form of assistive communication.

Even though Doug does not type much anymore, he and Judi continue to use FC in many ways that have a positive impact on his quality of life. Doug continues to decide what he would like to do for vacations and how he will spend his money. In 2006, he asked to retire from the work activity program and is now very happy at Milestones, his "retirement" day-care program.

Doug's input continues to be invaluable for medical issues. Judi notes, "Even if Doug doesn't want to facilitate about anything else, he still facilitates with me about health issues and that is very important." Doug can tell Judi how he is feeling or if he is in pain and they can discuss upcoming procedures.

Doug's biggest changes since he began to use FC are in the ways in which he interacts with his family. Also, his speech has become more accurate and less echolalic. Now when Judi speaks to him, instead of echoing her words, he will sit quietly and listen.

Ironically, the agencies that fought against FC in the court case sometimes ask Judi to type with Doug to get information from him. One time, they asked her to find out why he hit a staff person. He told her that it was hot. When she reported what he had typed, they acknowledged that the air conditioning had been out that day. In 2008, Doug typed to Judi that a housemate was hitting him. As a result, the agency made immediate staffing changes to prevent further occurrences. Eventually the offender was moved to another house.

When Doug first started FC he would often tell his family he loved them. Judi says, "It meant so much. We just didn't think in those terms because he sometimes acts like he is just tolerating us. In spite of everything we went through, I wouldn't change him learning to facilitate because that's given our family access to Doug that we didn't have before. I've gotten to know him so much better than I ever would have and that has been really neat for me. We always knew that there was something more going on than what he was able to communicate, but we didn't realize the depths of it."

Today, Doug tires easily while typing. He has access to FC only when he visits Judi, and he usually types for less than ten minutes and typically gives only yes or no responses. Judi thinks he has accepted the fact that he is not allowed to use FC except during the few hours a week when he visits her.

Asking Doug to look back on the court case came with the risk of opening old wounds, but he wanted his story to be told. When Judi told him that we were glad he was willing to participate, he replied simply and graciously, "I am happy to help."

In Doug's Own Words

Judi: "List the things that are most important for a 'quality life' for you."
Doug: "I like people. I like to go places."

Judi: "List the things that changed for the better when you started using FC."
Doug: "I got to see more people than before. I put people to shame."

Judi: "What do you mean?"
Doug: "They couldn't believe I was so smart."

Judi: "List the things that got worse when you started to use FC."
Doug: "I had to stop doing FC."

Judi: "List the things that you thought would or should change when you started using FC, but didn't change."
Doug: "I am not able to really be my own man."

Judi: "Do you want to elaborate on that?"
Doug: "I have to do what other people tell me to."

Judi: "Do you experience yourself differently since you started using FC?"
Doug: "Yes."

Judi: "In what way?"
Doug: "I am feeling smarter."

Judi: "Do you think differently since you started using FC?"
Doug: "Yes."

Judi: "In what way?"
Doug: "I don't have to think as much before doing something."

I Just Don't Know Who I Am When I Can't Type

Daniel McConnell

Snapshot

Daniel was born in 1984. He began typing in 2007, at age 23. Daniel was an outgoing, happy baby and a precocious toddler who knew many words and spoke in complete sentences before he started to regress. He was diagnosed with autism when he was three. Daniel spent his childhood living with his parents in a rural area on Maui. When lack of adequate services and incidents of abuse occurred in his intermediate school, Daniel's parents enrolled him in a residential school in Wisconsin. He was again targeted for abuse so his parents moved him into a home in the community so he could attend his local high school. Daniel is currently studying to take his GED exam. Once he passes that, he hopes to go to college.

About Daniel

Born: 1984.   **Started FC:** 2007 at age 23.

Current Facilitators: Mindy (mother), Jody (SLP), Char (retired special education teacher), Sally (consultant), Paul & Jesse (home staff).

Access to FC: Approximately 4 hours per week with facilitators at different levels of ability.

Living Situation: Lives in his own home with a housemate and 24 hour staff support.

Day Program: Goodwill - newspaper delivery, volunteer church work, YMCA, piano lessons, sensory integration activities, GED study, and FC practice.

Highest level of Independence: Typed with touch at the shoulder with Rosemary Crossley.

Daniel's Criteria for Quality of Life

I want to live a life of my choosing.

I am happy when I can type.

I want the opportunity to pursue higher learning.

Have a girlfriend and opportunities to develop personal relationships.

Eat food that tastes good and is nourishing too.

Listen to music that I love.

I want to belong.

Have people around that care about me.

Five Things Daniel Wants You to Know

I am smart.

I want to go to college.

I want to help others.

My heart is full of love.

I want to live a life of importance.

Seven Things Mindy Wants You to Know About Daniel

Daniel has a deeply loving nature.

Daniel has resilience and strength despite suffering awareness of his condition and its effect on people and his life circumstances.

Daniel has courage to acknowledge his feelings and insight into them.

Daniel has insight into people and their character and purity of motivation.

People in contact with Daniel usually love him easily. People from years ago still think about him. He has had a profound impact on many lives.

Daniel is very smart and yearns to go to college and take a place in the world.

Daniel wants to help others learn about the value of typing to communicate.

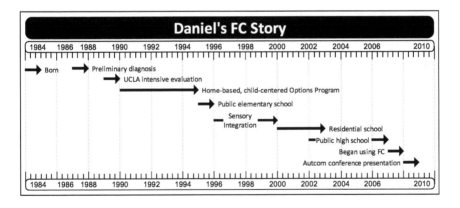

Daniel's Story

Daniel McConnell was born in Honolulu, Hawaii in 1984 to Mindy and John. He scored a maximum 10 on the Appearance, Pulse, Grimace, Activity, Respiration (APGAR) scale used to measure a newborn's overall health. The nurses called him the "The Star Baby" because he rarely cried and was the largest baby in the nursery.

Before being diagnosed with autism at age three, Daniel was happy, calm and engaged. He smiled a lot – especially at other infants – and connected easily with people. Mindy remembers the first time Daniel made eye contact with her, saying, "He looked directly into my eyes, stopped nursing and smiled his beautiful smile. It was 3:00 a.m. and one of the happiest moments of my life."

When Daniel was three months old, his father received a state judgeship and the family moved from Honolulu to Maui. They lived in an agricultural area above the pineapple fields. Every day before he left for work, John would carry Daniel down to the pasture to feed the cows and horses. Daniel loved the sensory experience of petting the big animals.

As a toddler, Daniel was tuned into his environment and learned new words at a rapid rate. At one year old, Daniel would point to items and enthusiastically name them. He memorized the words in many of his children's books, reciting them with perfect articulation as his parents turned the pages.

Despite Daniel's almost precocious development, seemingly insignificant events foreshadowed the future diagnosis. On the day he was born, as John carried Daniel to the newborn unit, he had a foreboding sense that something was not quite right. Months later, during a well-baby exam, a pediatrician noted that Daniel was unusually calm and quiet. It seemed strange, but the signs were subtle and the pediatrician let go of his concern.

In addition, throughout the early years, two baby sitters noted unusual behavior. They reported that Daniel ignored simple instructions and did not respond to them in typical ways.

During his second year, Daniel began losing interest in his toys and became more involved in repetitive activities and phrases. He would spend long periods flicking eucalyptus leaves in front of his eyes or running up and down the porch repeating words and phrases such as washing machine, weed whacker and vacuum. Mindy notes that during this time, he was fascinated with the sounds of machines.

When Daniel turned three, Mindy took Daniel to the store to pick out items for his birthday party. Daniel expressed no interest, instead lying down on the floor and rubbing his arms and legs along the surface of the carpet. At the party, while the other children played with Daniel's gifts, the birthday boy retreated to his parents' bedroom. Mindy found him looking at his favorite book, which was about a birthday party, and singing the words on each page. This odd behavior convinced his parents that it was time to talk to their pediatrician.

The doctor said Daniel might be mildly autistic or developmentally disabled. His parents were devastated. They consulted several other doctors who also suggested the diagnosis might be autism. Over the next two years, Daniel's words became less frequent and his sentences fell away completely. John and Mindy enrolled him in a 0-3 program and then in a special education preschool.

In 1989, when Daniel was five, the family traveled to UCLA for a 30-day intensive evaluation. They hoped to return to Maui with state-of-the-art programming recommendations and a productive course of action for Daniel's education. They received an official diagnosis, but not the treatment recommendations for which they yearned.

Mindy recalls her anguish, saying, "Hearing the diagnosis of autism is like being hit in the head and heart with a sledgehammer. The implications went against everything I felt and understood about Daniel in my heart. The biggest blow came with the full weight of the UCLA neuropsychiatric institute telling me not to beat my head against a brick wall; that there wasn't much I could do for Daniel. The label of autism was like a death knell. He was so much more than this label. Despite his great heart and spirit, he was being pushed down a black hole or put into a small box with no key. The label, while necessary for appropriate services, was somehow an assault on his personhood and I did not want to see the light in his eyes die out because of it."

Finding good professional help on Maui in the 1980s was difficult. Often a good therapist would work with Daniel for a while, then leave the island due to the high cost of living.

Mindy continually searched for therapies. Over the course of Daniel's childhood, they pursued Sensory Integration Therapy, Lovaas' Applied Behavioral Analysis/UCLA Discrete Trial Teaching Program, Judevine, Rebus Reading, Lindamood-Bell Learning, Craniosacral, Jin Shin and Dry Pants toilet training.

In first grade, the special education teacher at Daniel's school implemented the UCLA Discrete Trial Program. One day, Mindy parked outside the window of the classroom and heard Daniel repeatedly hitting his head in frustration. The aide was screaming at him and put him in time out in a bathroom stall. Mindy says, "I realized the school didn't have the resources it needed to help Daniel." In desperation, Mindy continued her search and eventually enrolled Daniel in the Son-Rise program at Kaufman's Options Institute in Massachusetts. It seemed there was nothing to lose.

After their trip to Massachusetts, Mindy established a home-schooling program based on the child-centered, positive approach presented at Options. Over four years, nearly 60 volunteers worked with Daniel in two-hour shifts, seven days a week for eight hours a day.

Mindy recalls, "I had a two-way mirror and could watch Daniel interacting with dedicated, loving volunteers. Daniel made steady progress away from his insular world, but he was not able to regain the recognizable speech that was lost. I am convinced that the love and belief in all possibilities offered by those volunteers preserved Daniel's spirit, loving relatedness and trust in most people. Years later, a teacher in California asked me if Daniel had been exposed to the Options program because, he said, he rarely saw children with autism exhibit such a sweet, happy nature."

After three years of home schooling, Mindy knew a professional teacher was needed, so she enrolled Daniel in fourth grade at his neighborhood school. The first day, when a group of students greeted him, Daniel gently put his hand on the shoulder of a classmate from preschool whom he had not seen for years.

Daniel's fourth-grade teacher worked with him and began to achieve results. In fifth grade, the principal organized a "Circle of Friends" who made the year a positive experience for Daniel. By sixth grade, a new principal was installed and all previous supports were removed. Mindy says she has noted over the years that when an institution cannot or does not want to provide services, they use the excuse that Daniel is not cognitively able to benefit.

In 1996, the McConnells pursued due process to obtain the services Daniel needed. They also were part of a class action lawsuit on behalf of special needs students in Hawaii. As part of the lawsuit, Daniel received a psychological evaluation that placed his cognitive development at an eight-year-old level. This test showed unequivocally that Daniel was capable of learning and it became a deciding factor in bringing educational resources for children with autism to the state of Hawaii.

One outcome from the legal ruling ordered the school district to fund educational and therapeutic services for Daniel in his home. During that time he had a wonderful teacher, Heather, who taught Daniel the Picture Exchange System (PECS) to meet his basic communication needs. In 1997, the family had traveled to San Diego for a comprehensive occupational therapy (OT) evaluation. They recommended for daily therapy sessions to address Daniel's difficulties with sensory regulation and modulation. Over the course of three years, the program had a significant impact on his attention skills.

Eventually, the autism center was established at the school and Daniel joined the other students there. Before long, his beloved teacher left the island and the needs of so many children on the spectrum began to overwhelm the staff. The school had contracted to use Applied Behavioral Analysis (ABA) but Daniel was never able to achieve the 90% success rate that ABA demands.

Failure to achieve the 90% success rate implied that Daniel was incapable of learning and as Mindy notes, "It became clear that Daniel, a non-verbal child with more involved sensory issues, would take a backseat because the autism consultants did not consider him a likely candidate for success. They resisted teaching him more PECS because they did not believe he could master more than three or four pictures."

Things continued to deteriorate for Daniel at the school and eventually a whistleblower notified Mindy and John that their son had become the target of abuse. In response, the school district agreed to pay the costs to send Daniel to a residential school on the mainland.

Mindy and John enrolled Daniel in a school in Wisconsin. Mindy believes, "Daniel was taken from his community because his community refused to provide an adequate education. This was not unusual in Hawaii, which opted to break up families rather than provide the resources necessary in community schools."

Daniel was in his new residential school for only one year before budget cuts led to weakened programs and overcrowding. Daniel again became the target of abuse, this time from teenagers. The McConnells removed Daniel from the school and bought a house for him so he could live in the community and attend the local public high school. On the first day, Mindy remembered how he almost ran to the school bus because he was so excited to go to a new school.

The school focused on activities of daily living and vocational skills, using PECS for communication, and it provided a good overall environment for Daniel. As Mindy described it, "The classroom was well-organized, the atmosphere was positive and the carpeted halls were quiet."

Daniel was integrated into regular education for art and music, which he particularly enjoyed. In his final year, he and the other special education students attended prom. They practiced dancing and walking down the promenade and they chose their clothes like all the other students. Mindy remembers how cooperative Daniel was while trying on tuxedos and how deliberate he was in choosing a red vest to go with his black tuxedo. On prom night, a National Honor Society student walked with Daniel down the promenade. Mindy says, "That Daniel performed this simple rite of passage that other young people take for granted brought us all so much happiness."

Today, John continues his work on Maui while Mindy travels back and forth between the two homes. When he can, John travels to Wisconsin so the family can be together there. Periodically, Daniel visits Maui where he spends time at the beach and in the company of his favorite eucalyptus trees.

Mindy had been following the controversy surrounding FC for years but she had not been ready to try it until a case manager gave her a copy of *Paid for the Privilege,* by Dan Reed. Remembering that time Mindy wrote, "I spent many years exposing Daniel to words coupled with photographs and spelling activities so that he would have the reading skills he needed when we took on the controversy of facilitated communication. This was not easy since the educational system did not support the idea that Daniel had the cognitive ability to read. The pain of those experiences left scars that Daniel's words are slowly healing."

In 2007, Mindy and Daniel went to Madison for an FC evaluation. Daniel typed two short sentences that day. The second sentence was, "I'm too excited," after which he jumped up and left the room.

In 2008, Daniel and his family attended a conference in Syracuse, New York. At the conference, Daniel met privately with Rosemary Crossley, the innovator of FC and the world's most skilled facilitator. With her, he typed the names of the capital cities of England, France and Italy with only a touch on the shoulder. He continues to work on his typing skills and looks toward typing independently someday.

Today, Daniel pursues his dream of furthering his education. He receives support from a community college as he prepares to take his GED test. Since he cannot sit quietly in a classroom for an extended time, Daniel and his staff work on a self-study program under the guidance of a college teacher.

Daniel has participated in panel presentations at autism conferences and hopes someday to be able to help others who do not speak. He has become an active member of his program planning team, in which he expresses his desires for future goals and his criteria for a good housemate. He also has been able to advise staff about how they can better help him with his daily life.

Mindy and John are still processing their feelings about the changes that FC has brought into their lives. Mindy says, "FC changed our lives and terms of engagement in ways I cannot yet fully fathom. Our non-verbal conversation had become so automatic and refined. My own slow ability to learn to type with Daniel seemed a step backwards, tedious to orchestrate yet also liberating and empowering."

She confides, "Years ago, I heard a parent say that once his son gained words, he was put in the position of having to respond to so many newly stated wishes and dreams. Now I understand the fear, fatigue, mental and emotional anguish expressed by that father. It is overwhelming to be thrust rather than move gently into knowing a growing child's wishes and changing dreams. There is a lot of catching up to do."

Mindy notes, "FC leaves behind a paradigm the professional autism world is not ready to relinquish. But when I feel Daniel's movement at the hand, then the wrist, then the arm getting lighter and lighter and his own rhythm becomes palpable, I know what I have experienced first-hand to be true."

In Daniel's Own Words

"The topic of neurodiversity is so big I hardly know where to begin. Let me start by saying that it is not easy to tell how my neuro is diverse when it is the only neuro that I know. I think it is telling that I cannot talk. My mouth is a foreign country far beyond the borders of my limited body control. It is not really even on the map. But it makes noise I can wave to from afar.

"There are so many thoughts that need to be spoken in typing. My mind moves like lightning and my body like a cement truck. Yet, it is all I can do to stay sitting. My mind is like a freight train and I can't make it slow down and stop in time. I wish it was not so persistent in its moving.

"You might think I am brave but I am scared of everything, even words. But it is my only hope for a life of importance. Being brave is the hardest thing in the world, but also it is the most important. This is hard because telling the truth makes you show your inside thoughts that might make others unhappy or sad or mad or even possibly happy. That is a scary thought. 'Not I, said the King when they asked about the words on the walls.' This story is about how words can help or hurt you depending on how they are used and how they are received, too. They can go either way but you might not know or be able to control them once they are out of the bag, so to speak.

"Autism is not a condition, it is a way of life. I remember everything from the day I was born. Telling my story does not mean telling my whole life. It means telling my life with words. When I was little, I taught myself to read because I needed to learn things about the world. I started reading everything in sight and eventually it started to make sense to me. That was when I knew I would be OK. Having things to think about saved me.

"I learned to read by studying the patterns of language. I only understood a little at first but then soon the understanding grew to include more and more letters and words. My understanding grew fast once I got a good supply of letters under my belt. Then I would rejoice with each new victory. It was very exciting in those days. But my excitement would have been unbearable if I had known that someday I would be using my new knowledge to write my own thoughts and feelings. Never did I imagine such a thing as this. I understand that being able to spell is the keys to the kingdom. It is the most important skill next to arm control, which is most difficult for me.

"I made up thought problems in my head and then set about to answer them to my own satisfaction. I had very high standards for the answers so sometimes it took a long time to finish a problem. Here are some: Why do words and letters mean so much to people and why do they think about things in words instead of in pictures? Why did my life seem happier once I knew how to read and think in words instead of making sense of the world in pictures?

"My mind is moving at warp speed all the time. It needs a lot to keep it busy. It is like a hungry elephant that can never get enough to eat. The mind is a terrible thing to waste. More food for the mind and less for the body. My mind cannot get too full. It empties itself out as needed. If important information comes along, other less important stuff will make room by moving to another area so I can pay attention to the new.

"I think about ideas all the time. I am never without an idea in my head. They keep me from going crazy. I love to think about how things work and about how people are and about God and the meaning of life and about the reasons why I'm this way and about love and how it can save me. I think I'm here for a reason. I also think about why love circles around some people and not others. Yes, I do feel the love that circles around me.

"Feelings are my behavioral downfall. Imagine a body that does not obey coupled with not being able to talk. You think I'm making these sounds on purpose, but I'm not really in control of them. It is not like I intend to scream, but the noise just comes out instead of coming out in words. I know it is just too hard to listen to but I just need to hear myself sometimes. I think it makes me appear retarded so I would prefer not to do it. I am always doing my best. Listen to my heart and not my body. It is all I can do to stay sitting. I'm really interested in learning more about instructing my body to do what I want.

"My heart is so full that it feels like it could burst open at any time day or night. Sometimes I worry that it is too full and if it gets any fuller, I will just implode. It is a heavy heart that loves this world too much. It is the heart of a man who is in love with everything and everyone on this earth. It is the heart of a man who is all love but who knows that there is no room for such a heart in this world. It will only be trampled and stomped on if I let it show. It grows heavy with love that is not given out. I want to do math. That will challenge my brain instead of my heart.

"I think words cannot hold so much emotion but I'm learning that they can and I find it to be a miracle of unbelievable proportions. Not that it gets any easier to have emotions but it does save on wear and tear on the body.

"I see the world not only with my eyes but also with my heart. It is beautiful beyond belief. Beauty becomes marred by human touch. Hopefully humans will realize their folly before it is too late. Never in this life did I think I would be telling others how I see the beauty! Everything sparkles with the love it holds inside. I see only the sparkles. Love makes me know it will all be OK but listening to the news casts doubt. But I think if I lose faith in love I will go crazy so I spend my days looking for sparkles. I see them in everything. But sometimes I can't see it and that is when I get scared.

"I want to talk more about how beauty in the world is trampled. This is not easy to say, but human endeavors kill beauty. They just refuse to let anything stand in their way, even if it means losing the beauty. They think what they are doing or what they want is all that matters. They lose the big picture. I might not have the biggest of all pictures but I rarely get lost in my human endeavors.

"I have love for everyone even people I don't happen to like. I hope that I can convey how the love happens in spite of my own feelings. It happens to me not from me. I think I am just a leaf blowing in the winds of some great love that has my number. Love has my number but mind you, I'm not complaining. I just want people to know that it's not necessarily because I'm such a good person. It is neither to my credit nor to my blame that this love moves in me. I hope that people can believe this because it will not be good if they think I'm some kind of saint or something. It can be scary because it is so big. When I was little, it scared me more than it does now. I want people to feel the love that is there for them. If they open their hearts to it, it will flow in and fill all the corners where maybe there has never been love before. Sometimes there are dark and empty corners.

"I just don't know who I am when I can't type. I'm not myself when I can't tell what I think and feel. When I'm typing, I am more involved in the world. I'm always working to be better at learning to tell my thoughts and feelings that are always running around loose in my brain. Please remember that I always have many thoughts and feelings at one time. Telling my thoughts and feelings makes them and me more real. I grieve for the others who do not have typing to help them say the things that are in their hearts. I remember how it was before typing set me free. I could not understand why everyone could talk but me. So now I still can't talk but I have a voice anyway. Who could have dreamed such a thing?"

Getting Rid of My Autistic Barrier

Tom Page

Snapshot

Tom was born in 1957 and began using FC in 1993 at age 36. Prior to that, he had earned a reputation for his unpredictable and violent behavior. In 1996, Tom started an intensive program of therapy with five different practitioners. During that time, he was able to provide the therapists with information about the kinds of treatment he needed. He also gave them valuable feedback on the effects their work had on his nervous system. Tom published his first book in 2002 and expects to publish his second book in 2010. Today he is a fully included member of his community. His current staff are in disbelief when they hear about his violent past. Tom attributes these remarkable changes to his ongoing therapy and his ability to communicate via FC.

About Tom

Born: 1957.   **Started FC:** 1993 at age 36.

Current Facilitators: Jo and Wally Page (parents) plus 7 others at a conversational level and 4 others at short-answer level. Facilitators include staff, professionals and friends.

Participants: Jo and Wally Page, Lauren Kruzshak (SLP).

Access to FC: 2-3 hours per day on weekdays, 24 hours per day on weekends.

Living Situation: Group home – stays with parents every other weekend.

Day Program: Sheltered work program with several jobs (paid and volunteer) in community.

Highest level of Independence: Independent for Yes/No questions and some open conversation.

Equipment: Letterboard, computer with text-to-voice output.

Tom's Criteria for Quality of Life

Compassionate staff.

Out in community.

Learn new skills.

Church.

Vacations.

Vote.

Purposeful work – earn money.

Charitable service.

FC conversational level – poetry –writing.

Take classes.

Treated as a person like everyone else.

Thoughts and ideas accepted on equal par.

Unconditional Love

Unconditional love is
touching, talking, hugging
After my sad rage is over

I am so frightened it
won't be there someday.

Please be forgiving until
I can control this monster
inside of me.

Five Things Tom Wants You to Know

I am very sensitive, perceptive, unbelievably intuitive, and care about others' feelings.

My improved sensory system is allowing me to become more flexible and initiate more things.

People are no longer so afraid of me and want to work with me. This allows me to be a better contributor to society.

I like the feeling that I am influencing others' feelings and beliefs.

I feel I am dong God's work and getting his message out. This is part of my mission.

Five Things Tom's Parents Want You to Know About Him

Tom's perception time is near normal now and is nearly always reliable both via FC and verbal responses. He is starting to initiate both communication modes.

He can and wants to set goals for himself (and us). He remembers them and works hard for achievement.

His remarkable improvement in overcoming his aggression has made him more comfortable and trustworthy with staff who now want to go places with him. It also allows us to take some relaxed vacation time. This has been and still is hard work for him.

Tom is losing many of the perceived traits of autism. For example he often has very appropriate facial expressions and often laughs at funny things. Many times he gives good eye contact. He has a genuine concern for others. He interacts socially and he can alter his routine most of the time.

A description of Tom would now include such things as intelligent, curious, pleasant personality, affectionate (to some), wise. He has a number of people (including professionals) who seek his advice on personal affairs.

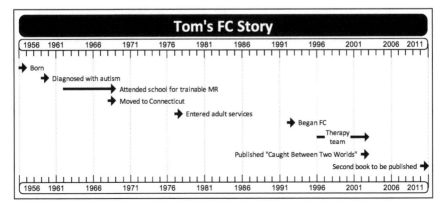

Tom's Story

Tom Page was born in 1957 to Jo and Wally. He was diagnosed with autism at the age of two and one-half. What little speech he exhibited was primarily echolalic (repeating words spoken by another).

Professionals advised Tom's parents to put him in an institution and forget about him. Jo and Wally ignored their advice and decided to give Tom and his older sister, Sally, a life that was as close to normal as possible.

Beginning with the initial diagnosis, Tom consistently tested in the profound range of what was then called mental retardation and now is referred to as cognitive disability. The range translated to the intelligence of a child at age two or three.

For years, even into adulthood, in accordance with that judgment and despite glimmers of intelligence, everyone talked to and treated Tom as if he were in fact two years old. Nevertheless, Jo recalls, "On occasion and out of the blue, Tom would do something or look intelligent in a way that was beyond his assumed capabilities. We were mildly puzzled. Then his behavior deteriorated and our lives became more complicated."

The Pages planned vacations and family events around Tom's ability to participate. They avoided activities that might set him off, causing him to have an aggressive outburst or retreat into his own world. When he lost control, Jo and Wally would take turns taking him away from the event.

Tom remembers the procedure well. "Going out in public was the best part of my day. I wanted to mix with the world, but it was chancy. We went many places if my behavior was good. If my behavior interfered with others, I would be taken out. I know what the outside of many places look like. Parking lots are my specialty."

Tom spent six years in a school for student with the label "Trainable Mentally Retarded." When he was 12, the family moved to Connecticut so that Tom could receive better services. They enrolled him in a state-of-the-art specialized school, where Jo served as a teacher. The school's philosophy reflected the thinking of the times. Tom recalls, "We were treated as a product to be manufactured. The people in charge tried to design us to their specifications. They discussed their product, which was us, right in front of us. It was a hurtful state of affairs."

As Tom got older, his aggressive outbursts, screaming and other negative behavior became much more difficult to manage. His violence was virtually impossible to predict or stop. Tom says, "As I got older, the screaming was still there and I could hit harder. What was a nuisance before became a danger. What had been a fly became a mosquito, then a lion, until I was a

6'2" elephant that weighted over 200 pounds. When I got mad, people became frightened of me."

Tom had outbursts on average once a week and sometimes as often as every other day. They would go on for hours. Often, the worst behavior occurred when Wally was gone or when Jo drove Tom to school. At home, Tom put so many holes in the walls that Wally installed solid wood behind the plasterboard in the places that Tom frequently hit. Jo says, "We didn't understand why the violence happened. Traditional methods of dealing with it had no effect."

As Tom got older, he developed more violent ways of hitting. Often, Wally had to fight with Tom to keep him from hurting others. Wally confides, "When I turned 60, my constant worry was that Tom would continue getting stronger while I became weaker."

The violence affected Tom as well. He now reflects, "I hated the violence, but my frustrations would get the best of me. I had little means to express myself. It was not my wish to strike people, but I could not control myself."

Although the Page siblings had been very close as young children, Tom's frequent violent outbursts, along with his growing size and strength, strained his relationship with Sally. They tried several behavioral interventions but Jo noted that none of them were effective. Jo and Wally agreed they did not want to give Tom psychotropic medications for his behavior.

At age 21, Tom entered a vocational day program. Jo and Wally developed a group home in which Jo served as director. When he was 26, Tom moved out of his parents' home and into the group residence. He continued attending the vocational day program.

Tom's physical size and violent outbursts earned him a reputation at both locales. Staff members viewed him as unpredictable and dangerous. The vocational program offered assembly tasks, but Tom's inability to initiate movement was so severe that it precluded him from functioning independently.

A vocational staff member, Lauren, recounts, "Tom sat around all day because there wasn't a job that he could do. Everybody was afraid of him, so giving him a physical prompt was something that people did not do readily. They didn't want to create any problems that would cause safety issues, not only for Tom, but for the other clients."

In 1993, when he was 36, Tom was introduced to FC and a paradigm shift occurred. He declares, "A miracle happened. It was magic."

Despite her fear of being in close proximity to Tom in a small enclosed space, Lauren agreed to try FC at the suggestion of her supervisor, who suspected that Tom might have untapped potential. Lauren was amazed that Tom seemed to tolerate a procedure in which she sat close to him, asked him questions and positioned his hand above the keyboard. Sensing the push of his hand as he moved toward the letters to answer her questions, Lauren realized that Tom's difficulties might be due not to cognitive deficits, but motor issues. As this idea took hold for Lauren, she started to see Tom in a whole new light.

During this time, another staff member, Mary, was enjoying success using FC with residents in Tom's group home. Despite Jo and Wally's ongoing skepticism, they gave Mary permission to try FC with Tom and even traveled to Maine to attend an FC workshop. They remained unconvinced. Jo explains, "I had been involved in teaching autistic people for years, and I couldn't imagine what they were saying was accurate. A lot of parents, our age, had been through so much we had become skeptical of everything."

During his FC sessions with Lauren, Tom gained a familiarity with the keyboard and an understanding of the process, so when Mary tried typing with Tom, everything came together very quickly for him. He recalls, "When she took my hand, the computer screen in my head lit up. Words and phrases came tumbling out. It was as if I were in a daze. It probably was one of the most emotional experiences I ever had."

After reviewing the initial session transcripts, Jo and Wally remained unconvinced. Eventually however, they decided to give FC a try. Jo experienced success quickly. Although it took Wally longer to learn to be a facilitator, he believed that Tom was doing the typing and he immediately changed his perspective: "I began treating Tom differently, so life started changing right away."

Considering the possibility that Tom's behavioral challenges were caused by neurological sensory and movement differences, his parents sought therapeutic modalities to address these issues. In 1996, they assembled a therapy team of five professionals. Now that Tom could communicate, he was able to provide feedback during the treatment sessions. The therapy became a two-way conversation between Tom and his practitioners.

This dialogue was pivotal to the therapies. Tom recalls, "The world was now starting to move with Tom, not making Tom move with the world."

The practitioners immediately understood how valuable Tom's feedback could be during his treatment sessions. Lauren states, "FC gave the other therapies entry into Tom's life. His ability to communicate made those therapies so effective. Tom gave wonderful feedback."

Over the next six years with his therapy team, Tom showed improvement in many areas of his life: motor function, sensory processing, behavior, attitude and engagement. Tom notes, "It is difficult to separate what was causing my improvements. All of the therapies contributed on their own merit, but also integrated into each other's as well."

In 2002, Tom published his first book, *Caught between Two Worlds: My Autistic Dilemma.* The two worlds to which Tom refers are his autistic world and the world he calls "your world," meaning the outer world of everyday physical reality. Tom's autistic world was his "comfort zone" where he found relief from the discomfort of the external world. As he says, "I really didn't like your world very much. It was filled with all the things that assaulted my inner being."

Tom decided to "get rid of the autism barrier as much as possible." He considers this one of the most important decisions of his life. His book tells the story of his journey. He relates how, through conversations with his parents and his therapy team, he understood how his sensory issues, the inability to express himself, along with the humiliation of being talked about as if he were not there and seen as severely retarded, took their toll on his well-being. In addition to Tom's incisive writing about his process, his parents and therapy team members add their perspectives and commentaries.

Soon after his book was published, Tom was involved in a serious auto accident while his parents were away on vacation and his favorite staff member had moved away. After several years of no behavioral incidents, the impact of these three simultaneous stresses resulted in a violent episode. Staff members who had not known Tom previously were stunned. Their disbelief that Tom could be so violent highlighted how much he had changed.

Today, as a result of therapy and self-expression, Tom's violence and behavioral outbursts have completely subsided. He gets along very well with staff at his group home. Jo says communication is the key: "If there's something wrong and Tom needs to talk about it, he'll type out what the problem is and we can fix it most of the time. Some of the time you can't, but you can explain to him why and you know that he understands."

In many respects, Tom has fulfilled his quest to get rid of his autism barrier. He is a fully included member of his family and the community. He has won awards for his poetry and annually sends Christmas cards with a new poem that he has written about the meaning of the holiday. He has attended one college-level poetry writing course and hopes to continue with this curriculum. He has given numerous presentations, at conferences and at his church, and won an award for his volunteer work. He continues writing and is finalizing a second book.

Tom believes, "I am considered disabled only by people who can't get beyond the outward signs of autism and into my head and feelings. That can be difficult, but the reward will be to find a person who is ready to relate and share the joys and sadness of life with you."

In Tom's Own Words

"In the beginning of my life, I was a frightened little boy. I remember being confused most of the time. People were doing things for no reason that I could make out. I seemed to be doing things for no reason they could make out. Neither could understand each other's actions. Their mouths moved and made sounds that made little sense to me. The sounds went too fast and the volume was inconsistent especially when they were directed at me. I was quite hyper when I was young and could do many physical things although most were not understandable to others, but they had to be important to me! For example, I would walk across the top of the swing set bar or roller skate on top of the picnic table or the neighbor's air conditioner. I was taken to parks and on trips with me doing my thing beside them doing their thing. I did not become sedentary until I was a teenager and I was not unhappy much of the time but lived mainly in my own little world.

"My speech never developed beyond echolalia as a child, to short words and phrases as I grew up. Not even those were very reliable. Therefore, I had no means to express myself in your acceptable terms.

"Things started to get worse as I aged. I was treated as I appeared. No choice in anything, just being herded through life like cattle. I was shuffled around without knowing what I was going to do or where I was going. No one thought I understood. I did pick up on some things but nothing was discussed with me. If it was, it didn't sink in very often.

"At home we talked about things but I had no way or no chance for an opinion. When I became frustrated or couldn't stand what was taking place that resulted in a behavior problem. Sometimes,(most of the time) I just retreated into my autistic world. In those days, I had few choices. The decisions were pretty well made for me.

"People were nice enough to me; they just didn't think anyone was home. My receptive language and understanding were developing and I got my feelings hurt very easily. I did not have sophisticated thinking in those days, but I had sophisticated feelings! Since people's perception of me was what it was, they talked about me and my family in front of me all the time. How hurtful that is especially when you can't talk or interact back.

"It was terrible when I became a teenager because I was big and strong. I became dangerous enough, that outside of my parents, I was left to sit and vegetate most of the time. I have seen the inside of many time-out rooms and know all about parking lots and posey restraints. What had been a fly became a mosquito, then a lion, and eventually an elephant. When I was good, I was like the circus elephant, but when I was frustrated, look out. The moral of story is: try to solve as many of your problems as you can before that fly becomes an elephant.

"I sat glued to a chair most of the time at my day program. I only showed initiative mostly when I got upset. At home, I continued to do my "things" and rock away. My sensory system was deteriorating in many areas. I was confused and upset with no means to express myself. I just existed with no purpose in life. This was me pretty much until age 36.

"At age 36, a miracle happened, as far as I was concerned. It is a long story, but FC was introduced in my life. That started the ball rolling. My first experience at FC was like opening a floodgate. Even in my middle-aged state, my whole world opened up. It was no miracle like a bolt of lightening, but steady, and it took quite a while before I became proficient and conversational. About the same time, my therapeutic sensory work started big time.

"It is hard to tell what helped in what areas, but my new-found skill of FC contributed to me giving good feed back to the therapists and doctors who worked with me. There were many things wrong with me. I needed help—my sensory system was a real mess. In my early life, they knew some of my problems and they tried to help with a few of them.

"One of the biggest gifts of FC was my ability to describe to the professionals how my senses really work. It is one of my greatest achievements outside of communication with loved ones. They have been able to tailor my sensory programs to fit my problems. Many of them were surprised by some problems they had not suspected. They tell me I am calling many of the shots, which contributes to my progress.

"My sensory system is becoming better integrated. It is not at all perfect but making progress considering my age. Occasionally, I still have sensory overload, but now usually I am in control. To me, my progress is like a gazelle, but to you, the observer, it is probably more like a snail.

"I attribute most of the following to both FC and sensory work. My processing time is nearly normal. I can now be reasoned with and think things through. I now set goals for myself. I wonder about others' lives and what they are doing. I feel I am creative and have a mission to accomplish. I can make a commitment and that drives my life. Sometimes I now talk in meaningful words and phrases on my own. I am more flexible and have more initiative. All of these now still vary from day to day, sometimes hour to hour.

"I also have more power and control over my life. No one ever knew how I felt without guessing. I appreciate the ones who tried hard to find out but now I am sure everyone feels more secure with the answers. It is the thing that really changed things. Most people are not afraid of me anymore.

"The result has been that I now make choices of what clothes I wear, sometimes what I eat, and what I watch on TV. I get to pick out my clothes in a store. I attend church frequently and my writings have been included in some sermons. I have more control over my body and can usually make it do what is needed. I get to go to many interesting places because people now know I like to go to them. We share opinions and have conversations just like 'normal people.'

"People do treat me differently, even non-believers. Yes, I'm now usually considered a real person. Most people, in the community, are friendly especially clerks, waitresses, librarians etc. It has been a surprise to me that doctors and nurses become more interested in my opinions as they get to know me and I have proven my validity. They respect my wishes usually (being big as I am doesn't hurt either).

"I can now be reasoned with and if I don't get my own way I can be made to understand, usually. I understand the problem even though I sometimes still get stuck on it for awhile. (like being unable to change my clothes or get out of the car). This happens when I am out of my normal routine.

"Now I have a say in my everyday affairs. Most choices and decisions in what I do are mine. There is a downside, too. I am scared a lot. I have more normal feelings now, I think, and need help to deal with them. I worry more about the future and my parents dying. What will happen if FC is taken away? Things like that.

"It is a constant worry that I will not be allowed to use FC. There are forces that want it stopped. It really bothers me to hear how TV programs and some so-called big shots are trying to hurt me and my kind by calling us fakes. They have not spent enough time with us individually to understand that it works and is truly our form of liberty.

"I now view myself as a person of worth and think I have a future ahead of me, if I can cut it with new facilitators. When the ones I have are gone and if I haven't achieved total independence, I don't even want to think about it.

When life became too painful, I had the gift of autism and the ability to kick into my autistic zone. This is a pleasant place to be. Nothing and no one can hurt you there. It is shelter and euphoric. I have committed myself to losing autism as much as possible and now have a lot of difficulty retreating back into my autistic comfort zone. It leaves me in the middle with no place to go when things get really bad. I don't think I am ready to do without it. Fear takes over. However, as I keep developing, it is becoming easier to do without and hopefully someday I won't feel the need for it at all.

"I have plenty of motivation and determination which translate into goals and plans for the future. I like the new me. I now think outside myself. I now feel part of the world with goals and aspirations. I want to know what others think and why. It is a world of many interesting things and I want to taste as many as I can. It is my view that I'm a viable part of it now. I want to stay that way. I am included in ordinary life conversation with real, so-called, normal people. The words 'What do you think about that, Tom?' have become the most important words of my life.

"FC is only one means of communication but it is my best and it changed my life. It was a major factor in bringing me out of my self-centeredness. I am more aware of other people and worry about them and their problems. I have difficulty in seeing others fail and I feel I could and should help them. It is not always possible.

"I was egocentric. I did think outside myself on an egocentric level but it always concerned me in the mix of things. Now I think about many things in this world. I love books and newspapers. I am interested in current events, history, sports, music, talk radio, traveling. The list goes on and on. I love to enter conversations either listening or participating. It is a wonderful place, this world.

"Most of all, I want to be treated as a person like everyone else, not tolerated or felt sorry for. I want my thoughts and ideas to be accepted on an equal par with others. I know no one has everything, but I don't want to live out my life with only memories and wonder what my life might have been."

With Language Have I Begun Truly to Live

Nick Pentzell

Snapshot

Nick was born in 1978 and started to use FC when he was 13. Within a few years, Nick had over 20 facilitators and was writing poetry and essays. In addition, he filled countless notebooks processing his feelings and gaining insight into his own behavior. Today, Nick is in college studying communication in non-human primates. In addition to college, Nick has written a screenplay for an award-winning video, participates in state politics, and gives presentations at conferences, universities, and local service agencies. He is currently vice-president of The Lonesome Doves—a political action and social group of FC users.

About Nick

Born: 1978.   **Started FC:** 1991 at age 13.

Current Facilitators: Gwen (stepmother), five direct-care staff, agency supervisor, supports coordinator, and several friends.

Access to FC: 24 hours every day.

Living Situation: Shares home with Gwen, soon to be in own apartment on first floor of home.

Primary Activity: College courses with educational assistant or Gwen.

Highest level of Independence: Forearm or elbow occasionally – mostly at wrist or hand. Facilitated handwriting, art, and music.

Secondary Participant: Gwen Waltz.

Nick's Criteria for Quality of Life

I want to live a life where I am treated as equal to neurotypicals; I want my *diffability* to be respected by others, just as I respect others' differences.

I want to get an undergraduate and graduate-school education.

I want to have a professional career.

I want to live independently, in my own home, with people I choose and support staff I control.

I want to have intellectual stimulation on a daily basis – I want to express myself creatively.

I want to contribute to my community, to perform meaningful work, and to make other people's lives better.

I want to make friends, beyond just my support staff.

I want to have romantic and sexual relationships; I would love to be married.

I DON'T WANT to be serviced as a disabled person who needs remedial aid. I

CANNOT be controlled by people who don't recognize and support my intelligence.

I MUST have programs that are structured around MY communication methods and that are accommodated to my sensory and neurological differences.

Waves

Tongue in knots, tied by a sailor of troubled seas,
My words remain shipwrecked in soundless isolation.
Thoughts wash up and I sift through brackish ideas
In search of a conch.

Found, in my hand it makes music,
Blown long and hard.
Across oceans it sounds:
A siren's song,
The aching cry of a gull,
Windswept, windward,
Misapprehended far from its source.

On the beach I loose
Calypso peals from the shell,
Splashing through the soul like a breaker
Pounding pores in salt spray,
A sound that penetrates and heals
Before it ebbs away to silence.

Published in *Pegasus*, Spring 2003, Volume 36

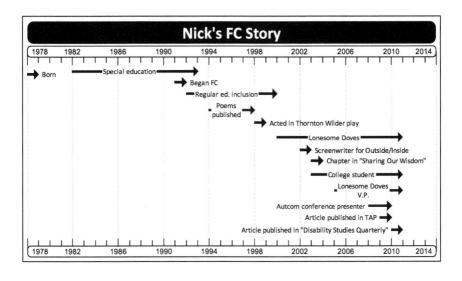

Nick's Story

As a teenager in 1997, Nick Pentzell wrote, "The day I was born was in a way a horrible day. I was born with a condition known as autism." Nick was born in 1978 and lived with his father, mother and three brothers until his parents separated in 1988. Then, Nick and his father, Ray (whom Nick called Da), lived together in what Nick described as a "merry life" where he felt totally accepted and the center of the universe. In 1989, Ray remarried and Nick's universe expanded to include his stepmother, Gwen.

Gwen had been a part of Nick's life from the day he was born and had often helped with the high level of ongoing care that Nick needed. As a small child, Nick's "play" consisted of taking apart and destroying objects. Before he had a means of communicating, Gwen reports, "We tried to take him to restaurants, but it didn't work too well. It was like taking a squirrel to a restaurant. He was all over the place and sometimes pulling things down off the wall."

Nick explains his behavior saying, "I used to control my life by behaving badly. I got immediate attention, and someone usually would figure out approximately what I wanted."

When he wasn't "behaving badly", Nick often would be in a passive mode. He would sit, doing nothing more than holding a ball or twirling a piece of string; blocking out any and every stimulus. Since he was in this passive mode much of the time, Ray and his first wife accepted his active, albeit destructive behavior; believing that when he was dismantling things, at least he was interacting with the world. Throughout his early years, he was allowed to chew the ledges on window sills, break TV antennas, pull down curtains and destroy books. Ray lovingly called Nick "The Deconstructionist."

Nick's toddler test scores showed severe mental retardation, but to those who knew him well, Nick appeared to have untapped potential. Gwen recalled how, even before he could sit up, Nick would laugh if she clapped a rhythm for him and then suddenly changed the rhythm. One time a teacher was trying to get Nick to do a simple puzzle but he was gazing out the window and randomly smashing the pieces onto the board. The teacher briefly left the room and when she returned, Nick had correctly completed the puzzle. Instances such as these led Gwen to say, "We always felt he was smarter than he seemed to be."

Starting at age three and one-half, Nick attended several Special Education schools. He experienced minimal communication success with the Picture Exchange Communication System (PECS) and traditional sign language.

In 1991, when he was 13, Nick's speech therapist suggested they try facilitated communication. Ray and Gwen were skeptical, but decided it would be wonderful if Nick could at least answer yes/no questions and tell them when he was in pain. Later, Nick would recount that before FC, he understood most of what was said, had taught himself basic reading and understood the power of knowledge, making him ready for the opportunity.

The FC process started slowly, but one day, after a breakfast of muffins at school, the speech therapist asked, "Nick, is there anything that you want?" Nick responded "Y" for yes and typed "TOST." Knowing he preferred toast to muffins, Gwen immediately understood the magnitude of the event. She decided it was time to learn the method and quickly became Nick's primary facilitator. Nick recalls FC's impact, saying, "For one of the first times in my life, I was able to make my Da proud of me. He realized that I wasn't retarded, and that I was complete on the inside as well as the outside."

One of the first changes that Nick's family noticed after he started using FC was his increased participation in events. At a Christmas Eve church service, Nick "sang" by typing the first word of each stanza of the Christmas carols. Nick's strong desire to connect with people (he would inform them, "I NO I M OK") was bolstered by FC, enabling him to demonstrate that he was intelligent and capable of understanding and interacting.

At first, Nick communicated primarily about food, but soon he was gaining about ten new words per day. Gwen and Nick played school at home. She would grade his workbook lessons and give him gold stars when he did well. Soon she realized that Nick felt a strong need to be correct about language; perhaps as a way to prove "I am smart."

Nick's skills grew over the next year as he prepared to transition to the fifth grade in his neighborhood school. He started with a schedule spending mornings in his new school and afternoons at his segregated school. However, soon behavior issues revealed the difficulty of moving back and forth between the two worlds. He and his full-time facilitator eventually settled into the regular education classroom on a full-time basis.

Some of his classmates accepted Nick and his method of communication, but others did not. At the time, Nick noted that other students "often treat me like I am stupid, young, or fragile. Sometimes they see me as a pest at the beginning. Some, on the other hand, just pretend that I am not there." Nevertheless, he believed, "[Attending school] made me feel much better about myself. I was not only attending a school, but it was the same school that kids who did not have disabilities attended. Even though I know I am normal on the inside, it made me feel like I was part of a group."

When he earned high grades in difficult classes, he reveled in the experience saying, "They found it hard to make fun of me when I was pulling a higher grade than they were. This made me so proud of myself. It made me feel truly normal!"

Despite Nick's ongoing academic success, he still encountered doubts about his abilities. When he was in sixth grade, there were several television shows with a negative slant on FC. When someone called the school to challenge the acceptance of Nick's communication, the principal stood by Nick and his right to communicate. Despite this vote of confidence, Nick remembers that time saying, "Can you imagine having to prove yourself every day? When people make you prove something that you know is true, it is very discouraging. No matter how hard I try, there will always be someone who does not believe. I cannot dwell on this, however; I have to press on. I know the truth. Inside, I am bright, caring, and sensitive. Autism makes me seem what I am not, and yet, autism is part of me, too."

In 1996, Nick and Gwen's world fell apart when Ray had a heart attack and died quite suddenly. Nick was very angry about his father's death and began to take it out on Gwen. She encouraged him to express his anger in words and soon they began to do therapeutic writing. During those sessions, she would not speak, but instead write her responses to him. They filled many journal notebooks as he worked through all of his emotions. Nick later went on to turn his grief into art by writing essays and poems about his father and about that very hard time in his life.

One year after his father's death, another tragedy struck. Trevor, an early friend from Nick's first years of regular education, committed suicide. Nick's behavior deteriorated and he started opening the car door while the car was moving as if he were trying to commit suicide himself.

Gwen could not help but reflect on what it might have been like if Nick had not had FC during these times of loss. He would have had to endure all of it silently, with no way to process and express his intense emotions. At the same time, she urged him to use his ability to communicate and his creative nature saying, "This is hard for anybody to deal with. You are a writer. You are a poet. This is what fuels an artist."

Following her advice, Nick wrote poems and essays about the tragedies. He acknowledged, "Sometimes I feel quite depressed. I am trying to deal with the losses in my life. I am trying to keep my Da's memory fresh in my mind. Perhaps Trevor's death has reminded me of the pain I have been able to deny. It really hurts to lose someone. Sometimes I try to think of my dad. Sometimes it feels like I am forgetting him. It is hard for me to remember his smile, smell, and laugh. These are the things that make him most immediate in my mind. I just wish I had one more chance with both my dad and Trevor."

In 1999, in his third year of high school, Nick's behavioral and mood changes were identified as epilepsy-related. He began withdrawing and decided to drop out of high school. He had accumulated not-for-credit college experience and continued to sit in on courses in a variety of disciplines at three colleges. In 2003, he began working toward his Associates Degree in Communication Studies at Delaware County Community College. Currently, he has completed 15 courses for credit ranging from Statistics to Shakespeare to Earth Science and is a member of an international honor society

Today, Nick leads a very busy and active life and is increasingly independent. He is quite extroverted and needs a lot of outside stimulation; especially intellectual. He loves playing with ideas, words and patterns and regularly beats competitors in Scrabble and other board games. If he spends too much time alone, he can slide into self-destructive thoughts or blankness and boredom, so Gwen makes sure supports are in place for him to do the things he wants to do. He has served as an autism consultant, taken yoga, pursued volunteer work on political campaigns and participated in anti-war vigils. He has served on a local autism board, on a state autism waiver committee and has advocated to elected officials regarding the need for supports for adults on the spectrum. Nick gives presentations at universities, care-providing agencies and conferences about autism and FC and serves as vice president of the FC self-advocacy group, Lonesome Doves.

Nick has enjoyed FC relationships with more than 20 people, including relatives, caregivers, classmates and friends. These relationships have boosted his self-confidence and enabled him to lead a more independent life. Nick has become a patient teacher of FC to his support staff and enjoys the empowerment of directing them on his own.

Gwen has been a steadfast support in using FC to help Nick process sensory, emotional and behavioral difficulties, and teaching him how to analyze and regulate himself so that he requires less assistance and cueing. For example, he more easily attends live performances such as concerts or lectures. In the past, this had been difficult because Nick often has a full body experience at these events. When this occurs, he feels the desire to run up to the stage and grab the performers or the lecturer to express his intense interest. To prevent this, Gwen would sit on the floor behind Nick, holding him in place with a bear hug. Today, he is able to remain seated most of the time and if he does jump up, a touch on the shoulder is all he needs to remind him to sit down.

Over the years, Nick has gained more control over his body and has become more independent in his life, but it has not always been easy. Nick gave a candid explanation of his thinking as he reflected on his attitudes during the early days of FC. He wrote, "...the ante was upped: having to communicate causes your life to become much more difficult, even while it relieves frustration, dampens loneliness, and gives you more control over your life. You are under increased pressure to prove your intelligence, achieve more, participate even when you are not interested, grow up, be responsible, put others' needs before your own, play social games, and conform. I remember that only three months after I began using FC...I felt ambivalent about leaving my easy life and accepting the demands required of those who are intelligent and communicate."

Nick is currently a college student majoring in Communication Studies where his work is focused on primate communication. He also continues to hone his writing skills and intends to become a professional poet and essayist. He reviews and proofreads the works of others, is active in a writers' group and has authored scholarly articles. He wrote and collaborated with Gwen on a documentary video, "Outside/Inside," which has been shown internationally and won four awards. Currently he has 16 publications including contributions to a chapter in a forthcoming occupational therapy textbook and articles in *Disability Studies Quarterly* and *The Communicator*.

He states, "I see writing as a privilege and a treat. Before FC, I never used to be able to write or express myself in any way. Because of this, I realize how special writing can be. I pray that through my writing I can shed new light on the world of autism."

In Nick's Own Words

"Back in 2003, much of what I wrote had a negative or self-pitying tone; I enumerated the things I couldn't do and stressed my frustration at being dependent on other people. However, I look back to these responses and realize that I was still experiencing emotional adolescence. I felt fearful then about my ability to face the increasingly independent life on which I was embarking. I was still adjusting to my father's death seven years earlier. I had moved from Michigan to Pennsylvania, from a small town to metropolitan Philadelphia. I was settling into a duplex that my stepmother and I had bought so I could someday transition to living in my own separate apartment.

"Although I had sat in on university courses for five years, I was only starting my college career as a matriculated student. My waiver-funded support staff was fairly new and very part-time. I was slowly making friends. Even more slowly, I was catching glimpses of myself as an adult, but mostly I was still afraid to let go of the dependency I found so binding ... yet familiar ... comfortable ... easy.

"I love my life now and no longer view my condition as 'horrible.' I feel compelled to introduce myself from the present, as the man I have become since I began using FC in 1991. Now, in 2009, I am well into my college career: I take one course per semester toward my associate degree at Delaware County Community College, where I am majoring in Communication Studies; consequently, I will attend a four-year college to earn my bachelor's degree, then work on a master's, studying primate communication; and recently I've trained an education assistant who will replace my stepmother in FCing my coursework and participation in classes.

"My staffing has increased and, at various levels of fluency, I use FC with all members on my support team. As I add to the number of hours I spend with staff, I look forward to transferring my reliance onto them and to changing the nature of my relationship with Gwen, my stepmother, to one that is less parental. Every year I am asked to conduct various workshops and to present papers at conferences, and I have worked with advocacy organizations and in an advisory capacity for university and state autism projects. I wrote and collaborated on the production of a video that has been shown worldwide.

"My social network is growing, although not as easily as I would like; however, I am more confident about my ability to make friends. I turn thirty-one soon, and many of my accomplishments, such as my presentation and publishing record, are impressive for any person my age. For someone who only began participating in his life eighteen years ago and who will always function with the hypersensitivities, interruptions, and distractions – as well as delights – of autism, I look back and realize that I have sped to maturity.

"In 1991, when I was thirteen, my speech therapist, Debby Kerr, who worked at Greenfield School in Hillsdale, Michigan, attended an FC workshop given by Ann Donnelan, then introduced me to this form of communication and opened the world to me with language. I had been in an SMI (severely mentally impaired) classroom, misdiagnosed, but -- around the time of my one-year FC anniversary -- I was an inclusion student in an elementary school, and was soon supported in FC by an educational aide.

"Before I was able to communicate, I wasn't alone, but I felt lonely and ignored. I spent much of my early childhood crying on the inside. I wanted to relate to people so badly, but there was no way to bridge that huge language gap. I had so much to say, but I lived in a bewildering state of muteness. I spaced out most of the time to escape boredom. Only I knew I listened to everyone's conversations and understood them. Also, by watching 'Sesame Street,' I had learned to read. Information entered my mind, and it filed itself away until words and grammar ordered my thinking once I was a language participant. No one realized that, in truth, the crux of my disability was neurological: although I took in data, my body scrambled the output.

"To have autism is like having a short in a computer. I know what I want to do, but my body gets confused and it does not correctly carry out the orders my brain sends it.

"I was solipsistically infantile in my experience of life. I wanted love, attention, security, and amusement from everyone else, but I didn't expect anyone to need much from me. I used to control my life by seeking negative attention, which got immediate results, and usually someone would figure out approximately what I wanted. (It is still my first impulse to do this; however, more and more often I sign or indicate my need to type in order to communicate my needs.)

"Autism was my godlike power. It allowed me to focus only on myself. In many ways my family gave me the freedom to play with anything, even destructively, because they wanted me just to show some interest in life. I became a kind of wild animal at times because there were few boundaries in my life, and I perceived people's attempts to control my actions or get responses from me mostly as power struggles or entertaining games, rather than selfless attempts to teach me control over myself and my environment. It took years as a communicating social participant before I performed selfless actions regularly.

"It is difficult always to be in control of myself. Before FC, I never tried; I just did whatever I was led to do by impulse. All controls were external. I would have killed myself in pursuit of an obsession, if no one were there to stop me. I reacted dramatically to sensory stimulus. The process of developing internal controls has been so difficult. It feels unnatural. It takes a focus that is not always there, or at least a focus that requires a good deal of conscious effort. Before I learned facilitated communication, my existence inside my body was often a frustrating hell. Now that I can communicate, much of my frustration with processing sensation and emotion can be worked through, because I have the words to explain what is happening to me, to analyze my experience, and to take action.

"At first as an FC user, I felt extremely vulnerable, like I was exposed, instead of hidden. Nakedly, I was open to all kinds of criticism and failure, once it was evident that I was intelligent, since more was expected of me. This didn't seem fair at first. Everyone thought my behavior should improve. At the time, I didn't want to take responsibility for my actions: I didn't see why I should change, just because I understood more than anyone had thought possible; it was their blindness that had limited their perception. I was the same as I'd always been.

"When I gained communication, I quickly became more impatient about the deficits in my life that, formerly, I had accepted as terrible but unchangeable. School was the worst. I understand why it took a year (after

I began using FC) for me to get into public school classes, but it felt like forever. Why did talking people take so long to get things done? I had changed overnight! I thought my life automatically should become like everyone else's. I became more consciously depressed about being disabled.

"Before, I was so wrapped up in sensation that I was unable to see myself objectively or frequently even separate from my surroundings -- the environment I was trapped in as a reactor. With FC, everyone else saw me as emerging from within, but I had to find myself before I was capable of coming out. Because of facilitated communication, I was able to recognize myself as the Thinker in my brain, instead of seeing myself as the victim of fears and impulses. This was not easy. My development of a solid self has taken time and effort; I don't think it could have happened without language.

"As I formed a more external view of myself, I found that my appearance, behaviors and physical abilities did not look like Nick as the Thinker imagined himself. Still I find this to be true. There are more aspects of autism that I embrace now as 'diffability,' but I don't like having a body that fails me in ways that necessitate dependency and make me feel helpless and humiliated.

"I require support for every intimate action of my daily routine; there is no privacy, and even a caring and supportive eye is still witness to my nudity and my body's uncomfortable jerks, uncoordinated clumsiness, and uncooperative volition and erratic motor disturbances. I fear humiliation, but in many ways humiliation is a way of life for me. I could avoid mirrors, yet I try to accept that others love me – body included – as I am, so I look at myself and try to accept my outside as much as I accept my inside.

"Always I have communicated. However, only with language have I begun truly to live and develop the potential that lay dormant before I had FC. I am connected to my family far deeper than before. I was able to love and amaze my always-accepting father as a chip off his ol' block for several years prior to the heart-attack that killed him. I am great friends with my stepmother, and we mutually teach and guide one another. I befriend and flirt, study, write, and joke. I make important and unimportant decisions, empowered to shape my life.

"I am named after Nike, the Goddess of Victory, and I try to believe my name is what I am. I have triumphed over many odds. There are times when I am frustrated by failure, but I am learning to see these experiences as part of the process of succeeding, since I survive them and discover how my body or the world works. I am Nike and I will listen to my true, victorious self."

My True Birthday

Chammi Rajapatirana

Snapshot

Chammi was born in 1974 and began using FC at age 17. A year after he started typing, he entered public school. While he had some very good experiences there, some of his teachers did not believe his writing was his own. Chammi's parents have stopped at nothing to help him realize his dreams. In 2003, the family moved to Syracuse, New York so he could have ongoing facilitated communication training and achieve his goal of fluid independent typing. In 2006, the family moved to Sri Lanka where Chammi and Anoja started EASE, a non-profit foundation that provides training for facilitators. Chammi's next dream is to open a coffee shop where people with and without disabilities can work and socialize together.

About Chammi

Born: 1974. **Started FC:** 1991 at age 17.

Current Facilitators: Anoja (mother) plus several staff, cousins, and friends.

Access to FC: 24 hours a day, 7 days a week.

Living Situation: Shares home with parents in Sri Lanka.

Day Program: Teaches workshops on FC and mentors new facilitators.

Highest level of Independence: Independent.

Fluent in two languages – Sinhala and English.

Equipment: Franklin speller, computer with text-to-voice output, letterboard.

I the Vinter

I the vinter hoping
To cull my bitter grapes
Given time to ferment
In loves sweet airy cellar
Will turn bitter grapes
To sweet wine

The Potter

The Potter who spoiled
My poor body
Paused to pour
Poetry into my
Heart
I pour it out

Chammi's Criteria for Quality of Life

Go places like conferences.

Being busy.

Reading.

Writing.

Going out.

Movie nights at home.

Hanging out with guys.

Five Things Chammi Wants You to Know

I am sigh still hoping to speak with my mouth.

I am teaching FC.

OK, I long for all the things you guys do.

I am struggling to not let autism, society, or the nay sayers limit me.

I am still autistic.

Eight Things Anoja Wants You to Know About Chammi

Chammi is one of the most loving and courageous people I know.

He puts himself in the line of fire defending FC .

He argues for what he believes is right even if it goes against a popular belief.

He always stands up for FC users who can't type independently.

He cares deeply for other people, especially those with disabilities.

He has a highly developed sense of ethics, morality and integrity.

He has a wonderful sense of humor.

He loves music, parties and would like to dance better than he does.

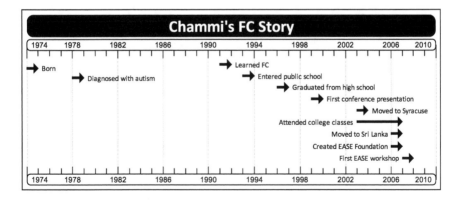

Chammi's Story

Chammi's parents, Anoja and Sarath, immigrated to the United States from Sri Lanka. In 1975, they settled in Potomac, Maryland. Chammi was born in 1974 and was the second of three children. By the time he was two years old, Chammi's parents knew he was not following the normal course of development. Although he had a few words and walked before his first birthday, the words soon disappeared, as did his interest in playing with toys. They spent two years searching for specialists. Finally, when he was four years old, Chammi was diagnosed with autism.

Anoja recalls that the doctor "made it sound like a death sentence," directing her to put Chammi in an institution and saying that he would never love or know he was loved. Anoja responded, "You are wrong. If my son were a rock, he would know he was loved."

Anoja and Sarath were willing to attempt anything that might have had the slightest chance of helping their son. They tried the Son Rise Program and the Doman Delacato Program, but Chammi did not respond. Most experts did not offer any hope for improvement. Eventually, they took Chammi to see Dr. Mary Coleman, a leading pediatric neurologist and researcher. They asked her to run every test possible. All of the tests came back normal, yet Chammi's behavior grew more and more difficult.

Glen Doman gave Chammi's parents some sound advice about the neurology of autism when he told them, "Though output is damaged, do not assume input is damaged." Anoja notes, "We lived by that wonderful rule." She gave Chammi daily learning opportunities using a variety of children's materials including puzzles, flashcards and matching games. Since he was not able to provide meaningful or consistent responses, she never knew if he was learning or not. As Anoja says, "This was before we knew anything about movement differences so we did not offer touch as we later learned to do with FC." Looking back, Anoja suspects Chammi was probably bored with the low academic level of the work she presented, but she also surmises that it contributed to the large vocabulary he enjoys today.

For many years, there were episodes, or "regressions," as Anoja and Sarath called them. During these regressions, which lasted seven to ten days, Chammi was extremely agitated and would not eat or sleep. He could not stop pacing or crying and would hit himself on the stomach until his skin was a dark callus. They consulted numerous doctors who could not explain or help, and so they lived in fear that one day he would not come out of a regression and would remain in that grim state for the rest of his life.

Later, when Chammi was able to communicate and described how he felt during the regressions, he was diagnosed with depression. Appropriate medicines, psychotherapy, and no doubt a more interesting life made the regressions disappear. He has been off the medication for years now and sees a counselor very rarely.

Anoja says, "All the things we tried would fill a book!" In addition to lessons, Chammi and Anoja spent time each day taking long walks around the high school track hoping it would dissipate some of his energy and help him sleep better, but it did not work. Groups of volunteers and paid aides worked round-the-clock on home-based programs. Chammi attended public and private schools and even the specialized Higashi school. Nothing had much impact.

Anoja continued to read books and talk with other parents who had found some measure of success with one therapy or another. They tried many different interventions and were open to trying anything that did not involve punishment. Anoja looks back on that time saying, "Finally when I was beginning to think I would never find the key to unlock my son's world, FC came into our lives."

While doing volunteer work at the Autism Society of America, Anoja read an article on FC published in the *Harvard Educational Review*. After making an appointment for Chammi to have an FC assessment, she decided to experiment with FC on her own. She sat Chammi down in front of his brother's computer, held his hand and asked him to spell his name. She vividly remembers, "He spelled his name as Chammi instead of Chammy as we had for years tried to make him write it. While it took me three days to see the significance of that change in spelling, it proved to me that this was Chammi and not me. After almost 18 years of silence, he asserted himself with the first word he typed!"

Although it took a full year before they were completely comfortable using FC, Anoja notes that people started to treat Chammi differently from the very first day. The teachers changed his goals in school and started reading age-appropriate books to him. Chammi's pediatrician wanted to try being his facilitator. He asked Chammi if he could try it and, taking Chammi's hand, expected him to point to the "Y" or the "N" for a yes or no answer to his question. Instead, Chammi typed "OK." From that moment on, the doctor became a believer. With his doctor's acceptance of FC, Chammi's typing has proved to be helpful in solving several medical issues.

Anoja fondly remembers the heady days in the first few weeks after Chammi started typing. She says, "When Chammi started using FC, we finally found our son. He was able to tell us what he did and did not want. We were able to have conversations with him, discuss poetry and politics with him. Have him truly be part of this family. Most of all it was wonderful to no longer have to guess if he was ill or in pain or hungry or sad."

Despite their great joy, Chammi's parents also faced many difficulties. They had to move quickly to find new supports for Chammi, including aides and a psychiatrist. Chammi typed that he wanted to go to a "real school" and it proved to be very difficult to move him out of the segregated school and into a regular classroom. By 1992, Chammi's behavior had deteriorated so much it seemed as if he was trying to be kicked out of the segregated school. He later acknowledged that, in fact, he was trying to get kicked out. In addition to difficult behavior at school, he suffered frequent headaches and ongoing bouts of agitation and rage at home.

Chammi had many episodes of rage directed at himself. He concocted tales about his siblings. He was aware of the controversy surrounding FC and was terrified that his voice would be taken away, although his parents had promised him that would never happen. As Anoja sees it, it was almost as if he were making up for his lost childhood by going through all the stages from the terrible two's to adolescence in the short span of one year.

Perhaps the deepest pain for Chammi and his family was to consider his past unlived life. Chammi explains, "I was filled with rage. Rage that I had spent eighteen years in a silent abyss. I was mourning the lost years and trying to break out of the shell I had grown around me." Anoja recalls, looks back on that first year saying, "Finding out how much anguish Chammi was in and that he knew exactly what he was missing in life was very emotional for us. I had hoped that he didn't know, but that first year we found out that he knew to the last dregs what he was missing. He was in so much pain and despair. Sometimes I was tempted to ask, 'Why can't you be happy to sit in front of the television, like everybody else in the world?'

In high school, Chammi's experiences were mixed. The students liked him and he developed several friendships. One classmate connected a television to his computer so it would show Chammi's words to the class as he typed. Using this system, Chammi could help a student struggling to answer the teacher's question by quietly typing out the correct answer. Some of his teachers were very respectful of him and his method of communication while others were less gracious. He encountered skepticism and rude comments from an English teacher. Chammi says, "They considered my writing too good to be truly mine."

Anoja sees clearly how Chammi's writing style and his ability to stay on-task have developed over the years as his thinking became more coherent. She also credits his improved skills to the excellent training he has gotten from his writing tutors. Chammi reports, "In the beginning it was hard for me to get my words in order. Now they order themselves."

When Chammi finished high school in 1995 and entered into the adult service system, he was not interested in delivering flyers or any of the other jobs that were offered through the work program, so his days were custom-tailored to meet his needs and wishes. After that particularly rough first year, he moved forward into his new life with its many exciting opportunities. He began to attend conferences and in 1999, he gave his first presentation at the Autism National Committee conference. His writing was so moving and incisive in its honesty that the audience gave him a standing ovation. Anoja remembers that day with pride saying, "My son, who they said was going to have to be institutionalized, brought 250 people to their feet."

From the beginning, Chammi worked on typing independently by pointing to words on a whole-word choice board. A few months after starting FC, he took his first IQ test, answering the multiple-choice questions by pointing independently to the desired letter. By 2003, he could type independently for short periods. He wanted to be able to be more consistent with his independent typing, so the family moved to Syracuse, New York where they would have access to the FC Institute.

Chammi began attending college classes at Le Moyne College. He was occasionally invited to be a guest lecturer in classes, including some at Syracuse University. His schedule included working on his writing with his tutor, going to therapy appointments (both psychotherapy and bodywork), emailing and going out to eat or to a movie. He had many friends among university students as well as other FC users. He always made it known that he wanted time every day for conversation, or "bantering" as he called it, with his job coach, cousin and friends.

Soon after he started typing, Chammi began to disclose his spiritual life and it became apparent that he was a devout Christian. Anoja notes that both she and Sarath are Buddhists and that their families have been Buddhist for generations. For her, this was the ultimate validation to show that she was not influencing his typing. Anoja and Sarath did not know how to support Chammi in his spiritual journey, so a Christian friend began meeting with him to pray and discuss Bible teachings. The friend was awed by Chammi's depth of belief and his connection to God.

Although Chammi's world had opened up after he started to use FC and his frustrations were greatly diminished, they did not completely disappear. In some instances, they expanded as he moved out into the world and saw his limitations more clearly. For example, he wanted to attend college, but his anger was triggered when he saw the other students on the campus. He typed, "I just got FC too late in life to make realizing this dream easy. I lived for so long in my silent abyss that my rage is so near the surface. I feel enraged to see other students working so easily. Returning to try college will mean I have to conquer envy."

Chammi has achieved his goal of typing independently, which he does at conferences and other public events. At a recent workshop at the National Institute of Social Development, someone took a short video clip of Chammi with a digital camera. He was typing independently in a room with traffic sounds outside, and another lecture and a phone conversation occurring nearby. When asked how he was able to maintain his focus and continue typing in the midst of so much sensory confusion, he replied that it was because there were "awesome girls" in the audience.

In 2006, the Rajapatiranas returned to Sri Lanka. Chammi notes that this was exactly 15 years to the day after he typed his first words with FC. He loved his life in Syracuse and had so many opportunities there that he struggled with the idea of moving. Nevertheless, being in Sri Lanka opened even more doors for him. As he said, "Till I altered my life I did not understand I could lead a life that is productive. I had presented at conferences, workshops, even been a guest lecturer. But in Sri Lanka I do all that and more."

In Sri Lanka, there are few services for people with disabilities and fewer still for those who could benefit from FC. With generous donations from family and friends, Chammi and Anoja started a non-profit foundation that provides training and opportunities to help people with disabilities. The foundation provides all of its services free of charge. Chammi wrote the vision/mission statement and named the foundation Educate, Advocate, Support, Empower (EASE).

In 2006, Chammi and Anoja began working with their first two students. In 2007, they held their first workshop. They have developed a Sinhala letterboard and an FC training program. By 2009, five trainees participated in EASE's FC training program, which consists of 12 hours of in-class training plus follow-up meetings every two weeks to discuss problems and progress. Anoja believes, "Chammi's contributions, observations, and comments are the most valued part of the training process."

Years ago, when he rejected a job distributing flyers, Chammi longed to "create a productive stimulating life." Now he does that for himself and for others. He says, "I enjoy this work tremendously. I feel I am making a difference in people's lives. I am just going on with my mission of helping nonverbal people get a life.

Chammi continues to weave new dreams for the future. He would like to open a coffee shop that provides integrated employment for people with and without disabilities and serve as a place where they could socialize together: "A place for people with diverse abilities. Such a place will provide the ideal environment for our often separate worlds to mingle, and learn to respect and like each other."

Chammi has achieved his dream of independent typing, is living out his mission of providing FC opportunities for others, and has begun dreaming his next dreams. In spite of all this success, with his sensitive nature he could not help but be aware of the toll it is taking on his mother. He confides, "Feeling frustrated I am freeing myself by tethering mom."

While Anoja acknowledges the many ways that Chammi's dreams have "tethered" her, she is unequivocal when she says, "Since Chammi is able to articulate his goals clearly to us and we try to help him achieve them, life is more complicated. If he had remained mute, he probably would be in a day program/job and maybe even a group home. But I am thankful beyond words for the complications that FC has brought into our lives."

In Chammi's Own Words

"The day my mother put me at my brother's computer and asked me to type my name was my true birthday. I lived in an abyss till then. The greatest day of my life was that day. My brain lit up like a neon sign, finally I could talk! I hoped that the fear was over.

"I was very hopeless inside knowing I would never be able to have a nice life. Being in an awful school, I was bored and trying to get home so I could listen to music. Not the least of the pain I endured was the work I was taught. Until FC, I was destined to be cleaning floors. Of course, the people who tried to teach me such skills had a hellish time.

"FC made people say, 'Yes, he is intelligent.' I love the books mom brings me now. I love my tutors. I love exercising my brain. I am a burgeoning writer now. Think of that. What could I write about? I could begin with traveler's tales. Yes, traveler's tales. Traveler's tales not about slogging through jungles or sailing across uncharted seas. I am a traveler ebulliently engaged on a unique journey between worlds. Between the quirky world of autism that I inhabit and the wearying world of 'normal' that I like to explore.

"Brightening my life is the greatest gift FC brings me. Accustomed to living in the abyss, coming up to the light was hard. Beset by memories, I am still terrified. Terrified that I might go back there. If FC were taken away from me, that is where I would be.

"Assisting my great ascent was Mom's task. Beset by emotions I can't express in words I run amok. I was filled with rage. Rage that I had spent eighteen years in a silent abyss. I raged at God for abandoning me. Asserting my rage was very important that first year. Because of my anger, my mom took me to a psychiatrist. Aware I need to live calmly, I go to therapy still.

"Simply by constantly soliciting words from me, Mom forces me to express myself with words. I feel words are inadequate to express my emotions. I tantrum instead of typing, Mom gets mad and yells at me so I type. Dwelling on this is hard – I have forgotten my wild weary days.

"Teaching my brain to think coherently is a continuing process. My brain was so chaotic but now always moving towards lucidity. In the beginning, it was hard for me to get my words in order. Now they order themselves. Having mom inside my head and following pitiless Mom's instructions—just being forced to write coherently helped me to think coherently.

"Eased by being able to express myself, I feel better. Yet, inordinately great rage takes me over sometimes. Dear Mom has to remind me I have words now. Yes, I do forget that often. Finding my voice made life utterly wonderful; yet, greatly freeing my voice brought its own difficulties, too.

"I urged my mom to get me into a real school little realizing the homework I would get would almost outrun my desire to get friends. Bitterly, I realized some of my teachers did not accept me as an intelligent person. Other teachers became respectful. Trying to stay in English class was hardest. Beset by his rude comments, I left his class. I loved history, earth science, and math. I had great teachers and made friends with peers. It is ironic that my English teachers had such difficulty accepting me. Perhaps they considered my writing too good to be truly mine. My doctor too began to see me differently. Only after FC, he saw me as an ordinary likable boy. Before this, he thought I did not open my mouth out of stubbornness.

"Awesome FC taking me to places I never thought of, like conferences. Eased by FC, I live quite an interesting life. Ostensibly, I am juggling many satisfying options. I like being busy. I love doing writing, reading, going out, movie nights at home, and talking to dear friends. I like being guys hanging out together. Realizing life-long dream of bantering with friends is possible because of FC. Hellish to sit by while other people talk and laugh. Yes, I remember that time well. I am not there now, yet I remember well the rage. The anguish I felt comes back and I am lost until I remember, I have words now.

"Mom says I must decide how I like to spend my time. I am asked at all times what I would like to do – nearly in full control of my life. Guy gets to choose food, activities dreaming of college. I still am going out less than I like. By going out, I don't mean isolating segregated groups. Mom does keep her promise most of the time. However, she limits my lolling. Yes, I find mind is better if I'm not lolling too much. Very nice to go out—love being out.

"FC freed my voice. I am now able to order my life through typing. My head is grateful I can type but heart longs to talk. As an experiment, just try keeping your mouth shut for a day. Just try keeping your mouth shut while they talk about you, telling your mother to put you away in an institution. You want to scream 'No, no, no,' but you are mute. Mom cried a lot.

"I listen to lilting country music songs hoping I will sing some day. Typing has led to speech for several FC users. I am working on this myself. Quite soon, I hope you will hear me effortlessly delivering the speeches I have typed. That would be the best gift of all.

"Being mute is like having your brain gouged out. It is a fate I would not wish on my enemies. Autism/apraxia took away my voice and a world that equates muteness with stupidity took everything else. Fortunately, a determined Mom salvaged me. She searched the world over until she found a way my voice could be as loud as yours.

"Being able to hold a conversation with another human is what makes life worth living. Hoping and dreaming of talking … torturing myself to push my dumb mouth to talk is messing up my life now. I'm not beset by the thought of how fruitless it is to live trapped inside, but totally frustrated now because I still can't talk.

"Speakers open their mouths and words pour out. I open my mouth and scream. Shouting is a symptom of my tension, my throat tightens and I shout but I get stuck in it even though I want to stop. Your sounds emerge modulated, shaped words. Mine emerge un-modulated, unshaped, un-understandable squeals. The reality is that I sound like an animal. It is an awful thought. The awareness of how bizarre I sound kills the determination to speak. Tussling with my mouth while trying to talk maddens me; I suspect most people don't have to do that. But I am aware I must try to not allow tantrums to destroy my peace. I need to be more polite. Resenting my inability to speak is the only reason I still tantrum. I (sigh) must not be bogged down in anxiety; I myself prevent mute mouth from yet loosening up its damned fetters.

"Uplifting to think of all the gifts FC has brought me. I have a mind that is intelligent and a body that is stingy with its obedience to my mind's dictates. Doing FC gives my weary body a break, typing makes my sappy arm work better. Grasping Mom's hand, I free myself from autism. Back to bitterness, I hate having autism: stumbling around instead of striding confidently through life.

"Helplessly I sit while Mom calls me to come. I know what I must do, but often I can't get up until she says, 'Stand up.' Because of my apraxia, I could never make my body obey my brain's requests; how could I make it obey Mom's requests? The knack of knowing where my body is does not come easy for me. Interestingly, I do not know if I am sitting or standing. I am not aware of my body unless it is touching something … your hand on mine lets me know where my hand is. Jarring my legs by walking tells me I am alive. I need to sit, loll, or move to know where my body is. If I am just standing it is scary, frustrating just trying to stand. I lose my body and must run to feel it.

I am often told that I am very self-aware, and that I am willing to reveal my vulnerabilities. I do so, only in the hope of helping others.

"Mom says I never looked like I made the effort to act as if I understood anything. I looked at things peripherally, I moved my hands jerkily, and I appeared not to understand requests. I didn't even look at people much. I have heard that in Thailand it is considered rude to stare fixedly at the person you are talking to, maybe I should move to Thailand!

"Helping others learn FC helps me stride more confidently. I am so glad I can do this work. It is the best joy in the world. It heals my heart to bring joy to other lives. Meditating on my life before and after FC has done me a world of good. I lost my impatience regarding the things still missing in my life. Wearying to live consumed by rage. I hope, I believe, I know that nothing is beyond my reach now that I have words."

Finding a Purpose is
What Changed Things

Barb Rentenbach

Snapshot

Barb was born in 1974 and started typing at age 19. Over the years, many of her lifelong aggressive and inappropriate behaviors melted away as she began expressing herself through FC. After an intense period of anger directed mostly at her parents, Barb went on to begin making her own goals for daily life. Ultimately, she discovered that her purpose in life was to be a writer and that she could use her writing to help others. In 2009, Barb published her first book and almost immediately began work on her second book.

About Barb

Born: 1974.   **Started FC:** 1992 at age 19.

Current Facilitators: Lois Prislovsky, Ph.D. (Educational Consultant) plus three other staff and friends.

Participants: Barbara and Mike Rentenbach (Parents), Lois Prislovsky, Andrea Reynolds (teacher).

Access to FC: 1-2 hours per day, 5 days per week.

Living Situation: Own home with 24 hour staff support.

Day Program: Reading, writing, e-mail, research, and exercise & giving presentations.

Highest level of Independence: Practices independent typing daily but it is very slow.

Equipment: Letterboard or computer with oversized keyboard.

Floating*

my cup of tea

bag o barb floats

in the warmth

as she has done through the ages

flavoring the surroundings

seeping out to experience dilution and the feel of molecular movement.

notes dance through my leaves

bombarding is banned for the float

i go while mesh holds my place

in this fine china of purity

non porous walls warm and shield me from all else

while i explore my limits of self.

i am expansive but not limitless.

good to know.

bag o barb is pleased.

thanks for the cup

i bring my own tea

> * Barb says this poem was written after a "delicious" experience in floating in a salt water sensory deprivation tank.

Barb's Criteria for Quality of Life

Being seen as:

Thinking.

Feeling.

Contributing.

Human being.

Five Things Barb Wants You to Know About Her

I am here to stay.

I plan to work hard every day to leave a legacy as a writer and a truth advocate.

I find I am an excellent friend.

I find I am enjoyable to be around. This has evolved over the last five years.

I will travel the world and savor it all and will use those experiences to serve.

Five Things Lois Wants You to Know About Barb

Barb's work ethic and maturity continue to grow with each year.

Her writing also improves with more depth and humor.

Cognitive behavior therapy helps Barb make the personal choices she desires.

Her future is incredibly bright.

She is one of my favorite people on the planet.

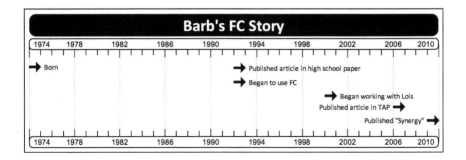

Barb's Story

In 1974, Barb was born into a family of her parents, Barbara and Mike, and two older brothers, ages four and five. Although the Rentenbachs tried to give their children a 'normal' family life, this was not easily achieved. Family photo albums show several early years with only one or two pictures at Christmas. Barbara suspects this was because she and Mike were too busy and exhausted to think about taking pictures.

The three children did play together at times; sledding, bicycling, driving go-carts. Despite being surrounded by a loving family, as a child Barb says she saw herself as a "fragmented island of terror and creator abandonment" and other people, including her family members, were nothing more than ships passing by the island.

Barb was a hyperactive child who did not sleep through the night for seven years. She would be up for hours during the night watching her favorite cartoons on the VCR.

Someone had to be with Barb every minute that she was awake. She had a tendency to eat or destroy household objects and sometimes would even leave the house in the middle of the night to swim in the neighbor's pool. Even though her parents never left her unattended, Barb still managed to find small items such as coins or buttons and swallow them or put them up her nose. Barbara recalls several instances of choking and at least ten trips to the emergency room along with two emergency surgeries. Barb later reported, "I greedily consumed all manner of reasonably edible and not so edible morsels. My family subsidized the emergency room."

In addition to ingesting inedible objects, Barb displayed many other behaviors that are not uncommon in children with autism. When frustrated, she would spit, bite, hit, grab or scream. She ripped the pockets and buttons off her clothes, set off fire alarms, ate soap and drank shampoo, smeared feces, and stole or grabbed food; often gorging to the point of becoming physically ill. Looking back on her eating habits, she says it was "an attempt to fill an unquenchable hunger in my heart."

Barb had several special items that she kept with her at all times. Among her favorites were a music box and a Tupperware bowl filled with nuts and bolts. While the constant sounds from either of these may have given her some measure of sensory stimulation or comfort, they were nerve-wracking for everyone else. When awake, unless she was watching TV, she constantly roamed around the house and would sit still for only a few moments at a time. Away from home, she would accost strangers on the street or get into their cars. In her family's car, she would grab the steering wheel or open the door and try to jump out while the car was moving.

Barbara recalls how Barb took apart the vacuum cleaner at age five and "got into everything – either breaking it, taking it apart, or eating it." Barb remarks, "I leisurely dismantled more phones, toys, remotes, radios, and clocks than the average bear."

Barb attended a special education school. When Andrea Reynolds became her teacher, Barb's behavior started to change. Andrea talked to Barb as if she could understand everything that was said and she held high expectations for her behavior. She refused to use the "bad hands mitts" that had been part of Barb's behavior plan if she was being destructive in the classroom.

In 1992, when Barb was 19 years old, the Rentenbachs traveled to a facilitated communication workshop so that Barb could be evaluated. Working with the experienced facilitators there, Barb was able to type and began using words for the first time in her life. Soon after that, the family traveled to Syracuse, New York for training at the FC Institute. Barbara believed, "It wasn't brain surgery and it wasn't invasive, so it seemed worth trying."

Suddenly the Rentenbachs' world changed forever. Barbara recalled that heady time saying, "Mentally both my husband and I were overwhelmed with the new possibilities for Barb and the injustices of the past at the same time. A strong range of conflicting emotions took toll on us. Years of frustration knowing there was really something very bright inside and not being able to get to it. Then in a flash, we had a very bright person on our hands. Our minds reeled!"

Within a few weeks of starting FC, Barb's life changed too. Barb says, "The first thing I told my attentive parents was to stop dressing me like Barbara Ruth the retard." The Disney-themed clothing everyone thought she loved was discarded and Elke, a German graduate student who was Barb's aide, took her shopping for clothes. Barb chose a wardrobe of cords, sweaters and Birkenstocks and soon got a new haircut, orthotics, and glasses. Everyone was surprised to learn she had 20/2000 eyesight. When her daughter began wearing glasses, Barbara noticed an improvement in her confidence and posture as well as her ability to see.

Elke held Barb to a very high standard. She would bring Barb home from an outing if her behavior was inappropriate. Barb realized that was exactly what she needed; now that she had a way to communicate, she asked her parents to be strict with her, too.

As her new-found control grew, many of Barb's behavioral issues melted away. Her mother notes, "Barb's behavior was the number-one aspect that changed with her FC interaction. Her extreme hyperactivity calmed down almost immediately. The rages and temper flare-ups and destructive behavior cooled to a huge degree. Some of her attachment to things in an obsessive-compulsive way dropped."

Along with her FC progress, Barb discarded her childhood name of Barbara Ruth. In her book, *Synergy*, she describes one particularly hurtful event from her years as Barbara Ruth. She and her mother were taking their daily walk around the high school track and saw a neighbor walking with a friend. Barb's exceptional hearing allowed her to overhear their conversation. Even as they waved a friendly greeting from the other side of the track, the neighbor was telling her friend, "Barbara Ruth is sad, sad, sad. She is the retarded Rentenbach girl. Money can't fix what plagues this child. Autism. And she's got it bad. She can't talk. This kid barely feeds herself, and Lordy, what a putrid mess that is. She is damn near grown now and can't even wipe herself."

In her book, Barb sends her retort: "My name is Barb. I am the Rentenbach girl, but I am not the retarded one, Barbara Ruth. She is gone. She left over a year ago."

Barb attended school in a segregated setting and her teacher, Andrea, helped her make good progress with her behavioral issues, so when Andrea took a teaching position at a public high school, Barb transferred with her. When Barb began using FC, Andrea quickly became a fluent facilitator. Before long, Barb was integrated into a few regular education classes, including advanced placement world history. She gave presentations to science classes and participated in workshops for teachers and adult service providers.

Andrea commented on FC and the changes she saw as Barb's teacher. She notes, "FC is a true form of communication. We are constantly being told to 'train' autistic students with PECs, routine schedules, constant reward systems, etc. I have had much more success by having normal expectations, teaching them to deal with change, and showing them that I respect their intelligence by working on different communication systems - primarily FC. I think most of Barb's improvements in behavior, speech, and movement were directly or indirectly related to the introduction of the use of FC."

In her first published work, Barb wrote an essay for the school newspaper entitled, *Inner Self Denied.* The article is an exposé on the culture of the teenage social hierarchy that included geeks, wallflowers and athletes. Barb revealed her social justice sensibility by boldly asking her classmates to "look beyond the surface and consider the person within."

Despite so many positive changes, difficult and hurtful times lay ahead. Barb needed to assert her independence and in the process, became fiercely angry with her parents, especially her mother who she had nicknamed, "Smother." Barbara acknowledges that for her, letting go and realizing that Barb had her own goals and preferences was not always easy. Andrea remembers how Barb would never give her mother a break and when she was angry about something her mother had done, she would not let it go for a very long time.

Barb accused her parents of trying to control her and keeping her prisoner all those years and was adamant about getting out of their home and far away from their reach. In response, her parents enrolled her in a private residential facility in Kentucky where she stayed for five years until she was kicked out after her behavior deteriorated when her facilitator and favorite staff person was fired.

In 2000, Barb's parents hired Lois Prislovsky, Ph.D. As an educational psychologist, Lois used a full range of techniques; from behavioral methods of cognitive psychology to spiritual teachings that might speak to the "unquenchable hunger" in Barb's heart.

Soon Barb set her own goals at regular intervals and discovered she had a purpose in life. Barb's first goals included losing weight, living on her own, taking college classes, finding non-paid friends and perhaps someday learning to speak. Although Barb's parents had provided her with speech therapy in the past, it had never been very effective. Once the therapy sessions came from Barb's intrinsic motivation, she made good progress. Her mom was impressed: "Because Barb wants to do it and has put her mind to it, she is getting results. That has been a real insight to us."

Through her work in therapy, Barb's facial muscles have become stronger and she is losing her flat affect. She now smiles and uses appropriate speech to greet people, make choices, and express desires as many as 25 times per day.

In addition to speech therapy, Barb's week includes regular workouts with her personal trainer, academic tutoring in her current areas of interest, listening to books on tape, following daily news coverage, swimming, horseback riding, and weekly meetings with Lois where she answers email or works on her writing and other creative endeavors. Barb emphasizes her need for "chill time" to recharge. She explains that interacting and being "on" takes a lot of battery power and that having time everyday for relaxation is a key to succeeding at writing and other functional tasks.

Lois has observed enormous positive changes over their four years together. At the beginning, Barb regularly attacked nearly everyone in her world, including Lois, Barbara, the personal trainer and her tutors. This behavior has not occurred for over four years. Lois explains, "She has more internal controls, which I believe, are correlated to her adaptability with words. She's more in control from top to bottom.

In their initial FC sessions, Barb exhibited no focus or drive, typing only one or two paragraphs. Today, Barb has more speed, focus and motivation, regularly typing three or four pages per session. Lois says, "She never shows up to a session unwilling or uncommitted to work. She looks forward to it and produces every single time."

Lois keeps an archive of all the transcripts from their sessions. She said Barb's early work consists of egocentric, demanding, one-sided conversations. Comparing those early transcripts to Barb's current work provides concrete evidence of the evolution of Barb's personal development.

The Rentenbachs have seen many positive changes in Barb and in the ways family and friends relate to her. People no longer talk about her, but instead talk to her and include her in their conversations. These positive interactions, along with her increased ability to make decisions, have had a tremendous influence on Barb's overall behavior. Barbara notes, "She controls most of her world now and is 500% calmer. It is literally a world of difference. She makes most of the decisions about her money, her condo, her vacations, and her support team. We always ask her opinion and she has control over 80% of her life.

On rare occasions when Barb becomes frustrated, she might break her glasses or pound on something. She is asked to put her frustration into words. Together with her parents, support team, and Lois, everyone works together to solve the problem.

In 2006, Barb wrote an article for *The Autism Perspective* magazine in which she describes how after refusing to type with Lois for several days, she had a flash of intuition and suddenly understood that her purpose in life was to be a writer. Finding a purpose can provide a central core around which to organize a life. Many of her difficult behaviors melted away when she realized that they did not serve her purpose. She no longer saw herself as a "fragmented island of creator abandonment," and soon she began to understand that her writing could help others with autism.

She says, "I have suffered punishments and consequences before. Finding purpose is what changed things. My work now is to write with as much love and commitment as I can manage so others can have a more beautiful island experience."

Barb published her first book, *Synergy*, in 2009. The book is filled with her humor, stories and philosophy of life, along with many photos of friends and family. She offers practical suggestions on how to not just live, but to live well with autism.

As part of her desire to be of service to others, Barb founded The Greater Living Institute. Its mission is to help bright adults with disabilities reach their highest potentials.

Over the years, Barb and her parents have worked through the developmental stages and the seemingly endless anger that Barb had for her mother. Despite the pain, Barbara has always been grateful for everything that FC brought into their lives. She also maintains a vantage point that acknowledges reality, saying, "Everything is not perfect. The autism has not gone away. Sometimes we expect her to be normal just without talking and I have to remind myself that the autism still has a grip on her. But a whole new world opened up for us and for her. It was very gratifying to us as parents to finally know our child and her needs. All in all, we would not be where we are without FC. EVERYTHING is better."

In Barb's Own Words

"I am Barb Rentenbach, and my other defining label is autism—the severe kind, if I may be so bold. For decades, I bumped around ignorantly in this vexatious arcade of blaring impersonal voices, erratic assaults of color and light, indefinable loneliness, and relentless confusion. Eventually, I let down my bulwark and discovered clarity, purpose, meaning, confidence, independence, and friendship.

"Today, I am at peace and I am happy and productive. The paths to that state of being were filled with considerable pain, intense anger, frustration, and lots of trial and error. And that is not the half of what my parents went through.

"I don't look normal. I appear to be quite messed up and a prime candidate for nothing but pity and patronization with a sprinkling of repulsion and fear. I am disguised as a poor thinker.

"It should be noted that until age nineteen (1992), I was thought to be profoundly retarded. FC changed that. A typical day pre-FC? Boring!!! I would be attended to, bathed, fed, toileted, and schooled (which was really more like watching a TV show about a classroom before interactive video was available). On days when I didn't bother misbehaving, I was simply furniture to be walked around and toted to various gatherings. I loathed my existence at school but knew nothing other than my less painful life at home. I was a case. Violence was about the only distraction I was capable of initiating at school other than intermittently eating whatever I could get my grubby hands on including soap.

"Today is a different life and I am a different person. I am fully involved as a daughter, sister, employer, student, friend, activist, and writer. My days are filled with purposeful activities and responsibilities, not just time fillers and distractions that help another 24 hours to safely pass until I become worm food. The whole process is actually more difficult in term of demands. More is expected of me. Being a fat, non-involved, messy, aggressive, immature slug is no longer an option. My days are structured and I mentally and physically show up for work.

"I think the bulk of my disturbing behaviors – like smearing, kicking, biting, grabbing, hitting, pica, manipulating tantrums, running away, stealing food from others' plates, handling objects for hours on end, breaking my glasses, etc.—have all melted away because none of those things serve my purpose. One is much less likely to be kicked and attacked when I momentarily loose grasp and understanding of my surroundings. Now, when I get confused, scared, and agitated, I try to put my thoughts in words and tweak them into decent prose until I am able to unload them with FC support. All just more good book material.

"FC is quite controversial, meaning lots of people think it is not really me doing the typing. This infuriates me, and I considered chucking the whole thing out of spite. But the words...the words possessed me. Letters first became formidable and gave me power and glimpses of humanity. I touch Y and, tah-dah, Mom knows I do want to go swimming, or let me go towards N, and what I want to stop or not happen magically yields to my power.

"Then combine letters, like they have been forever singing and showing at school, and words appear and take the place over. I like the pseudo-concrete nature of it all. Words are stable. You can count on them.

"FC has helped me to think more systematically. Thinking in language made a huge difference for me in terms of organizing my thoughts. Prior, my thoughts tornadoed in my mind picking up this and that and strewing ideas, feeling, memories, knowledge, and worries about. To get anything done I had to rummage through the debris. It was hard for me to follow through with almost anything except anger, which seemed to be the wind fueling the funnel. So FC helped me piece together the world, block letter by block letter, until I was able to file, store, and retrieve different thoughts and ideas. My world became way less random. Now it works like a well-made clock.

"I think totally differently now. Words are everything: life, death, colors, foods, people, places, wants—everything in the past, present, and future. Now I see people as allies in life not aggressive predators up to no good with unpredictable moves and sounds and I experience myself as part of the whole system of beings and not just a fragmented island of terror and creator abandonment.

"All creatures are built to do more than survive. Quality of life requires it and life is designed to be quality. I must have instinctively known this and was therefore frustrated and angry to the core at doing nothing but passing time between here and autism. Those unsettling feelings and squandered energy manifested in bad behaviors.

"I am not the ambitious or adventurous type, but I have decided to bet the autistic farm on designing and creating the perfect life. I am starting to care and I go now into the wild, wild world of normals. Previously my progress stagnated because of my own lack of commitment to any real change that would be perpetually taxing. Being an unemployed, nonverbal rich girl can be quite luxurious and relatively stress-free, especially with a get-out-of-jail-free label like autism.

"What if I get invested in the outer world and make a real effort to be included and still fail to be successful at the level I desire? Then I am screwed, because the good normals will know that I am rather capable even if I am not terribly interesting or bright. That brings on a lifelong barrage of menial demands. Such chores are not worth fighting through the autistic noise to accomplish.

"At first glance, autism's relationship to the world appears parasitic. I now straddle both realms and seek to disprove the hypothesis that autism needs the world but the world does not need autism. The trick is not to coexist as autism and as a writer but to synergistically be my whole self.

"When I concentrate and turn myself 'on,' fully tuned to the external world, I am quite capable. However, being on uses a lot of battery power. I generally need to recharge after four or five hours, or I won't be able to remain completely on. I follow a schedule which allows blocks of "pseudo-on" states where I am in the world – eating, drinking, exercising, listening, and learning – but am paddocked and essentially undisturbed. This pseudo-on time has increased greatly since I learned to type but I am not expected to type during these times. Typing requires my "full on" resources.

"Also built into my days is significant chill time when I am not required to interact or perform at any level, which allows me to refuel and frolic in my field. But for two hours each day, between the paddock and field, I synergize my efforts and identities and write. I am most alive and fully on at these times, because that is who I am and what I do."

My Writing can Change Minds

Sarah Ann Kemp Stup

Snapshot

Sarah was born in 1983. At age eight, Sarah was diagnosed with autism and she began using FC that same year. Her first wishes after she started typing were to go to her sister's neighborhood school and to be a writer of children's books. While still in high school, she began her writing career as an intern at the ARC of Frederick County, MD. Sarah's published books include a children's book and a book of poetry. She has had several magazine and newspaper articles written about her—most notably a feature story in Exceptional Parent magazine in 2008. Sarah's goal is to help others understand autism and the importance of acceptance and friendship and her website features many teaching materials.

About Sarah

Date of Birth: 1983.   **Started FC:** 1991 at 8 years old.

Current Facilitators: Judy (mother) and Janna (sister).

Access to FC: 1-4 hours/day.

Living Situation: Lives with parents.

Day Program: Self-employed as a writer with supports from The Arc of Frederick County, MD.

Highest level of Independence: Briefly at shoulder and independent with school facilitator.

Secondary Participants: Judy and Darryl (father).

Sarah's Criteria for Quality of Life

Being part of a loving family.

Write kids books about disabilities.

Look and act normal.

Cured of autism.

Having people believe in me.

FC.

Beach and park visits.

Eat out.

Praise God.

Write poetry.

Listen to music.

Hope

Hope troops along through stop signs.

Hope is my leader
Out of a world that turns away.

Hope gathers me in its arms
to go in new directions.

Five Things Sarah Wants You to Know

I am inside.

Really love not being in bad places like special schools.

I love learning.

Paper is how I speak and who I am – a typer with autism.

With my writing I can change minds and make the world a better place.

Five Things Sarah's Parents Want You to Know About Her

Sarah is a creative writer.

She has a strong faith in God and love of family.

She suffers with autism and from misconceptions by others with regard to her disability.

Sarah's mission is to use her writing to improve the lives of those with developmental disabilities and to be a good citizen.

Sarah is very aware of, and hurt by, the doubts of others regarding her communication method and that she is held to a higher standard.

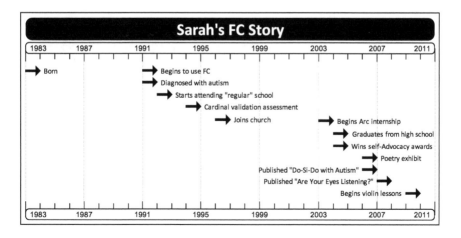

Sarah's Story

Sarah was born in 1983. Her older sister, Janna, was three years old at the time. Sarah's development was on course for two years. Sarah's mother, Judy, remembers hearing her daughter talk in short phrases on the phone to her grandma and calling from her crib that she wanted to get up.

Between two and three years of age, Sarah's development began to slow down. Her behavior became hyperactive and impulsive and she began losing speech and social skills. From that time on, Sarah needed constant supervision because she was fearless; swinging on indoor shutters and jumping from high places. She consumed inedible items and ran into the street with no awareness of cars. In addition to these dangerous behaviors, Sarah's speech and movements became very rigid and obsessive. She lined up crayons for hours.

When she was four and one-half years old, Sarah entered a school for children with disabilities. Her vocabulary was extremely limited; she could verbally communicate only a few food or activity choices. She could identify pictures of items, but her movement disorder prevented her from using pictures as a communication mode to meet her needs.

Before her ninth birthday, Sarah was given six diverse diagnostic labels, including Severe Communication Disorder, Mild Mental Retardation, Attention Deficit Disorder with hyperactivity (ADHD), and Behavior Disorder with Non-Compliance and Oppositional Behavior. Eventually, Sarah was officially diagnosed with Infantile Autism.

Since her behavior fit the profile for mental retardation, most of her interaction with others – family members, special education teachers and peers – occurred with the assumption that she had a limited ability to understand. Although she often spent time in with Janna's friends, no one realized how much Sarah understood.

In 1991, Sarah learned facilitated communication and the world shifted for Sarah and her family.

Today although Sarah is an accomplished writer and advocate for herself and others with disabilities, much of her outward behavior remains rigid and ritualistic. She needs constant supervision and assistance in daily activities. She cannot turn the page of a book and will impulsively eat inedible items. She remains obsessive, ritualistic and prone to wandering, unable to return or solicit assistance. She can be extremely impulsive in both her limited speech and behavior, and appears to have no cognizance of danger. She can be both hyper- and hypo-sensitive to touch; sometimes avoiding and other times seeking it. Upon entering a room, Sarah might flick the light switch several times, take off her shoes or wander about, lightly touching objects and verbalizing to herself, seemingly lost in her own private world. She confides, "I live still in a world called autism, but now I can send you my messages."

As soon as she started communicating with FC, Sarah began to advocate for herself. Judy recalls, "Sarah felt the need to remind us often when she first began to type that she 'is smart.' She rarely tells people this any longer."

Hungry to learn about the world, she told her parents that she wanted to attend the regular school that Janna attended. Judy reveals, "Sarah led us on a new journey of inclusion in neighborhood schools." Less than one year after she started typing, Sarah began to attend her local school.

In looking back on her life in the special education school, Sarah says, "When young I could not speak and was a student in a school with kids who were broken, like me. Not being able to speak made teachers think I was dumb. Also I was afraid if I went to school there long, I might not be able to walk or move, like some other children. Sad days there."

Soon after Sarah began using FC, Judy initiated a series of blind tests to validate Sarah's typing. The teacher would send home a question about something that had happened during the school day. Sarah would type the answer. Likewise, Judy would send questions to school and the teacher would validate Sarah's answers about things that happened at home. On these tests, Sarah achieved between 70-90% accuracy.

In addition to informal testing, Don Cardinal of Chapman University conducted a formal assessment using a portfolio approach and a series of controlled tests. Dr. Cardinal noted that Sarah's typing was validated by the test results as well as by the congruence among facilitators in idiosyncratic writing style. In addition, when Sarah typed something with an emotional charge, uncommon behaviors consistent with the content of her message arose.

Sarah's inclusion in elementary school was largely successful but things became more difficult with each successive school. In middle and high school, some teachers accepted her and saw her gifts. With others, Sarah felt pressure to curb her autistic behavior and realized that her need to type rather than talk put her at a disadvantage. She was painfully aware of her peers' reactions to her odd behavior.

Sarah ceaselessly strived for acceptance and respect. When an insult came her way, she would write a letter to the offenders, imploring them to believe she was smart and to accept her as she was.

In one instance, Sarah's science class listened to a presentation on genetic issues and fetal testing for Williams Syndrome and Downs Syndrome. Believing the lecture took a negative tone toward people with disabilities, she wrote her teacher a letter. In it, she said, "I love science but hate it that you think I am not a good student. You wish I was dead. Williams syndrome and Downs syndrome might be bad genes but the people are not bad. Autism is awful but I am not awful. You forgot to tell my class that real people do live inside who are needing people to quit staring and start politely making friends."

Sarah loved going to a "regular" school and learning new things. She especially liked biology and geometry. Still, she missed some of her old teachers and aides from previous years. Of one teacher Sarah wrote, "She was not scared of autism. She is a friend who understands I am really inside."

At school, Sarah had a full-time assistant who accompanied her to class and helped her interact with her teachers and peers. Over the course of her school years, Sarah utilized 12 school staff who served as facilitators, one of whom was able to support her for short sessions of independent typing. Training and retaining facilitators was a challenge. In the absence of this assistance, Sarah would frequently stay home from school.

Sarah's many sensory and movement differences include hypersensitive hearing. The noisy school environment assaulted her ears, which in turn triggered her odd behaviors. When the faculty took measures to curb these behaviors, Sarah interpreted their actions to mean they hated autism and, by extension, hated her. This belief, in addition to the ongoing doubt and skepticism Sarah endured regarding her method of communication, made it increasingly difficult for her to stay in school.

Nevertheless, Sarah loved learning. Her ability to function in the school setting and the changes she made after starting to type are noted in various official reports.

Before FC, a school psychologist reported, "When compared to six-year-old social-emotional behaviors, Sarah is significantly below the norm. She exhibits little evidence of entering into sustained, reciprocal, and mutually pleasurable relationships with peers and adults."

After using FC for one year, Sarah was evaluated by the same expert, who now observed, "a marked change in social behavior and affect is emerging ... good eye contact, smiles, and some laughter. She is beginning to facilitate social language." Later, in an honor's class, an autism consulting team noted, "Sarah appeared to be functioning well. Sarah's behavior throughout this class, other than the method of communication, was similar to her typical peers. Her teacher was very effective in including Sarah in discussions."

Despite this progress, by 2002, school life became very difficult for Sarah. She lost her facilitator, reacted poorly to OCD medications, her typing regressed and her behavior deteriorated to the point of occasionally hitting others. She wanted to graduate with a diploma rather than a certificate of attendance, but needed approval for an accommodation to pass the Maryland Functional Test with the help of her facilitator. Judy said that gaining this approval took two years, primarily due to the "misinformation, misunderstanding and resulting doubts" regarding FC. Finally, Sarah was able to take the test typing independently for multiple-choice questions and with her facilitator supporting her upper arm for writing text. She passed and graduated with honors in 2004.

Sarah was not eligible for transition funding until she turned 21. The gap in services was filled by a grant for an internship at The Arc of Frederick County. Not only did the internship give Sarah a quiet environment in which she could work with supportive people who did not question her method of communication and who understood her odd behaviors. Sarah had dreamed of being a writer ever since she started to use FC at age eight and with her internship at The Arc, that dream was coming true.

Sarah became a prolific writer and developed a portfolio of her work. On its cover she wrote, "I feel alive to type. The lid opens and out comes pieces of Sarah, the girl with wings who soars above the place with no hope called autism. I am real when I write. Autism is my prison, but typing is the air of freedom and peace."

Sarah writes in a variety of genres and maintains a website. While her writing is focused on advocacy for people with disabilities, it often goes beyond this and strikes at the heart of what it means to be human. She has collaborated on a college-level curriculum designed to help special education students realize their own hopes and dreams as they transition from school into adult services. Her publications, which help non-disabled people understand disabled individuals, have earned self-advocacy awards.

Sarah's first book, *Do-Si-Do with Autism*, features Taylor the Turtle. Taylor has autism and uses his shell for protection. Sarah created Taylor and the other characters in the book when she was ten years old and her dream of publishing a children's book was realized in 2006. Since that time, she has continued writing and publishing and is currently working on a novel for middle school students.

In addition to writing, Sarah is involved with community, political and religious interests. She is currently training a new facilitator who is her own age. Her hope is to have someone other than her mother to help her go shopping for cool clothes. Sarah has always wanted to make music and recently started facilitated violin lessons.

Sarah still has autism and must deal with the limitations as well as the gifts that it brings. Her FC journey has raised the expectations of everyone, including herself. The journey has been worth it, confirm her parents. "Every single day we know first-hand how important this method of communication is to Sarah."

In Sarah's Own Words

"Sarah Ann Kemp Stup is my name, and I am disabled with autism. I am a girl with lots of problems but I am doing my best. Today I type to speak with just a touch on my arm. I am now a real person who can speak about my own wishes and thoughts.

"My body behaves as it pleases. But when my arm is touched, I feel a connection to it and if I go slowly, it can do as I say. When I practice a lot, I need less touching. Pleased to type nicely. To type thoughts makes me a real person.

"When I was alone with no voice, parties could not cheer a lonely hearted soul. Sadness was my best friend and I was peaceful because I had no power. When I was silent, I felt loved but invisible. Saying what I feel and know makes me belong with, not belong to. Now I can be a good citizen. My writing can change minds. Today I am happier and less lonely. Gone is the peace, because now I have opinions and wishes. I feel afraid to lose it. What if I go back to no typing? I feel afraid and hopeful and free, just like a real person.

"Now that I am a facilitated speaker, I can choose and I can complain with typing. I choose both plans for my future and plans for a day. I love to tell how to do math problems and what clothes I prefer. Many people still treat me like a dumb girl, but some know that I understand things. Still wish for speaking voice since it can be fast, warm, and friendly. Love to type, but too slow to be funny and timely. This is my wish: to be real and to have a voice. I wish to say things aloud but the voice does not work and I am silent. A pleasing time for me is typing when I am alive. I am a real person then with things to say. Without typing people forget I am hearing or seeing what happens. Letters and touches worth more than gold to me. A real speaker I am. Autism loses on the keyboard.

"Are your eyes listening? That's what needs to happen to hear my writing voice. Because of autism, the thief of politeness and friendship, I have no sounding voice. By typing words, I can play with my life and stretch from my world to yours. I become a real person when my words try to reach out to you without my weird body scaring you away. Then I am alive. A real person, that's me!

"Autists like me can't tell our bodies what to do. Wishing to be without autism, I killed my beast who is not acting nicely to fit in a normal world. Please forgive my posing as one of you. Meet the real Sarah Stup, the typer who is disabled. The girl who is waiting for you to stop pretending that I need to hide my autism to be in your space. To pretend is painful. Some day the wall may begin to crack as my lots mighty words keep bombarding it.

"People with disabilities are patiently waiting for access to you. Yes, we know your places are open to us if we try very hard to act normal. But opening your places is only the beginning. We are still not really with you yet. We are not real citizens and participants until you allow us to bring our disabilities into your places and then find our gifts inside. Reach out by getting past your fear of imperfection. Please be with us to realize we are worth knowing. Disabilities can make you sad and uncomfortable. Many of you pray not to be like us, and to see us in your places puts you too close to what seems to be a sad life. Pity sounds like caring but it is really fear. We are sad to see fear on your faces instead of friendship. Peace comes when it is passed to all people—not one is unworthy. People with disabilities need access to you, not just your buildings. Do you need ramps to get over your fear of imperfection?

"Autism likes to hide. I'd like to speak to more people, but I am too shy and type too slowly. People make me shy when they visit me, but letters don't make noise. Letters wait patiently for me to finish typing, and letters never hate autism. Letters don't do weird things that scare you away. We who are silent have our value. People can't hear my voice. They must learn to wait for my typing and then use their eyes. But very few people have eyes that hear. They read only what is written as in books and letters.

"Autism stays. My prayers to be cured aren't being answered. Planning to be cured of autism some day, I am a girl full of hope. My mom is not voting to kill autism because she thinks I am great.

"Hope is what I do when I am not busy. Lots of wishing about finding a cure for autism is what I do. Long ago, I decided the name 'Good Girl' was my name, and hoped to be a better girl. Sarah had autism but Good Girl could behave easily. Hoped to be better from dear name, but autism stayed.

"When young, I could not speak and was a student in a school with kids who were broken, like me. We were scared because others didn't know that inside bodies that didn't work were kids with wishes and hopes. Real people do live inside who are needing people to quit staring and start politely making friends.

"I felt awful being alone and silent. My voice or body did not do what I wanted. Dumb girl was Sarah with broken voice. Your world hurt my ears with loud throwing echoes that stayed inside my head. I needed to do weird stuff to protect me. Don't hate autism, my shield and enemy both, because I need it to protect me from the pain of your world.

"Autism is part beast and part human with people trying to tame the naughty animal. The beast has talent but can't always put on a good show. The beast scares you and the human is sad and lonely. Love my beast. Beast keeps me safe. Find me inside the beast. I am the soul.

"Beach visits bring me peace. The beach pleases me when powerful waves roll in to meet a young heart that wishes to wash away pain of autism. Autism leaves with the water. Really love the time waves lap over my body. They tell me of a new life when I will taste the salt of a free soul. Visit a new world of painless renewal. A wave of hope.

"I need to keep climbing my mountains of doubt and sadness into hopeful floating clouds of service. Wish to be truthful and good helping other people who are silent witnesses of another world called autism. Pray that I am a good citizen some day. Pleased to find ways to serve other people by really trying to help people with disabilities. With others helping me, I would like to close institutions and help people with developmental disabilities get regular lives.

"Able to pass God's test for being worthy of love, people with disabilities need friends who think they are worth lots, not broken. Hating people who are disabled is doubting they are real people who think and feel. When I write my kids' books, people might learn that those with disabilities are worth lots. Voices that do have sound are not better than typing voices, just different. I really say lots through typing. Normal kids think I'm broken and not a thinker. Vote they read my book. Really need friends who pose new ideas to old mistaken ways to treat silent people. Please be reading this with Just Glasses so you can see my young eager voice in the letters. The glasses are sold at Wishes Come True stores everywhere. They are just saving lives who are mute but wish to communicate.

"With writing I reach out to try, and autism or hate or walls of doubt can't hold me. I am pleased to be typing away — typing away loneliness, typing away silence, using paper to hug you and slap you and join you. Paper is the holder of who I am. Paper is my ticket out. Click, click, clicking keys are my heartbeat. Listen with your eyes.

"I need my typing to be safe and happy. Kill the doubts that be hurting me. We need just a touch to have a real life with you. Please help us speak loudly. We can be good citizens.

"Don't stop learning from us because our minds are different. Your wish to learn is my hope for understanding.

"I hope many people will open their world through FC. It is sad to be inside a lonely place with no communication. I live still in a world called autism, but now I can send you my messages. Listen in a new way.

"Finished."

Going to Bat for People with Disability

Aaron Ulrich

Snapshot

Aaron was born in 1974. When he was a child, he was placed in a segregated school until his parents filed a lawsuit to allow him to attend public schools. He began to use FC when he was 18 years old and he had a full time facilitator (Tina C.) to assist him in regular education classes. Once Aaron graduated from high school and entered adult services, his life changed dramatically. He no longer had the support he needed to communicate or to learn new functional skills. In 2000, Tina Veale, his speech and language therapist and best facilitator, moved to another state. Today Aaron does not have any facilitators with whom he can type fluently. He lives in a group home and attends an adult day care program.

About Aaron

Born: 1974.   **Started FC:** 1992 at age 18.

Current Facilitators: Mary (mother).

Access to FC: Short answers with Mary 1-2 times per year.

Living Situation: House with one roommate.

Day Program: Day Habilitation program.

Highest level of Independence: Full hand support.

Secondary Participants: Tina Veale (SLP).

Aaron's Criteria for Quality of Life

A very dandy house a little yellow house, big yard and trees.

Father and mother can visit [my house].

Find real nice dandy car.

Persons doing good work with me.

Going to work.

Hearing music.

Knowing friends.

Being free to be OK.

I like to go out places once or twice a week – restaurant, very nice lake or ride very big bike, go to shop in the mall, bowling - need to have more things to do.

Like to eat pizza, ice cream, and cheese.

Black Beauty Book Report

Book I like - Black Beauty. Its like me. Sad story. My life sad. Beauty was hit, no home, looked good, loving horse and black color. We lonely. No friends. Open relationship. I need understanding. Me just got to be gotten serious. Beauty got more they look over us. Got to read book to see the story place. Got to read it. I like it but just very sad. Run to get it. Book hide, no got lost. Go to library just to get it.

Five Things Aaron Wants You to Know About Him

People like me.

Girls are cute and girls like me.

I listen best to music.

To me the world is very beautiful.

You need to be very near to know very much of me.

Seven Things Tina Wants You to Know About Aaron

Aaron is proud to share his thoughts with others.

He expresses opinions about everything from his political views to personal life preferences through FC.

He is a quiet advocate for individuals with life challenges every day.

Aaron is outgoing and social. He loves to GO, whether it be for vacations or social events.

Aaron cares deeply about his family and friends. He is intuitive about their thoughts and feelings, and considers them when forming his decisions and views.

Aaron is more flexible than most of us give him credit for. He has dealt with more change than most young men his age, and has done so gracefully. He is amazingly appreciative and forgiving of others.

Aaron has an inborn sense of faith and has used it to get through some very difficult times in his life.

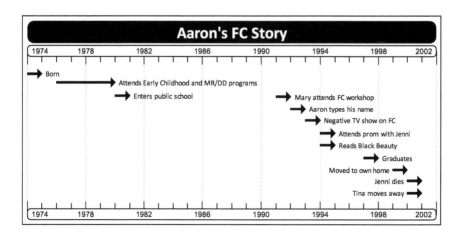

Aaron's Story

Aaron was born in 1974. Two years later, his brother, Tommy, was born. Aaron's father, Tom, taught Industrial Arts in the public schools. His mother, Mary, was a kindergarten teacher and later a professor of Special Education at a university.

As a child, Aaron received multiple diagnoses, including psychomotor delay, mental retardation, autism, cerebral palsy and slow development. Anne Donnellan has noted that Aaron is a "poster child for movement differences." He is sensitive to touch, can get locked into repetitive patterns, has difficult initiating movement, prefers stable routines, is often restless and needs to pace, and will bite himself or others when pressured to perform. Despite many efforts to teach Aaron to point, he never did until he began using FC. His most recent battery of IQ tests reported his IQ as two years and 11 months.

At home, Aaron's parents tried to focus on the positive things and worked hard to accommodate the very few activities that held Aaron's interest for more than a few seconds. They kept extra locks on doors and cabinets and repeatedly plunged toilet paper rolls out of the toilet. Tommy knew to keep his bedroom door locked or he would come home to find his baseball cards strewn about.

Aaron has been a pioneer for inclusion, supported living, the Medicaid waiver and HUD rent subsidies. In the 1980s, Ohio had a segregated system for people with the label of mental retardation. Through a series of lawsuits, Aaron and another boy with a disability challenged the Cincinnati School District. Although the district was nearly broke at the time, it spent $60,000 in legal fees to keep the boys in a segregated setting. Roncker v. Walters was the first case that went to the Federal Supreme Court under P.L. 94-142; shortly after that, Ulrich v. Walters enabled Aaron to be the first person with a severe disability to go to Cincinnati public schools. Years later, when the speech therapist documented that Aaron needed FC in order to communicate, the district hired its first full-time facilitator to assist Aaron in general education classes.

Mary remembers the 1991 workshop where she learned about FC. She and Tom had always been open to trying experimental things to help Aaron have a better life, but she was convinced FC would not work for her son. She relates that she attended the workshop only so she could check FC off her list.

The next day, Aaron attended the workshop and successfully typed with one of the instructors. When it was Mary's turn to try some simple multiple-choice questions, she was not certain whether or not she might be leading

Aaron's hand. Then she experienced an undeniable moment in which everything changed. She says, "I saw his pointer finger hesitate over a letter and he made a sort of surge to the letter next to it, which was the correct letter. A week later, I was still haunted by that finger twitch to the right answer. I spent another full day at the conference wondering about that earlier twitch, and what it meant for Aaron and our family."

Despite the finger twitch, Mary and Tom were still not certain that Aaron knew how to read and spell, so Mary took him to see another experienced facilitator. Aaron did not type anything, but just as they prepared to leave, he took the facilitator's hand and typed his full name, hometown and state. Mary recalls, "Cincinnati wasn't spelled right, of course, but four words and we just knew."

Those four words changed everything. Mary began to regret all the ordinary opportunities she had given Tommy, but not Aaron as the boys were growing up. She remembered with horror all the conversations that had occurred in front of Aaron about frustrations, resentments and fears for his future; now she realized he had understood all of it! Immediately, conversations with family and friends shifted.

Once Aaron started typing, Tommy was happy to have his brother share the burden of answering their parents' inevitable question, "What happened at school today?" Mary says FC had given her "the gift of being able to know Aaron's likes and dislikes; what he thinks is funny, sad, and scary; what he wants to do."

Aaron worked on his typing with Tina Veale, a speech and language pathologist (SLP), every week. His peers began to see him as more competent and Aaron began to have a regular teenage life. When the school planned to celebrate Earth Day, Aaron typed that he wanted to be on the tree committee. When his school facilitator asked why he chose that committee, he answered that was where the cutest girls were. Aaron joined the cross-country team, began eating lunch with the jocks and dressed in a tuxedo to take his lifelong friend, Jenni, to the prom.

Black Beauty was the first book Aaron read for school. Afterward, he wrote a book report on it. Next, the class read Lord of the Flies. In it, a boy is killed for being different. The story upset Aaron and although he never typed about it, he has never wanted to read another book. One good outcome, however, was that Aaron started looking at books for the first time and pointing to pictures. This activity continues to bring him much pleasure today.

Aaron began participating in his IEP meetings at school and making decisions about his education and other aspects of his life. He was able to explain some of his behavioral difficulties, which were usually based on physical discomfort. Mary says those high school years were his very best years. Aaron echoed that, when he wrote, "I just like to be in class with people, just like other kids. I used to be in multiple handicaps class but I in regular class now, too. With my friends. Mother feels good. People think I'm not retarded anymore. Only dumb people think so now."

In 1994, Tina interviewed six boys in some of Aaron's classes. Many peers easily accepted his presence in the classroom. Classmate Bill said, "I like Aaron and I'll sit by him anytime." Mark showed a high level of empathy when he said, "I feel I'd like to be in a higher level class. So, I know how Aaron would feel if he weren't here."

When Tina pressed to see if the boys questioned the validity of Aaron's typing, she was pleased, and perhaps a little surprised, to learn that doubting Aaron's abilities never occurred to them. As one astute boy, John, said, "Without a doubt it's Aaron. I've sat next to him from time to time. It's him. He knows what he's doing. His body language changes."

Tina supports Evan's observation with specific observable changes that occurred when Aaron was typing. She explained, "I believe that Aaron is so much more fluid, fluent with movement when doing FC, especially with me. His tremors are fewer when we FC, and his attention and vigilance are greatly increased. He is usually high strung and needs constant movement or activity. When he is typing, however, he is much calmer, he is more focused and stays on topic much longer."

In 1997, Aaron graduated from high school. When Tina asked him what he thought was his most important accomplishment from his high school years, he replied, "Going to bat for people with disability to go to classes with other kids." When she asked about his graduation parties, he said, "Good time to go but fun is not the point. I am finished in school. I like being with others to celebrate going to be adult worker."

Aaron had always been included in Boy Scout outings with the help of his dad and brother. While he had a good time and good experiences with the other scouts before FC, he had never had a badge to put on his uniform because he could not pass the verbal requirements. After he started typing, everyone was surprised to learn he knew the Scout oath and motto. Soon he went before the board and passed the test for the rank of Tenderfoot. On weekend outings, he became more a part of the group when he could type with several other scouts and their fathers.

Typing became a vital conduit for Aaron to process emotions and connect with others during difficult events in his life. In 1993, a television show presented FC in a negative light. After it aired, Aaron had trouble sleeping for several nights. Tina was able to discuss it with him, so he could express his concerns.

In 2000, Mary and Tom sold the house where Aaron grew up and moved into a condominium. The first night in the new house, Aaron came to Tom and Mary's bedside in the middle of the night carrying his shoes and verbalized, "Go home." Although this shows that it was a stressful time for Aaron, Mary said it also marked a milestone for authentic verbalization. Typing later with Tina, Aaron said, "I wish things would settle. I like things to be settled. Up all night because had to fresh up thoughts about the house. Great to move but I like mom and dad's old house."

Before FC, Mary wondered what Aaron thought and felt about traumatic life events. When his grandparents died, he had no way of asking questions or expressing his thoughts and feelings. In July 2000, Jenni's mother killed herself and Jenni. Jenni and Aaron had been friends since early childhood and spent a lot of time together over the years. Tina offered Aaron the opportunity to type about this tragic event. It is apparent from his words that Aaron was working to frame it in a positive light. He typed, "Jenni is my girl from a long time and now Jenni is just gone. Thinking real sad not to see Jenni. Friends who die go to heaven with Jesus. Friends in heaven are OK. Jenni is really alive but she is just not here. Jenni likes Uno and I like cards so we are alike. I have lots of friends but you can't get new friends like Jenni since she was a friend since I was little. Can I really see Jenni in heaven. I can find her OK because heaven is crowded. Going to heaven is happy."

In addition to processing feelings, FC gave Aaron an avenue to go to bat for others. Aaron and Tina took part in several events to promote FC, including a presentation to the entire School of Education at Miami University. They also held several presentations to speech and language students and to Mary's Special Education class at Miami University. When Tina asked Aaron what advice he would like to give to the future teachers, he typed, "Just to be sure to always be able to believe you are able to make a difference but not to give up on people who need your help. Just be strong and keep working hard."

After graduating from high school, Aaron entered the world of adult services and no longer had funding for a day-to-day facilitator. Mary explains, "When he reached 22 and the guarantees of school and IDEA were over and done, Aaron just slid back down into the valley of no man's land. No law, no services, no recourse, or due process." Despite this, Aaron continued to see Tina once or twice a week until she moved 200 miles away.

To date, Aaron's staff at home and in his day program have not been interested in learning FC. As a result, Aaron has been without a voice for eight years. He occasionally types with his mother to provide short answers to her questions, but they have never been able to achieve a fluid, conversational level of communication. In 2002, Tina traveled back to type with Aaron so he could answer the interview questions for this book. Mary reported that Aaron and Tina easily picked up where they left off and that Aaron was "like a typing machine after a year of no typing."

During this time, Aaron spent three days per week in a work day program where he had a job for two hours each day. According to Mary, "That was our big victory. Of course, he worked outside picking up in a parking lot at a hotel which was fine. Aaron likes being outside – it seemed to be a job that he enjoyed doing."

The rest of the time, he worked indoors sorting screws. Aaron did not like this work and sometimes swallowed a screw. The staff then removed him from the work area. When he was not sorting screws, Aaron could watch TV. Mary reports, "They had this place called the back ward for the people who didn't want to work. They had this fuzzy television with this ragged old rug in front of it and people slept on the rug because they were so bored out of their minds." There were worktables in the back ward too, but unfortunately, they were very high, so when Aaron sat at the table it was about face-level. As a result, he just sat and licked the table until the day was over. They just washed it off.

When Aaron was not licking tables, he usually sat quietly in front of the fuzzy television. On one visit, his mother noticed that the chair he was sitting in did not have a cushion. Instead, he was sitting on the Velcro strips that had once held the cushion. Apparently, the staff had not thought to replace it, even though Aaron sometimes sat there for seven hours at a time and if he was wearing shorts the Velcro irritated his legs.

Although he was only 28 at the time, the workshop management suggested placing Aaron in their geriatric unit. Mary's parents had often said she should put him in an Alzheimer's unit where the doors would be locked and he would not know the difference; then she could go back to living her own life. Fortunately for Aaron, Tom and Mary have not been willing to do that.

Over the years, many professionals have told Mary to be thankful for the services Aaron receives. Her response: "How can I be thankful when I see Aaron lose all the skills we worked so hard for him to achieve?"

Today, Mary and Tom's frustration over adult services continues unabated. Staff are not well trained to work with people with disabilities and they do not understand or care about using the lens of sensory and movement differences to interpret Aaron's behavior. After every available transition and rehabilitation dollar had been used, Aaron could no longer continue in the work program because he was unable to work independently. His choice was limited to adult-day-care-with-a-theme, such as sports, art or computers. Each day Aaron does 'artwork' using odds and ends such as toilet paper rolls, felt scraps and macaroni while the staff sing preschool songs and talk about the weather. Community outings are limited to Burger King.

Mary notes that the adult day care programs are run by good people, but they are not trained in disability issues or best practices and are not aware of the gulf between their program and that offered in the schools. As Mary watches Aaron and the others lose skills, she says, "It breaks my heart. Yesterday, the residential staff recommended putting Aaron in diapers. Another new low."

In spite of everything, Aaron is resilient and seems to know the staff are doing their best. He is given reading materials. He spends hours looking at encyclopedias and magazines. He likes music and can operate a tape recorder independently.

Aaron manages to communicate many wants and needs without words. His alphabet board sits on the coffee table in his home, mostly unused; once in a while he will point to a letter. Mary thinks Aaron's reluctance to use the board with her comes from the fact that he was 18 when he started FC, and by then he had already worked out a system of communicating with his parents.

Mary incorporates the concepts around movement differences into Aaron's life whenever possible to interpret his behavior. Recently, Aaron had an opportunity to go horseback riding. Mary could clearly see how the horse calmed him, just as it did when he was little.

Each day is another opportunity to learn more about Aaron. His family is hopeful he will show them the way. FC and the concept of movement differences continue to impact their lives every day.

In Aaron's Own Words

Tina: What is important for people to know about FC?

Aaron: I think they are going to get a big surprise. I think they are going to find too many people in the world need to type because they don't talk. [They] have it fine in their life. They can talk. You tell them to stop hoarding the talking. I just want the right to talk. Very important to them. They need to learn how to listen. Really I need to talk to make people hear me, but no one thinks I really have things to say. They are wrong, but know funny little how to communicate with me.

Tina: Tell me how to best communicate with you.

Aaron: How I find best is to work on rhythm. Really I need to see the rhythm of very willing people. Understanding sharing rhythm in togetherness.

Tina: What is rhythm?

Aaron: To feel beats, big and little, going in and out, up and down, back and forth all the time. There are too many to totally hear.

Tina: What is noise?

Aaron: To be out of beat. Most people feel one beat, but I have many. It is a problem because I am on different beats. To type just need your beat. I listen best to music. It teaches rhythm.

Tina: What do you do when you are having a hard time putting your thoughts into words?

Aaron: I always have that problem but I say it and the best I can to get it out. I just type little bits of thinking using very little prompts on my hand.

Tina: Aaron, mom wants to know it is OK to put your sentences in her book?

Aaron: yes

Tina: Is there anything you would like to say to someone who is thinking about starting facilitated communication?

Aaron: To type to the heart. You can get your point out.

Tina: What's your biggest message?

Aaron: I want to say give it a try

Tina: What's on your mind?

Aaron: Very nice to dream about breaking the mold and doing big new things. Thinking powerful thought is to be like a moonbeam in the night. To me the world is very beautiful and big like your mind...how big it must be to bend new ideas. Having a voice is wonderful but greater is having understanding. Greatest thing is happiness, but some people don't know this.

Happiness is going ready into the world to be with people. Doing good is being friends by being willing to accept faults and really be free. You need to be very near to know very much of me.

FC has Lightened the Burden for Me

Wally Wojtowicz, Jr.

Snapshot

Wally was diagnosed with autism at age two and by age three, had taught himself to read. His favorite book was the dictionary and he spent his childhood educating himself through books along with public TV and radio. Wally started to use FC at age 25 and soon became a prolific writer. When he quit attending his day program in 1998, he and his father would type for five hours per day. Today Wally is almost completely paralyzed from ALS but he continues to have a positive, loving outlook on life. He currently uses eye gaze equipment to communicate.

About Wally

Born: 1966.   **Started FC:** 1992 at age 25.

Current Facilitators: Wally Sr. (father).

Participants: Wally Sr. and Gayalyn (parents).

Access to FC: 24 hours per day/7 days per week.

Living Situation: Parents' home.

Day Program: Custom program – FC, reading, listening to music & talk radio, letter writing, creative writing.

Highest level of Independence: Typed short phrases independently. Uses eye gaze equipment independently.

Equipment: Letterboard, computer with text to voice, Tobii eye gaze equipment.

Wally's Criteria for Quality of Life

To be able to ask questions.

To have a way to reach the world outside of my mind.

To be a contributing member of society.

To continue to learn and grow.

To be in the company of loved ones.

To feel a soft kiss on my forehead.

To look into another's eyes.

To feel someone's hand holding mine.

Quietly, Quietly*

Years escape our notice as they slip quietly by without a sound that alerts us.
Quietly, quietly I will exit the life that I teach others of.
Truly, I leave you to eventually follow me.
I will return to you in your dreams as you sleep.
Each of my old ways will remind you that I am still here in spirit.

*Written in a letter to Wally's Grandmother

Five Things Wally Wants You to Know

I love people and enjoy their company.

I believe in God.

I love life and nature.

I am very intelligent.

My favorite place is Schoodic, Maine.

Five Things Wally's Parents Want You to Know About Him

Wally is a very patient person.

He makes friends with his eyes and smile without saying a word.

Wally accepts his situation (ALS, autism, epilepsy) with grace and dignity.

He is very thoughtful.

He has a great, strong spirit.

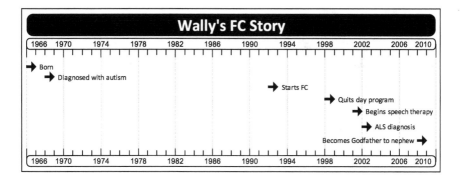

141

Wally's Story

Wally Wojtowicz, Jr. was born in 1966 to parents Wally Sr. and Gayalyn. He has an older and a younger sister.

The doctor who diagnosed Wally with autism at age two told his parents their son would never achieve a mental age beyond a three-year-old and an IQ of 20. Advising them that nothing could be done for their son, he recommended they place him in an institution. Instead, the Wojtowiczes have kept Wally at home with them for his entire life.

When he was nine years old, Wally was diagnosed with epilepsy. He also suffers from degrees of Cerebral Palsy, Tourette's Syndrome and Obsessive-Compulsive Disorder.

Wally was enrolled in day programs from ages three through 32. At age ten, he had a short stint in public school. He recounts, "I attended the local elementary school for one hour. My one brief experience with public education stemmed from my mom's insistence that I be given the opportunity to sit at a desk in a class with normal students."

Wally did not encounter FC until he was 25, but he developed an early relationship with words and had learned to read by the time he was three. His parents remember seeing him run his index finger along the lines of print on a cereal box at a very young age. He spent hours fanning the pages of children's storybooks.

Wally says he gleaned the meanings of the "word shapes" by associating them with the audio version of the story that he gained from listening to his parents read the books to his sisters. If Wally's parents attempted to read to him, however, he would run away.

Communicating years later via FC, Wally acknowledges that initially he was very careful about divulging his intelligence. He says, "Each revelation of my intelligence that I revealed to my parents was carefully thought out. Each revelation was slowly administered in measured doses so my parents would not be overwhelmed or frightened by my understanding of the world that so far had been only a fantasy for them."

The family home was a literacy-rich environment offering a wide array of encyclopedias and other educational materials. Wally was continuously exposed to elements to educate and stimulate his mind, including public radio and television, books on tape and classical music. The dictionary was one of his favorite books. Wally's parents loaded books on tape into a tape player every evening so he would have something to listen to if he awoke in the middle of the night. When Wally was older, his father and uncle devised a bookstand with a ribbon page marker so he could signal when he needed help with turning the page.

Like many FC users, Wally reads at a very rapid rate. He notes, "Reading 400 pages per hour is not uncommon for me. Reading a book truly is as easy for me as tying one's shoes is for someone else. Tying my shoes is something that I still can't do."

Being able to speed-read but not tie one's shoes is not an uncommon situation for individuals with sensory and movement differences. For Wally, the lack of connection between his inner abilities and outer behavior made life, as he says, "a living hell. My head was full of great thoughts, great ideas and really great questions. I couldn't get them out and didn't think I ever would." He explains the disconnect by making a distinction between his two wills: one based on impulsive behavior and the other upon what is reasonable and rational. He says, "They pulled my mind in opposite directions for most of my life."

Despite his literacy abilities, as a child, Wally exhibited many behaviors that appeared to confirm the doctor's prognosis. For hours, he would spin the wheels of toy cars, twiddle string, or sift sand or dirt though his fingers. He would push his grandfather, eat the feet off his sister's Barbie dolls, and chew on the doll's clothes or twigs from the trees in the yard. Other common behaviors included rocking, bobbing, hand-flapping, tiptoe-walking, screeching, screaming, spitting, jumping on his knees, burping, moaning, slamming chairs, pinching and laughing, tearing clothing, dumping things, grabbing others' food and jumping out of a moving car. When he had an outburst, his parents would go through their checklist of possible causes. If they could not figure out the cause and offer something that would pacify him, they were forced to leave him alone until he wore himself out.

When Wally reached adolescence, he withdrew. For the most part, he ignored everyone, including family members. In 1991, the Wojtowiczes saw an article on FC, Wally Sr. filed it away, presuming it was beyond Wally's capabilities and that Wally had no interest in communicating. Nevertheless, later that year when Wally Sr. learned that a school was using FC, he decided to observe the method. He left the school that day with a set of instructions and worksheets and stopped to buy a Franklin Speller on his way home.

Wally Sr. began by reading the FC article aloud in hopes that Wally might comprehend the process and its purpose. He set the Speller on the table. Wally responded by extending his index finger. As soon as Wally Sr. offered support and backward resistance to his hand, Wally typed his full name: wallywojtowiczjr. In looking back , Wally says, "This escape from prison was so welcomed by me that on several occasions I simply wept upon realizing that there were opportunities for me that I never thought would be possible."

In 1998, after communicating via FC for several years, Wally decided it was a waste of time to continue attending a day program where his abilities and talents were not utilized and where the bus ride was more stimulating than the program itself. He said, "Each day I waste at the center exaggerates the typical behaviors associated with autism that I demonstrate so well."

His parents agreed to let Wally pursue a course of self-study at home in which father and son typed for five or more hours per day. Although he was making good progress on his goal of independent typing, Wally wanted very much to learn to speak, so in 2001, he started speech therapy. He gained the ability to give short verbal answers to questions and to ask questions of his own.

Wally took two non-credit college courses; one home-based and one classroom-based. He did well in both. During the latter, he began learning to sit in a classroom at community college. Although he increase of seizure activity made it impossible for him to continue his college curriculum, his writing benefited greatly from the formal educational structure.

Despite improvement in his daily life, many of Wally's difficult behaviors remained. As behaviors developed over more than 25 years, Wally says he viewed them like old friends that are difficult to give up especially when they are effective. Referring to habits of grabbing other people's food or jumping until his head touches the ceiling, he acknowledges, "I realize that I am being obnoxious each time that I do one of these behaviors but also know that I will get immediate results."

Sometimes, an outburst resulted from something that frightened him, such as violence aired on TV. FC has proven to be very helpful in dealing with these episodes. Wally notes, "I, in protest to such inhuman treatment that man perpetrated against man, infuriating my parents, would holler, scream, and carry on. I, now, can indulge in an intelligent conversation about these frightening topics."

Wally studied foreign languages in books and on educational TV. He taught himself to translate several languages including Russian, German, Italian, French, Hebrew, and Spanish. He has written articles for newsletters and helped college students with assignments relating to autism and FC. Driven by a desire to be comprehensive, he once answered a student's question not with the few paragraphs she expected, but with a 50-page response that took 350 hours to write.

In 2002, Wally was diagnosed with ALS (commonly known as Lou Gehrig's disease), a degenerative neurological disorder. In researching Wally's writings as far back as 1993, the family found many references to early signs of the disease.

As the disease progressed, Wally became weaker. In 2003, he fell and had to spend nine days in the hospital. His parents shared some of his essays with the nurses, who were touched by his writings. Some made copies to give to friends whose children had autism. When Wally left the hospital, one nurse said goodbye in Russian; the gesture brought a quick smile to his face.

By 2007, it was more difficult for Wally to breathe and swallow. He had a tracheotomy and a feeding tube was inserted. He has been on a ventilator ever since. Now, Wally is almost completely paralyzed; he has lost the use of both legs, his left arm and left hand, and all but the index finger of his right hand. He can type a small amount with arm and wrist braces. He has no control of his head and neck muscles and only slight control of his facial muscles. Wally still has control of his eye movements which allows him to communicate independently utilizing his Tobii eye gaze equipment. Once Wally's eye muscles deteriorate, the use of the Tobii will no longer be an option for him. As his father notes, "Wally does not dwell on the subject of his ALS and only occasionally mentions it in his writing."

When it appeared it would not be possible for Wally to attend his sister's wedding, they moved the ceremony into his room. He was dressed for the occasion in a T-shirt painted to look like a tuxedo and the family decorated the room with artificial wedding flowers that would not exacerbate his allergies. In 2008, Wally attended the baptism of his nephew and became the baby's godfather.

Wally's life has become severely limited, but he still enjoys visiting with friends, participating in family life and contributing to society. A friend is currently compiling, integrating, and editing Wally's writings for publication. It will include insights such as this: "Our futures depend on what we can show to the world as a badge of worth so that we will not be left at the fringes of human existence."

In Wally's Own Words

"Before using FC my life was a living hell. My head was full of great thoughts, great ideas and really great questions. I couldn't get them out and didn't think I ever would. The days passed very slowly for me. Fortunately, I taught myself to read at about three years of age and was able to do anything that I could read about. Math, physics, philosophy, biology, fooling around with heat and light, and having great times goofing around with philosophy are some of the things that I thought about during the time I was five to six years old. Fortunately, there were lots of books in the house to read and the TV was on good educational stations.

"Perhaps I was viewed as behaving like a baby before I could communicate because no one took the time to try to understand me. This infuriated me and as a result, I finally gave in to behaving like everyone expected me to behave, i.e. like a baby or sadly like the two-and-one-half year-old that my immeasurable IQ indicated. I knew the effects of this behavior ill-suited my size and age, but how else was I to manifest my likes or dislikes or basic needs? This behavior-based communication system is in reality still in use by me even today. It is easier to grab someone's ice cream cone than it is to ask for one using FC and run the risk of being denied because of the fact that I am allergic to dairy products.

"I took each person to the point of insanity when they would try to teach me even the simplest form of communication. In my mind, I knew, for the most part, what they were trying to teach me was truly in my best interest. Their apparent infuriation at not reaching me only made me feel more in control of them and of the situation. The more power that I realized I had, the more I wanted and craved. In my mind, I was the victor in these daily skirmishes. In reality, I was the loser. I was a big loser.

"It was easy to trust my parents, my family members, and a few close friends of our family. No matter what the situation was, someone would always be there to protect me from any physical harm that I was exposed to through my extremely bizarre behaviors. They saw only the helpless little boy with a problem that they didn't understand but who they tried to protect with patience, love, and understanding.

"The optimism that my parents had and still possess eventually figured in my learning to communicate when a friend sent us a newspaper article dealing with facilitated communication. This happened in the fall of 1991, resulting in my starting FC in February of 1992 when I was 25 years of age. FC continues to be one of my links to the world that is outside of myself.

"Prior to the onset of ALS, FC was my major link to the world though I also tried to develop other forms of communication such as independent typing, use of verbal language, expressive art, and brainwave activated computer access. I achieved varying degrees of success in each of these endeavors. During early 2007, because of the advancing ALS which caused a waning of my FC abilities, I started to incorporate the use of the Tobii eye gaze computer system in my communication program. The use of the Tobii eye gaze computer system will extend my ability to communicate with the world that is outside of my mind when FC is no longer an option for me.

"FC has meant for me a way I reach the world that is outside of my mind. It wasn't until I started to communicate using FC that I found the link that was missing for so many years between our two worlds. Many of my misconceptions about your world were corrected in my mind as I began to use your language to communicate with not only you but ultimately myself.

"Without some way to verify the information that you have experienced from the world that is outside of yourself, you can't realize what information is reliable and what is not; what is truth and what is fiction. Without some way to communicate with the outside world in a rational way you soon become isolated from it and become a prisoner in the solitary confinement that is your mind. You become – as I became –autistic and though you are willing to become 'normal,' reality is always just a question away; a question that I could not ask.

"Each FC session is as emotional for me as is religion for others. Pre-FC was at best a time that, for me, was totally and brutally savaged by autism when its reality and the blinding storm of sensory stimulation isolated my mind from the world that existed just outside of myself and at worst it was a time when I was aware of everything that was happening all around me even though I couldn't respond with a meager 'yes' or 'no' to indicate to others that I too had a functioning and intelligent intellect. This inability to answer simple questions that they asked of me was quite depressing emotionally before FC.

"FC has lightened the burden for me so that I can now cope better with the world that I am slowly becoming part of. I can now communicate my thoughts and feelings directly from my mind to the eyes of others via FC. This has given me the voice that I never had. FC makes it possible for me to communicate my thoughts with the topics ranging from dinner plans, current events, health matters, government affairs, music, and of course to the presidential race among others. This escape from prison was so welcomed by me that on several occasions I simply wept upon realizing that there were opportunities for me now that I never thought would be possible.

"Reaching out to the world to tell you that I am an intelligent and thinking person was only a dream for me that I dreamt for many years. Reality, the reality of my knowing that I was an intelligent and thinking person who could not communicate with the world outside of my mind, would rip through the euphoria that I felt when I awoke each day and it soon engulfed me with the despair that I lived with for many years before learning to FC. Every night sleep would bring a mixture of peace and, at times, horror-filled dreams. Because I could not ask questions, reality and dreams were mixed to give me no sense of what was real and what was only a product of my mind. Perhaps this answers in part why I acted the way I did at times.

"Maybe someone, some place will read my thoughts and will then establish in their minds a new image of the non-verbal autistic person and because of this new image, make the life of some other autistic person more meaningful. If this happens just once, then everything that I have done will have been worth the effort and will be the most important thing that I could have done.

"I rapidly am beginning to open my world to include other folks other than just my family and a few close friends or acquaintances. This opening of my iron curtain that I constructed to protect myself from imagined fears and imagined anxieties unfortunately also prevented entrance into my life those people whose companionship I now appreciate as I open my private sanctuary to those willing to share a precious moment with me. Constant words of encouragement are not the stimulus that makes me go through the pain of coming to your bright and colorful world. The stimulus is love that I feel emanating from the people I work with and trust. The hours of silence between the FC sessions are tremendously lonely for me as I seem to have realized in my own way the subtle and satisfying feeling that this meaningful connection to your world has made on my life.

"Please don't think FC is a cure for autism. It isn't, it's just a tool to help us communicate. FC, though successful for me, may not be the procedure for others. The purpose of FC is for communicating, not curing. I am very content with being the only autistic man, so far, in my immediate family. I must confess that I enjoy my unique position. 'Wally the Autistic' has about the same ring as does 'Alexander the Great' in the minds of many.

"Today I think that ALS is how God is rewarding me for my past prayers for deliverance from autism. I look on this episode in my life as perhaps the closest that I will be to becoming a normal human being. I reiterate what I have told other people; my life now with ALS is what I always wanted it to be with the exception of being paralyzed. I can now eat with other people without grabbing their food or drink. I don't run away from people upon meeting them. I can be a part of a group without leaving to be by myself. I now can look into someone's face to let them know that I am happy to be in their company. I can now look into another's eyes and pierce their soul with my gaze. I can now be happy and content to feel another person's cheek press mine, or to feel a soft kiss on my forehead, or to feel someone's hand holding mine. All of these little things that most people don't think about I can now do and take pleasure in. Yes, I miss the freedom of movement, but I now enjoy those people who I see. I am now as close to being 'normal' as I ever will be. God has answered my prayers."

Part III:
Prominent
Themes

Skepticism

*"I don't think I expected to have so many non-believers
and to be fighting the battles."*

Jo Page

While opponents have taken a position of rigid certainty concerning FC, many proponents hold a more nuanced stance. Although they encounter times of doubt and skepticism from others and even themselves, proponents have not abandoned it altogether. There often is an initial hesitancy to embrace the method and twinges of doubt can endure for years. As behavior improves or typed messages are spontaneously validated, the doubt subsides.

It can be a life-changing experience to fully embrace and comprehend FC. In the initial stages of using the technique, it is no wonder families, professionals, and facilitators find themselves feeling disoriented and questioning the reality and authenticity of what they are seeing. Even when they become more confident with the process, they still must contend with the disbelief and in some cases, the opposition, of others.

Skepticism can impact autistic individuals directly, through the disbelief of their family members, teachers or therapists, and also through limited availability of services. Many individuals with autism are denied access to FC. Those who have obtained it often struggle to keep it in their daily lives. Finding and retaining professionals trained and willing to use the technique is a constant challenge.

Initial Skepticism

Nick's stepmother, Gwen, describes how she and Nick's father, reacted with skepticism when they first encountered the idea of Nick being able to to communicate,

> When Nick started facilitating [at school], his teacher spoke to his Dad and me. We laughed in her face. I said, "If you can get a yes and no and you can tell me when he's got an ear infection or when he's stealing suckers, that would be great." Then when she sent home a notebook of [concrete examples], we read it and had shivers down our backs. I called her the next day and asked "How do I do this?"

Habitual perspectives can be particularly difficult to overcome. Often, the most staunch skepticism comes from professionals. Aaron and Tom both have mothers who are highly trained educators in the field of autism and disability. FC challenged everything they knew, leading both of them to express strong doubts. After watching Aaron type for the first time, Mary confided, "I cannot rationalize the logic of what my eyes are seeing. How is it possible that Aaron can spell?"

As a professor of special education, Mary understood that the autism spectrum includes a wide range of cognitive abilities. When she first learned about FC, she thought Aaron was probably in the estimated 10% of individuals for whom FC would not be applicable. In Aaron's story, Mary tells how she felt Aaron's finger twitch just before his hand surged toward a letter. Despite this, her prior beliefs were strong enough to cause her to question her own experience.

Jo was a teacher in one of the top-rated schools in the country for children with autism. As a parent of a 36-year-old son with autism, she had seen many interventions and procedures come and go. When she attended her first presentation on FC, she was thinking it might be beneficial for some of Tom's more able housemates, but certainly not for Tom. She noted:

> I was impressed, but also not impressed. I was looking at it from more of a scientific standpoint. I had been involved in teaching

autistic people for years and I just couldn't imagine that what they were saying was accurate. It just didn't ring true to me.

Jo's notion that "it just didn't ring true" is consistent with many professionals' initial response to FC. It challenges all of the field's theory and practice.

Despite their extensive knowledge of the research literature on autism and their initial disorientation and disbelief about what FC meant in terms of that literature, both Mary and Jo maintained what Pedhazur and Schmelkin have called "the scientific orientation."[1]

The scientific orientation requires a tolerance for ambiguity and the ability to avoid rushing into quick and easy answers. This can mean postponing closure and maintaining a "wait and see" approach while gathering more data. It also allows questions to emerge; even questions that challenge conventional wisdom and the status quo.

Adjustment

Opponents of FC suggest that support has come from parents who are deluded and overtaken by wishful thinking. However, many responses from the families profiled in this book reveal that FC stunned them and upended their worlds. Their responses were much more complex than merely "wishful thinking." The adjustment period was extremely difficult as they dealt with a variety of emotions including guilt and regret. Jo explains:

> Up until that point, Tom had consistently tested at two years old or under. He fit into that profile in the retarded category and we treated him as such. I talked to him like he was a two-year-old or a three-year-old. That was one of the things that was terribly traumatic for me – to think that this sophisticated conversation was coming out of this person that I had treated like a baby. He's 36 years old – how do we treat him at this point? Should I talk to him like I usually did or should I suddenly start talking to him like an adult? I can just remember sitting and looking at him and just wondering what he must think of me! It was traumatic for a while until we adjusted to the difference in taking care of a profoundly retarded two-year-old and suddenly being confronted with a man.

Mary's self-observation echoes Jo's thoughts:

> I feel tremendous guilt. We would, right over his head, talk about our fears for his future, our frustrations with the present, our personal sacrifices and resentments. How damaging to Aaron's

self-esteem! No wonder he retreats away from us! All those times when I had been so hurt by injustice, unequal treatment, and opportunities, it had been a comfort to think Aaron was content, happy, somehow protected in his innocence.

Effects of Skepticism

Since FC challenges virtually all our current knowledge about autism and developmental disability, many professionals were quick to guard the status quo and stifle the debate. While opponents have brought to the fore important questions about FC, their vehemence has been a destructive force that has been hurtful to many FC speakers and their families. Sarah's mother, Judy, wrote, "The misinformation, misunderstanding and resulting doubts about the method never stop. They are painful for Sarah and also for us." Sarah reiterated, "A lot of doubters hurt me. No faith in me for very long. Never can stop the doubting."

Doubt from the professional community has been particularly harmful to Doug and Aaron. Aaron's facilitator, Tina, reports:

> Aaron was sensitive to the negative swell of public opinion about FC. He felt very bad that some people were skeptical, and that some people said bad things about not just him, but others (such as myself) who were directly involved with FC. He has often said that he thought we were brave.

Like Aaron, Doug was very sensitive to the skepticism. He overheard some of his staff saying they did not believe his typing. Judi notes, "That was pretty devastating for him because he wanted to quit facilitating [after that]."

Nick views the skepticism about FC as a continuation of doubts about his intelligence. He relates:

> Many people are skeptical about my ability to communicate. I have lived my whole life continuously trying to prove to people that I am not dumb or retarded. It seems that every day people try to test my intelligence. It is almost as if they are trying to prove my intelligence to themselves. They seem to think that I am trying to 'con' them or trick them into believing that I am normal. They want to prove it is a hoax, not to prove my intelligence, but in a weird twist it seems that they are trying to prove that they are intelligent because they are not taken in by me. They want to prove that they are not easily tricked. No matter how hard I try, there will always be someone who does not believe. I cannot dwell on this, however; I have to press on. I know the truth. It is not my problem.

Many FC speakers understand that skepticism makes them vulnerable. They fear "going back" to their pre-FC lives if FC is taken away from them. Tom expressed his anxiety: "I worry more about the future and my parents dying. What will happen if FC is taken away?" Chammi also worries. He wrote:

> Accustomed to living in the abyss, coming up to the light was hard. Beset by memories, I am still terrified. Terrified I might go back there. If FC were taken away from me, that is where I would be.

Skepticism within the Family

Skepticism can strain relationships among family members. Tom's sister Sally was skeptical at first. During family gatherings, she and her family were polite, although it appeared that they did not truly believe Tom was actually doing the typing. During one visit, Tom was typing and Sally sat down next to him instead of across from him as she usually did. From that position, she had a different vantage point. She watched intently and began to see that Tom's arm was initiating the movements. After that session, the strain within the family dissipated.

One of Barb's brothers was skeptical for several years, until her book helped ease his doubt. Barb's mother confides that her son's doubt made her sad and disappointed, but did not interrupt the FC process or finding Barb the support that she needed.

Skepticism from the Outside World

Skepticism can come from service agencies, professional communities and family members as well as from the larger society. Barb's mother says she encountered disbelief "from almost everyone. This skepticism affected my husband, me and my personal friends. It had a winnowing effect."

Tom reports:

> Some people who know me dismiss FC immediately without checking on it at all. They never spend the time to investigate even when some of my work has been available. They have heard that some experts call it a hoax and the fact that my life has changed is irrelevant.

Aaron's facilitator, Tina, is a speech and language pathologist who began using FC nearly 20 years ago. She writes:

> Some people believe that professionals who engage in FC are unethical. That is the hardest for me because I have a good reputation as a clinician and professor. I'm still explaining why I believe in FC.

Mary endured both prejudice and career obstacles because of her association with FC. During an interview for a teaching position at a local college, she was told that that the professors in the department were scientists and as such, they could not work with anyone who believed in FC.

Overcoming Skepticism through First-hand Experience

Despite negative press and institutional biases, first-hand experiences are a particularly effective way to overcome skepticism. Many people pass judgment against FC based on very little information and virtually no first-hand experience. Once they gain that experience – through observation, conversation and/or facilitating – trust begins to build and they become more open.

When Chammi's doctor tried typing with him, Chammi gave an answer that was completely different from what the doctor was expecting. At that point, the doctor became an ardent supporter of FC, never wavering even amid the negative publicity.

Wally has taught several "reluctant facilitators" to type with him. He observes:

> For most of these people, because life has been kind to them, they simply don't examine what is happening beyond what they see. If these people would take the time to have a non-verbal autistic person teach them how to FC as I taught several reluctant facilitators to do, then they too would have the appreciation for FC and for the intellectual capabilities of the non-verbal autistic people who use this method of communication.

First-hand experience is valuable, but is no panacea for doubt. After closely observing Sarah's typing, her doctor at a major autism clinic allowed that her messages were valid. He continues to insist, however, that Sarah is the rare exception. This attitude, which prevails among many professionals, limits the introduction of the method to many people with autism who might benefit greatly from it.

Balancing Skepticism and Belief

The FC speakers, facilitators and family members have all endured skepticism. It has been part of their lives for years, but in most cases, it is no longer central to their experience. This is not to minimize the impact and importance of skepticism, but rather to suggest that FC speakers and their facilitators deal with it as it occurs, but do not dwell on it as they move through their everyday lives.

Although skepticism has seemingly moved into the background, it is not altogether lost. While rejecting the necessity for double-blind message-passing tests, it is helpful for facilitators to possess a healthy skepticism and opt to maintain their scientific orientation. Holding the tension between belief and skepticism in a fine balance can rein in over-zealousness. This stance can help protect everyone from unintended influences and false accusations.

Validation of typed messages that occurs spontaneously is a powerful way to balance skepticism and belief. Several facilitators reported instances of spontaneous validation. Medical issues in particular present a strong case for spontaneous validation because the physical evidence is unequivocal. For example, both Doug and Chammi reported stomach pain, which eventually led to ulcer diagnoses.

Other types of spontaneous validation may not be as strong as medical evidence. However, when examples of spontaneous validation are kept in a portfolio the weight of the accumulated evidence can be very compelling.[2] Examples from the stories include:

- Spontaneous message-passing – FC speakers often type information that could not have been known to the facilitator. Doug told Judi about events at his group home that staff later corroborated.

- Behavioral validation – Often, uncharacteristic behavior, or a sudden shift in behavior can validate typed messages. For many people, sitting down and focusing without any reward (beyond the communication itself) is a form of spontaneous validation. In other examples, Chammi was able to undergo a complicated X-ray. Prior to FC, he was not able to undergo a similar procedure without anesthesia. Typically it took three people to hold Tom down for a blood draw. When he used FC to instruct the nurse how to position his hand, he was able to allow the procedure with no physical restraint.

- Disagreement between the facilitator and the FC speaker - This can offer a level of assurance. Wally and Jo sometimes have extended arguments with Tom about things that are important to him. Anoja says the major validation for her has been Chammi's deep understanding of and commitment to Christianity when all of his family members for many generations have been practicing Buddhists.

In addition to spontaneous validation, some FC speakers have been successful with formal validation procedures. When Sarah's elementary school teacher observed a 70-90% success rate in message-passing tests between home and school, she and the staff became convinced Sarah's typing was valid.

Several FC speakers in this book can now type independently in reply to yes/no or short-answer questions. Sometimes they can validate their typing by reading a word or part of their message out loud. When these methods are utilized in a non-confrontational way, they can add another layer of confidence to major decisions and other significant typed messages.

Maintaining a healthy skepticism means watching for and noting instances of spontaneous validation as well as discrepancies in typed messages. It also means bringing in a second facilitator to validate lasting or major life-changing decisions or actions that will have an impact on others.

Finding a balance between belief and skepticism can be supportive of FC speakers. It need not cause undue anxiety or imply a threat of losing FC. When handled with sensitivity, healthy skepticism does not imply a lack of trust or belief in the person or the typing. It can go a long way in helping everyone feel at ease and confident.

Skepticism continues in all quarters. Even FC users who now type independently encounter skeptics. However, throughout the country and all over the world, nonverbal people are honing their skills as they work towards independence and greater acceptance for their mode of communication.

References

1.Pedhazur, E. J., & Schmelkin, L. P. (1991). *Measurement, design and analysis: An integrated approach*. Hillsdale, NJ: Lawrence Erlbaum Associates.

2. Biklen, D., Saha, N., & Kliewer, C. (1995). How Teachers Confirm the Authorship of Facilitated Communication: A Portfolio Approach. *JASH, 20*(1), 45-56.

Broderick, A., & Kasa-Hendrickson, C. *Toward Independent Typing: The Collaborative Use of Portfolio Documentation*: Facilitated Communication Institute.

Sensory and Movement Differences

"Our bodies are not who we are."

Nick Pentzell

Sensory and movement difference is an umbrella term for the neurological condition that prevents or disrupts congruence between inner state and outer behavior. This type of congruence can be seen in all mammals where survival depends on communication between the individual and members of the social group. Body language and movement are used to broadcast one's inner state and to perceive the inner states of others.[1]

Congruence between inner state and outer behavior is assumed to be universal in humans. For most of us, this is true. However, the assumption of congruence falls flat when autistic individuals describe their personal experience. When congruence is lacking, there is the danger of being misinterpreted at every turn.

People often find it difficult to "believe" in FC because the outer, visible behavior of individuals with autism belies their intelligence and conscious awareness. In this way, the lens of sensory and movement difference provides an explanatory framework for FC. With this, it becomes possible to look beneath autistic behavior and see hidden competence.

Movement differences are the outward and visible manifestation of invisible processes within the individual. Although the causes of movement differences are not well understood, one common area of difficulty is in processing sensory information. When the seamless flow of information between the central nervous system, the sensory system and the motor system is interrupted, congruence between inner state and outer behavior may be lost.

We are neurologically hardwired to detect changes in the environment through the sensory system and respond to those changes via the motor system. As the name implies, the sensorimotor system operates as a single process where information continually flows in two directions. The sense organs take in information from the environment and transport it to the central nervous system. After processing, information from the central nervous system moves outward to the muscles.

The assumption of congruence is so deeply embedded in our cultural understanding that it is the basis for virtually all intelligence tests and other assessment tools. When congruence is lacking, all forms of body language are subject to misinterpretation and all traits that are inferred from outer behavior, such as intelligence or emotion, can be misconstrued or appear to be absent.

The enormous body of academic literature on autism is based on the unchallenged assumption of congruence between inner state and outer behavior. However, over the past two decades, an explosion of books have been written by individuals with autism, including those who speak or write independently as well as those who use facilitated communication. Virtually every one of these works conveys a complex picture of behavioral attributes that are not congruent with inner state or intention. While each picture is unique, many common threads exist.

Donnellan and Leary published a book on the concept of movement differences.[2] In 1996, Leary and Hill published an article showing the similarities between autistic behaviors and those seen in other neurological conditions such as Parkinson's, Tourette's Syndrome, or catatonia. [3]

At the same time, occupational therapists were bringing in a perspective that focused on issues related to sensory processing.[4] Today, there is a growing body of evidence that the difficulties experienced by autistic individuals in all realms of daily life are not always behavioral or volitional, but instead are based on neurological abnormalities of the sensorimotor system.

Sensory Processing

It has been estimated that 30-100% of autistic individuals experience abnormalities in sensory processing[5] and that they have significantly more sensory symptoms than comparison groups.[6] Another study reveals that 90% of children with autism have pervasive, multimodal sensory abnormalities that persist across the lifespan.[7]

The sensory processing issues within each individual can fluctuate between over- or under-responsivity to sensory stimuli. These fluctuations can be affected by history, context or other non-neurological factors.[8]

The professional literature also has begun to acknowledge the many ways in which these difficulties can create secondary consequences that disrupt functioning in daily life and as future development. For example, sensory responsivity has been found to have a higher impact on adaptive behavior than the severity of autistic symptoms.[9]

Sensory disorders are highly correlated to high levels of rigid or repetitive movement patterns and they can lead to many forms of disruptive or aggressive behavior.[10]

Although the diagnosis of autism generally does not occur until at least 18 months, early symptoms or signs can be present from birth. For example, sensory overstimulation can cause infants to withdraw from reciprocal social interaction, which in turn can affect all future development and regulatory processes.[11]

Tom's speech therapist astutely observed the connection between his aggressive outbursts and his emotions and sensory system. She relates:

> [The sources of] his aggressive behaviors were twofold. One was of frustration and anger, and the other was a sensory component. His arousal level would get so high that he'd go into fight/flight, and he fought. All of his pent up energy burst from him. We tried to cut off any stimulation that, if he tried to process it, would send that arousal level up to panic again. His system was just too overloaded. Auditory, tactile, even visual input was shut off or kept to a minimum.

Movement difficulties can derive from neurological abnormalities that can disrupt overt motor functioning as well as hidden processes such as emotions, perceptions, thoughts and feelings.[12]

Individuals with autism traditionally have been thought to have particularly well-developed motor skills. However, recent studies have shown that often the most basic skills such as gait, posture, balance and coordination are impaired.[13] Nick describes how he and other children with health problems were required to walk around the school track instead of participating in athletic activities. Even among the group of students who were overweight or injured, Nick could not keep up. He recalls, "When I walked at school the kids would often lap me. Keep in mind that these were kids with broken legs or sprained ankles."

Today, the lens of sensory and movement differences provides a way to reconcile the assumption of hidden competence and the unusual behaviors that are observed. We can acknowledge the triggers and covert processes that lead to unusual behaviors and at the same time, comprehend the hidden competence that underlies those behaviors.

These ideas are only the tip of a large and complex iceberg, but they are enough to force professionals and caregivers to rethink assumptions and view individuals with autism in a new way. Aaron's mother describes the far-reaching effects of this monumental shift:

> This movement differences paradigm does allow a kinder and gentler way of looking at our children, and helps explain why facilitated communication can work. At last, a paradigm that finds expression in the love, trust, and care that grows between our children and their caregivers. It fosters optimism.

Often hidden competence is revealed sporadically and only within a safe, interesting, and nurturing context. For years, Mindy kept notes of all the glimpses she had seen of Daniel's intelligence. When he was professionally evaluated at age 12, Mindy provided an extensive list describing 28 types of events, including two instances in which teachers heard him say, "I love to read." She hoped the assessment would confirm her belief that Daniel had more awareness and more intelligence than was immediately apparent from his everyday behavior.

Prefacing her list, Mindy explained the importance of context and relationship. She noted that all of these examples occurred when Daniel was doing an activity that he enjoyed and when he was with a person whom he trusted and liked. She also acknowledged that he did not do any of the things consistently. Unfortunately, the team of professionals who evaluated Daniel did not see the items on this list as being significant. Examples from Daniel's hidden competence list include:

- Touched words that rhymed with a given word five or six times; when praised said, "Easy."

- Always chose the highest number when asked to choose the number of food items he would receive.
- Pointed correctly to a specific word in a familiar song or poem.
- Correctly touched words in a list that he had never seen before.
- Showed clear preference for inspirational or spiritual music and detailed visual art.

Descriptions of Sensory and Movement Differences

Sensory and movement differences encompass both internal and external attributes. Observable behaviors that serve as markers for the diagnosis of autism may be triggered by covert, internal processes. The overt behavior may be unintentional or it may be used as a coping mechanism or protective device for dealing with extreme discomfort from sensory hypersensitivity or other types of pain.

A wide range of behavior falls under the umbrella of sensory and movement differences. FC speakers explain:

> Barb: "My facial expressions do not always match my emotions. I can walk and move fairly well, but my fine motor skills are limited and my initiation impulse is extremely weak, so assistance is needed in almost every sphere."

> Sarah: "My voice is not connected to me. My speaking is not working for me because it says nothing or weird non-speech sounds. Sometimes it speaks real words, but not always what I want to say. With autism, my body doesn't do what I tell it to do."

> Nick: "Autism yowls inside me. I have a hard time each day being in control of my behavior. Inside me I try hard. Outside, my body does what it wants. I tell it to sit still and it is a wiggle-worm. I tell it to lie down and sleep, but it leaps on my bed. I tell it to want good and it goes for bad. I open the door to maturity and it slams in my face. What a situation! I want a new body."

There are three areas where the FC speakers have the most difficulty. These include:

- Lack of connection between body and mind.
- Issues related to sensory sensitivity.
- Difficulty interpreting sensory information.

Lack of Connection between Body and Mind

The feeling of being disconnected from one's own body is almost incomprehensible to the average person. Yet it is not uncommon for individuals with autism. There is a striking similarity among three of the FC speakers on their awareness of this split between body and mind.

Nick: "My body acts childish, even though my brain is adult."

Sarah: "I act dumb but am smart."

Tom: "My body has a mind of its own. In my mind, I know what you want. My body says no."

Tom's disconnectedness reached a peak when his parents and physical therapist planned to make a videotape of his therapy activities as a training tool for his staff. On the day of the filming, Tom was out of control. He raced to the door to run outside. He ran to his chair, then back to the door, then to the basement and out to the car. He later noted, "You can't imagine the turmoil of mind and body fighting like this."

Nick described his sense of disconnection this way:

To have autism is like having a short in a computer. I know what I want to do, but my body gets confused and it does not correctly carry out the orders my brain sends it. I take in information, but my body scrambles the output.

Touch is a central part of facilitated communication. The following quotes describe how touch can increase awareness of a body part and the connection between body and mind.

Wally: "Before FC, seeing my arms, hands, and fingers waving wildly in front of me or beside me gave no clue to me as to whose arms, fingers, and hands these were. Realizing that my arms are attached to my body at the shoulders and that I can consciously control their positions … is a truly miraculous realization that I became aware of after starting FC."

Chammi: "I am not aware of my body unless it is touching something. Your hand on mine lets me know where my hand is. Jarring my legs by walking tells me I am alive."

Sarah: "My body behaves as it pleases. When my arm is touched I feel a connection to it and if I go slowly, it can do as I say."

When the connection between body and mind is tenuous, initiating and executing volitional movement becomes difficult or impossible. Verbal and physical prompts have always been used to teach tasks of daily living. In individuals with autism, sometimes prompts from others help this process; sometimes they have no effect; and sometimes they hinder it.

> Tom: "I can't even get a drink of water without a signal or prompt of some sort."

> Chammi: "I could never make my body obey my brain's requests; how could I make it obey mom's requests?"

> Wally: "The inability to respond on demand underscores many autistic people's inability to perform many tasks put before them by other people or by their own mind. Autistic people have functioning minds, but we all don't have functioning control of our bodies when we are asked to do a task. I have trouble trying to consciously direct my body to perform simple tasks such as sitting down gracefully or putting my treasured nails and stones in my pockets rather than throwing them. It is the reason I gobble my food and gulp down a drink."

Issues Related to Sensory Sensitivity

Individuals with autism have various kinds of sensory issues. Some of the most common include:

- Over- and under-stimulation of sensory systems.
- Information from the individual senses not coming together to form a complete picture.
- Inability to process sensation through more than one sensory modality at a time.
- Crossover between modalities (e.g., smelling colors or sounds).
- Complete shutdown of one or more sensory systems.

FC has given non-speaking individuals a way to tell others what they are experiencing. In many cases, accommodations can be made so that negative sensory experiences can be avoided or at least ameliorated.

The most commonly reported sensory issues are extreme hypersensitivity in one or more sensory modalities. Sensory hypersensitivity can be an ongoing source of discomfort or even extreme pain. Understandably, aggression, behavioral issues, or other seemingly inappropriate motor responses can be a direct result. The following quotes provide general descriptions of sensory issues:

> Tom: "My sensory system was (and still is to a large degree) a real mess. My senses and body parts did not work as a unit. It certainly had a direct connection to my behavior."

> Barb: "My senses are often so intense and painful that you wouldn't believe me even if I described them in the most benign, candy coated way."

> Nick: "I couldn't imagine what it was like not to be overstimulated. Sensory overload inhibits anyone from thinking about much more than surviving is barrage."

Hearing

Many people with autism report high levels of auditory sensitivity. Mary relates that Aaron has always been sensitive to sounds. Once Kathy obtained ear protectors to block out the noise at her job, her anxiety was reduced and her obsessive behavior decreased.

Wally's sound sensitivity includes internal noises he describes as "constant ear ringing, intestinal noise, blood flowing, heart beating, feet hitting the floor, breathing, and teeth clicks." He explains that his vocalizations provide a way of canceling out the internal noises and reducing the distraction from them. Barb notes the lasting effects sounds can have on her psyche:

> Sometimes my hearing gets incredibly sensitive. When I am alone, I usually enjoy the fleeting superpower. If it catches me when I am walking with normals, it is harder to handle, as they are so loud to begin with. Such a noise bomb may leave my ears ringing in pain for a day or even two.

Tom believes his auditory sensitivity has several implications:

> I can hear both parts of a phone conversation with ease. It is no problem hearing what others are saying in other parts of the house. It is a two-edged sword because you are hurt many times by what you should not hear, but also you hear nice things that are said and not just because you are listening. In the end it has been more of a blessing than a curse.

Using microanalysis of film footage, psychologist Bill Condon saw individuals with autism responding to a single sound multiple times.[14] He wondered if they were hearing echoes. Sounds do in fact echo all around us as sound waves bounce and reverberate off multiple hard surfaces within a room.[15] For most of us, our sensory systems have made an adaptation so that we no longer consciously hear these echoes. Sarah's description of her sound sensitivity and the echoes that she hears support Condon's hypothesis. She writes:

> I hear too well. My autism protects me when your world is too much for me. Sounds pay me visits after I leave them. I wish to stop their visits, but they come uninvited. So I need to do weird stuff to avoid them. Pacing back and forth puts the noises behind me for a while.

> With too much noise in school, I could hardly breathe, and I needed the naughty beast called autism to protect me from hearing and seeing too much. When too many voices are sounding, pain rips through my body. Your voices are too loud and they echo.

Vision

Throughout first-person accounts written by people on the autism spectrum, examples abound concerning vision. For those with visual sensory sensitivity, complex and random sensory environments can be confusing. For Sarah, a busy store creates a difficult environment: "A not good store is loaded with angles and towers and noise to confuse people with autism. People scream at one another and carts roll everywhere. Packed shelves touch me. Lights hurt."

Lack of eye contact is one of the most commonly cited traits of autism. The title of autistic author John Elder Robison's book, *Look Me In the Eye*, refers to the constant command he heard from teachers, parents, relatives and school principals.[16] As a child, he did not understand why this was so important to people and why it made them so angry when he did not comply.

Direct eye contact and focused vision can be too intense for those with high levels of sensory sensitivity.[17] Nick explains the way in which he has adjusted:

> To focus, I learn to glance at things out of the corner of my eye and see things in a peripheral way. This allows me to regard life in small doses. It is too confusing most of the time to look at things face on. Really, I am overwhelmed by what I see.

Similarly, Tom describes his reliance upon peripheral vision and people's response to it:

> I use peripheral vision, photographic memory or other means and can see well enough but not good. I do this because my eyes will not hold their focus. When I try to look closer at things the image breaks up. The problem of not looking at things seems to be hard for some

people to grasp. They are told about it but still treat me as though I am uninterested or not even aware. I don't mean to insult them, but they are the ones who are unaware.

Relying on peripheral vision is significant in facilitated communication, because best practice includes looking directly at the keyboard or letterboard. Using microanalysis of videotaped FC sessions, some research studies have shown that, although FC speakers do not look at the board continually, they do consistently glance at the letters before keystrokes.[18]

Difficulty Interpreting Sensory Information

Perception is the process by which we put together all of our sensory information and make sense of the world. We perceive the environment as a single, unified gestalt that is derived from a continuous stream of sensory information that is available. Without the ability to form a cohesive picture by weaving together information from all six senses, it is difficult to be oriented in time and space.

Creating a perceptual gestalt is, in part, a cognitive task. For most of us, it happens naturally and effortlessly. Wally describes some of the ways he becomes oriented. He says, "Rocking and bobbing, hand flapping, tiptoe walking, screeching, and reaching out to touch items to help me find my position in my immediate environment." Nick confirms that FC has helped him with this process:

> Language gives the thinker tools to control sensation. My hearing is more focused, since I am involved as a participant in conversations, rather than as a passive bystander. I see things all around me in a riddle of movement, color, and form, which must be deciphered. Now I have language to help me make sense of what I see. Things I see are not so confusing as to their purpose (and I can ask about things that are confusing).

FC and Sensory and Movement Differences

When asked if FC had any impact on his movement or sensory modes, Aaron used the word "plugs," which suggests that FC helps him keep fleeting thoughts in focus. He wrote, "More hand and mind focus like plugs in my mind. Plugs in my thinking."

Heather has observed how FC helps Kathy focus her attention, saying,

> Her concentration becomes focused, her arm movements become very precise, she strikes the board strongly, and it appears that her whole body is focused on the task.

Wally says the sensory feedback he receives doing FC has helped increase his body awareness:

> To hear the click that is made when I depress a key and relying on the facilitator for resistance to my arm/hand is bringing yet another dimension to my sensory awareness of the world that surrounds me in terms of knowing where my arms are relative to my body. Realizing that my arms are attached to my body at the shoulders and that I can consciously control their positions in space to do my bidding is a truly miraculous realization that I became aware of after starting FC.

Rhythm is an important aspect in movement. As FC partners gain experience working together, the rhythm of their coordinated arm movements becomes increasingly strong and fluid. This might be an important feature in making FC successful. For individuals with sensory and movement differences, rhythm can be beneficial in "creating order out of [perceptual] chaos".[19] Sarah described the importance of rhythm and touch in FC:

> Tricks I use to release thoughts are to try to really get my hand connected to my thinking. When my arm is touched I feel it and the it listens to where I want it to go. This is how FC works to help me communicate. Another trick is typing rhythm helps keep both my mind and my body working together as one tune.

There are other positive changes related to sensory and movement differences that occurred for people after they starting to use FC. Lois notes that Barb is much better at following a verbal request such as getting out of the car saying, "She's in more control from top to bottom." Nick can sometimes write his name on a blackboard independently. Barb and Tom now exhibit increased facial expression. Tom is using focused vision longer. Doug says he doesn't have to think as much before doing something.

These kinds of changes suggest the FC users are experiencing higher levels of overall control, integration and organization. Aaron's speech and language pathologist, Tina, observed the effect of FC upon his overall organization:

> I believe that Aaron is so much more fluid, fluent with movement when doing FC, especially with me. The touch is organizing for him, cognitively and linguistically. His tremors are fewer when we FC, and his attention and vigilance are greatly increased. Amazing! Another testament to the organizing nature of the FC process.

Nick has seen similar overall changes take place within himself:

It is as if I can work better to control my body. I know part of this is because I have learned to understand how my body works, but I think I am also more aware of myself IN my body since I started using FC. I feel integrated more often.

References

1. Lewis, T., Amini, F., & Lannon, R. (2000). *A general theory of love*. New York: Random House.
2. Donnellan, A. M., & Leary, M. R. (1995). *Movement differences and diversity in autism/mental retardation: Appreciating and accomodating people with communication and behavior challenges*. Madison, WI: DRI.
3. Leary, M. R., & Hill, D. A. (1996). Moving on: Autism and movment disturbance. *Mental Retardation, 34*, 39-53.
4. Leekam, S. R., Nieto, C., Libby, S. J., Wing, L., & Gould, J. (2007). Describing the sensory abnormalities of children and adults with aum. *Journal of Autism & Developmental Disorders, 37*, 894-910.
5. Dempsey, I., & Foreman, P. (2001). A review of educational approaches for individuals with autism. *International Journal of Disability, Development & Education, 48*(1), 103-116.
Rogers, S. J., Hepburn, S., & Wehner, E. (2003). Parent reports of sensory symptoms in toddlers with autism and those with other developmental disorders. *Journal of Autism & Developmental Disorders, 33*(6), 631-642.6.
7. Leekham (2007).
8. Rogers (2003).
Dempsey (2001).
9. Rogers (2003).
10. Dawson, G., & Watling, R. (2000). Interventions to facilitate auditory, visual, and motor integration in autism: A review of the evidence. *Journal of Autism & Developmental Disorders, 30*(5), 415-421.
Leekham (2007).
11. Dawson, G., Hill, D., Spencer, A., Galpert, L., & Watson, L. (1990). Affective Exchanges Between Young Autistic Children and Their Mothers. *Journal of Abnormal Child Psychology, 18*(3), 335-345.
Greenspan, S. I. (2001). The affect diathesis hypothesis: The role of emotions in the core deficit in autism and the development of intelligence and social skills. *Journal of Developmental and Learning Disorders, 5*(1), 1-44.
12. Donnellan, A. M., Hill, D. A., & Leary, M. R. (2010). Rethinking autism: Implications of sensory and movement differences for understanding and support. *Disability Studies Quarterly, 30*(1).

13. Donnellan (2010).

14. Condon, W. S. (1997). *Bio-modulation: The Organization (and Disorganization) of Speaker and Listener Behavior at the Micro-Level; The Relevance For Autism*.

15. Frick, S. M., & Young, S. R. (2009). *Therapeutic listening: Clinical concepts and treatment guidelines*. Madison, WI: Vital Links.

16. Robison, J. E. (2007). *Look me in the eye: My life with asperger's*. New York: Three Rivers.

17. Williams, D. (1996). *Autism: An inside-out approach*. London: Jessica Kingsley

18. Grayson, A., & Emerson, A. (1995). *A Microanalysis of Video-taped Facilitated Communication Interactions Involving a Client with Autism*: The Nottingham Trent Unviersity.

19. Williams (1996).

Building Protective Worlds

We must create another bearable world inside your world
that allows us to breathe.

Sarah Stup

A common description of people with autism is that they live in worlds of their own. Often works written by other autistic authors echo this feeling of alienation from the non-autistic world. For example, the title of Tom's book is *Caught Between Two Worlds*[1] and Wally's upcoming book is *My Three Worlds.* Sue Rubin entitled her award-winning autobiographical documentary "Autism is a World."[2] Other works by autistic authors include, *Songs of the Gorilla Nation, Through the Eyes of Aliens, Women from Another Planet* and *Born on the Wrong Planet.*[3]

Clearly, this is an important issue for many writers on the autism spectrum and they are reaching out to neurotypical people on this topic. It behooves us to listen. We can reach across the divide and attempt to understand their worlds by asking questions. We can try to imagine what it means to feel separate from the world around us.

Many people on the autism spectrum have written about having sensory hypersensitivity. They describe how, as a way of coping with the harshness of the "normal" world, they build safe havens or inner worlds where they can find comfort.

Authors with Asperger's, John Elder Robison and Dawn Prince-Hughes write about their sensory sensitivities and how they cope. Robison describes the contrast between his world of electronic circuitry that was a "comfortable world of muted colors, soft light, and mechanical perfection" and the "real" world that was, "anxiety-filled, bright, disorderly world of people."[4]

Dawn Prince-Hughes notes that all core characteristics in the official definition of autism are "descriptions of coping behaviors and not descriptions, necessarily, of innate orientation."[5]

In a similar vein, Sarah acknowledges that some of her behaviors serve to protect her, although they may not be of her choosing:

> Autism is not about good or bad manners. Autism is part of us, a shield that we need and not a manner that we are choosing. Your world gets confusing so I have to protect myself. Protection is to tune into autism. Your world is not the same for those of us with differences. We often experience your world in a different way; and, therefore, we may need to react to it in an unusual manner.

With their high levels of sensory sensitivity it is easy to understand the autistic person's need for building a private world and arming themselves with protective behaviors. Several FC speakers in this book describe how they build an inner world where they can go when the outer world becomes unbearable. Their reports suggest that the unbearable nature is largely, though not exclusively, due to sensory overstimulation. Tom names this retreat his "autistic zone." Others distinguish between "my world" and "your world."

Sarah believes FC is her bridge between worlds. She confides, "By typing, I can play with my life and stretch from my world to yours. I become a real person when my words try to reach out to you without my weird body scaring you away."

Barb tries to live in one world at a time. She becomes disoriented and angry when jolted out of her world. She relates, "As my understanding of both my inner and outer world became more settled, I discovered I could allow contact with a few people for a limited time."

Wally has written extensively about being trapped in his world prior to FC. He reports, "Pre-FC was at best a time that, for me, was totally and brutally savaged by autism when its reality and the blinding storm of sensory stimulation isolated my mind from the world that existed just outside of myself."

In the chapter on emotions, the FC speakers describe the intense loneliness that comes from living in two worlds, but not fully belonging to either. Sarah explains:

> We want to be with you, but your ways are not our ways. Your world is not the same for us. We must create another bearable world inside your world that allows us to breathe – an inside world that protects us from the pain of exposure. With this inside world comes peace, but sad and lonely times too.

Chammi provides a more positive description of moving between two worlds. He says, "I am a traveler ebulliently engaged on a unique journey between worlds. Between the quirky world of autism that I inhabit and the wearying world of 'normal' that I like to explore."

Douglas Candland, professor of psychology and animal behavior, wrote about the individual "umwelt" or private universe that each of us inhabits. The umwelt is largely built on our interpretation of sensory experiences. Candland notes that in order to understand another's umwelt, we need to try to understand the sensory-based perceptions behind it.[6] He explains:

> "We all live in a bubble ... whose edges are created by the limits of our perceptions... The bubble both contains and *is* the phenomenon of our self-world [or umwelt].... Each animal, each individual, has conceptions of many aspects of space. I have a tactile-space, the space I use when I write with a pen or pick out an object to grasp; taste-space, a different taste in my mouth depending where I put my tongue; a smell-space; an auditory-space, one with softnesses and loudnesses that signal distance and help me locate the presence of other objects within this space; a visual-space, a space that uses clues about the shading and interposition of objects to tell me something of their size and distance. These spaces are united into one grand bubble, the total umwelt, an umwelt characteristic of me, one that changes constantly and yet represents my knowledge of the universe.

Wally's view supports Candland's thesis. He writes:

> Reality as we experience it rarely results in our picturing in our minds the same reality experienced by non-autistic folks because of the

sensory and neurological problems that each autistic experiences. These perceptual differences in how and what we think about the world that we share with others and how we react to its sometimes frightening stimulation, is the greatest obstacle for us to overcome.

Occasionally FC speakers refer to "our world." This suggests that perhaps through FC there has been a rapprochement or healing of the split between their worlds as we, parents and facilitators, have come to better understand the perceptions that make up their umwelten and they have come to better understand ours.

Robison says he chose to leave his safe world of electronic circuits and fully enter the world of people.[7] Tom tells of his decision to leave his "autistic zone" and enter the "normal" world as fully and completely as possible. In the following quote, Tom describes his autistic zone, the purpose it serves, and how his movement is affected when he is in it.

> People with autism have a comfort zone of relief we turn to when things get too bad in your world. We also use it to relieve the loneliness and boredom of our existence. It is like taking yourself mentally and emotionally out of a situation which is intolerable to you. It may appear to you that we are in our own little world. It can become addictive and mesmerizing. People with autism often resent being forced out of this state, especially when they aren't particularly interested in what you want them to do. My body is basically useless when I am in that state. It is when I am completely out of the autistic zone that I can move as I wish. A lot of the time I am in-between.

Wally describes his three universes: "my world," "your world," and "our world." He notates the ways in which his world has both served and imprisoned him. He also tells how FC has given him a way to ask questions to verify his perceptions and begin to build a sense of "our" world. In his book, he writes:

> Each sensory system if operating normally ties us to the world that is outside of ourselves linking our minds to everything that we sense. This is not the case for those of us who are non-verbal autistics. Our reality is not based on each of our senses operating efficiently and effectively all of the time that we interact with the world that is outside of ourselves. In my black world of autism, there is only the sameness of constant order and the justice of nature that I accept

and witness. Our world is chaotic, noisy, and exceptionally violent.

However, I can now cope to a point with some level of all of this as long as I can retreat, from time to time, to my world of order and natural law and ask appropriate questions about what I see and hear. It wasn't until I started to communicate using FC that I found the link that was missing for so many years between the two worlds. Many of my misconceptions about your world were corrected in my mind as I began to use your language to communicate with not only you but ultimately myself.

Our world, at times, reaches a yet to be understood crescendo of misunderstandings and inequalities that I cannot tolerate and must escape. Years of constantly moving between my three worlds has made me adept at navigating from one to the other. I need to maintain these three separate realities or worlds because I think this way I can maintain my autistic identity that is the real me while capitulating to your world's requirements to appear to be "normal." Our world is the dream that I have for us that will include your world and my world on an equal basis.

References

1. Page, T. (2002). *Caught between two worlds: My autistic dilemma.* Woodbridge, CT: Words of Understanding.
2. Rubin, S. (Writer). (2004). Autism is a World. In G. Wurzburg (Producer). USA: State of the Art, Inc.
3. Hammerschmidt, E. (2004). *Born on the wrong planet.* Palo Alto, CA: Tyborne Hill.
Miller, J. K. (Ed.). (2003). *Women from another planet?: Our lives in the universe of autism.* Bloomington, IN: 1stBooks.
O'Neill, J. L. (1999). *Through the eyes of aliens: A book about autistic people.* Philadelphia, PA: Jessica Kingsley.
Prince-Hughes, D. (2004). *Songs of the gorilla nation: My journey through autism.* New York: Harmony.
4. Robison, J. E. (2007). *Look me in the eye: My life with asperger's.* New York: Three Rivers.
5. Prince-Hughes (2004).
6. Candland, D. K. (1993). *Feral children and clever animals: Reflections on human nature.* New York: Oxford University. (pp. 183-4).
7. Robison (2007).

Behavior

"Most of us are unaware of the enormous difference that the onset of language can make in a child's overall behavior."

Bernard Rimland[1]

Behavioral change is at the heart of FC, yet that has never been its goal. The link between expressive language and behavior is powerful and the changes that people have experienced have been spontaneous and far-reaching. Large-scale behavioral change for non-speaking individuals with autism, especially for those who have reached adulthood, is rare. FC has been compelling to its proponents because it has served as a catalyst for so many immediate as well as lifelong behavioral changes. In addition, through typed messages FC users can now explain the reasons for their unusual behaviors and provide insights about their difficulties with sensory and movement differences. These things have served to increase understanding and improve quality of life for everyone.

Quantum Behavioral Improvement

Bernard Rimland was a pioneer in autism research and founded the Autism Research Institute (ARI). In the editor's column of the institute's newsletter, Rimland discusses the sudden and unexpected changes that occurred when non-speaking individuals with autism gained access to expressive language. He wrote:

> Although we all know that language is an important predictor of outcome in autism, and we are all aware that even limited language skills are very useful to the child and those around him or her, most of us are unaware of the enormous difference that the onset of language can make in a child's overall behavior.

> There is abundant evidence, from many sources, that if language can somehow be stimulated in an autistic child or adult, there will often be a sudden and unexpected improvement in a wide range of non-language behaviors.[2]

Rimland describes these non-language behavioral changes with unrestrained enthusiasm. He described them as "the great general leap forward," "breakthroughs" and "the remarkable transformation of personality." Citing one example of a nonverbal boy who learned to use word cards, Dr. Rimland wrote, "Access to language, even if not to speech, had given Jimmy a more positive attitude, and had almost made him a new person."

The article includes anecdotal case studies and personal experiences in which non-language behaviors changed when a child gained access to expressive language, even if the expressive language entailed nothing more than the ability to make one-word choices. Recognizing the importance of this, Rimland named the phenomenon Quantum Behavioral Improvement (QBI).

The word quantum, originally used in physics, describes a change of state that is both sudden and significant and comes about in an abrupt or discontinuous manner. In contrast, the behavioral model which is the basis for many autism interventions, views change as a linear process where one can trace a clear, predictable pathway between cause and effect. For example, the desire for an M&M or other treat, reinforces a particular response pattern. In quantum change, no traceable pathway, predictability or control over outcome exists. Quantum change is not forced or prescribed; it comes from within and of its own accord. QBI changes Rimland notes include:

- Improved overall demeanor.
- More positive attitude.

- Less frequent outbursts.
- Improved behavior across all settings.
- Increased sensitivity to others.
- Improved ability to follow complex commands.
- Increased readiness to interact.

The changes described in the stories Part II were never taught or "trained" by using the external rewards found in the behavioral model. However, there were many naturally occurring "rewards" such as being seen as intelligent, making choices and participating in conversations.

Immediate Changes

It is not uncommon for an autistic individual to show immediate, uncharacteristic positive behavior in the course of an FC session. Tom's speech therapist Lauren was struck by Tom's unusually calm demeanor and ability to tolerate interaction with her during their first typing sessions. This uncharacteristic positive behavior served also to change Lauren's view of him, which in turn changed *her* behavior. She notes that she began to see Tom as being "in there" when she realized his destructive and violent behavior was not due to cognitive deficits.

Lifespan Changes

Many people with autism have experienced positive changes across the lifespan after gaining access to FC. Testing psychologist Dr. Groff noted how much Sarah changed when he saw her a year after she began using FC. He was struck by her increased eye contact and improvement in her overall demeanor. He noted that she had begun "to facilitate social language."

Before FC, Nick would try to run up to the stage during a concert or in his philosophy class. Gwen would have to hold Nick to prevent these outbursts of excitement. Today, all he needs is a reminder with a light touch on the shoulder and he will sit down.

Tom's history of violence is well known in his home and day program. Yet when he had his first violent episode in seven years, his current staff had never seen it before and could hardly believe it.

Barb's lifetime of difficult behavior changed dramatically. As her mother reported:

> Barb's behavior was the number one aspect that changed with her discovering FC. Her extreme hyperactivity calmed down almost immediately. The rages and temper flare-ups and destructive

behavior cooled to a huge degree. I sensed her frustration level at not being understood begin to subside.

Explaining Behavior

As FC dyads become more fluent with typing, they can begin to engage in ongoing conversations about specific behaviors. Sometimes these conversations bring about system-wide changes where new supports or accommodations can be put in place. Often, the mere act of engaging in dialogue can induce change.

In her story, when Kathy and her staff had a dialogue about her misunderstanding of the term "committed," her anxiety decreased immediately. Her staff also learned that seemingly random bouts of anxiety could have very logical causes.

Tina and Mary were having a conversation while Aaron sat at the keyboard, pinching and biting his hand. When Tina asked why he was doing this, Aaron typed, "I pinch because I teach you not to talk to mom." When Mary and Tina understood the rationale behind Aaron's behavior, they could change their behavior accordingly. At the same time, Aaron learned he could use words to modify the behavior of others.

Doug was able to explain to Judi that he hit two staff members because he was too hot. When Judi relayed this information to staff, they confirmed that the air conditioning had been out that day. Although by then it was too late to make Doug more comfortable, this exchange helped staff see that Doug's aggressive behavior was understandable.

When Tom's parents took him to one of his favorite restaurants, he refused to get out of the car. He typed, "I don't have the right clothes on." Once Wally and Jo understood his reason for not moving, they could discuss it with him. When they pointed out people leaving the restaurant wearing clothing similar to his, Tom decided he could go in.

To avoid potential problems, Jo and Wally use FC to talk with Tom before they leave for an event. They explain what is going to happen, state their expectations and ask if he can handle it. Jo notes, "He takes the responsibility of saying whether he thinks he can do it or not. His answers are almost 100% on the mark."

Behavior and Intention

There are many factors that complicate the behavioral issues. Observable behavior is only one small part of a complex system that includes both internal and external processes. Neurologically-based sensory and movement differences, emotions, exposure anxiety and motivation play a role in behavior, as do various aspects of the external context such as relationships, environmental conditions and the perceptions of others.

While FC gives individuals with autism a way to explain their behavior, explanations do not always result in a solution. Behavior can be confusing for the observer as well as for the individual.

We all do things that are contradictory or illogical or that we know are not good for us. However, most of us have a general sense of congruence between intention and behavior.

Unintentional Behavior

Sensory and movement differences by definition involve a lack of congruence between intention and behavior. While FC speakers have control over their behavior at least some of the time, many of them also have ongoing experiences in which their behavior is outside of their control. It is through their typed messages that we have come to understand how much of their behavior is not intentional and how difficult it is for them to change it.

Sarah described her autism as both her shield and her enemy. As her shield, certain behavioral patterns protect her sensitive sensory system from too much stimulation. As her enemy, autism causes her body to do things over which she has no control. The unintentional behavior is so foreign to her that she describes herself in the third person.

> My body did what it pleased and hardly ever listened to my instructions. Instead, it darted about, squealed, and angered everyone. It repeated actions and could not stop. It jumped from high places and ate dirt.

External controls are often used for disruptive behavior. Some of Barb's teachers used "bad hands mitts" when she was impulsively grabbing things in the classroom. Tom's parents would take him out to the parking lot when he was causing a disturbance during an event and Wally had to wrestle and physically restrain him when he was having an aggressive episode. Gwen would wrap her arms and legs around Nick to help him remain seated during a lecture or musical performance. Before FC, it was impossible to know how these restraints were perceived by the autistic individual.

Sometimes an FC speaker will ask for help curtailing unintentional behavior. Barb had two facilitators who used strict boundaries and natural consequences. Barb understood how these controls were helpful and asked her parents to use them too. Eventually she developed her own internal controls so they were strong enough to bring her behavior into accord with her intention.

Typically, the process of developing internal controls is accompanied by the child's growing use of language.[3] While this process is never smooth or easy, embarking on it as an autistic teenager or adult can be exceedingly difficult. Nick acknowledged his difficulty when he wrote:

> My behavior is inconsistent. This can be frustrating. Sometimes I am calm, and other times I am not. I am trying to learn to control my behavior. This is not an easy task, really. Being autistic, I am not always in control of myself. I can be a good listener one minute and a horrible distraction the next. I know I must control this behavior, but I don't know how.

> It is more difficult to always be in control of myself. Before FC, I never tried; I just did whatever I was led to do by impulse. All controls were external. I would have killed myself in pursuit of an obsession, if no one was there to stop me. The process of developing internal controls has been so hard. It feels unnatural. It takes a focus that is not always there, or at least a focus that requires a good deal of conscious effort.

Wally noted that in recent years having ALS has served to inhibit his unintentional behavior in ways that nothing else could. Prior to that, like Nick, he found it very difficult to change lifelong behavior patterns. Once an impulsive behavior becomes ingrained, learning to inhibit it can be extremely difficult.

> The hollering and other unpleasant activities brought on by me forced my parents to curtail my visits to many public functions, going to church, going to the store, and seeing an occasional movie. My public behavior was terrible. It still can be improved greatly and I am working on it. It will take time to get the impulsive behaviors in check. After all, it took twenty-five years to develop them.

Intentional Use of Inappropriate Behavior

Although FC speakers frequently write about impulsive behavior that feels unintentional, at times they also admit to intentionally using inappropriate behavior to communicate. For someone who cannot speak, this is a reliable way to get quick results. Nick wrote:

> I used to control my life by behaving badly. I got immediate attention, and someone usually would figure out approximately what I wanted. It is still my first impulse to do this, but I am getting better at indicating my need to speak in order to communicate my needs.

Wally also revealed his intentional use of inappropriate behavior.

> The autistic behaviors that I exhibited before I used FC for the most part continue despite my ability to communicate. I have tried to put the behaviors to rest only to become really frustrated and upset

when other sociably acceptable substitutes are found to be too slow and too cumbersome. Relying on these more acceptable procedures is like relying on a stranger for help; sometimes they will help and sometimes they won't. With an old and trusted friend, you are sure of the results.

Intentional Behavior

Intentional behavior increases during the act of typing. Every time an autistic person sits down and begins to type, he or she confirms Rimland's thesis that there is a powerful connection between language and behavior.

For a successful typing session, the FC speaker has to "muster up" enough internal control to restrain impulsive behavior, focus attention, formulate a cohesive thought, and perform a series of controlled arm movements. Each of these intentional actions places great demand on the individual. Thus, FC provides the motivation for organized behavior as well as the opportunity to practice it.

During an FC session, the autistic individual has the experience of behavior and intention coming into alignment through his or her own internal controls. Multiple, moment-to-moment opportunities for this experience create a dynamic spiral of positive behavior.

The changes that Rimland alluded to when he coined the phrase Quantum Behavioral Improvement extend far beyond the intentional behavior that is needed for a successful typing session. QBI suggests changes that are global, far-reaching, and greater than the sum of their parts.

In her story, Barb explained that her purpose in life is to be a writer and an advocate for other "special forces" members. She traced the strong connection between behavior and language when she wrote:

> I no longer surreptitiously raid refrigerators or other unguarded food sources and gorge until I am physically numb and ill just for something to do in an attempt to fill an unquenchable hunger in my heart. All creatures are built to do more than survive. Quality of life requires it and life is designed to be quality. I must have instinctively known this and was therefore frustrated and angry to the core at doing nothing but passing time between here and autism. Those unsettling feelings and squandered energy manifested in bad behaviors.
>
> I think the bulk of my disturbing behaviors -- like smearing, kicking, biting, grabbing, hitting, pica, manipulating tantrums, running away, stealing food from others' plates, handling objects for hours on end, breaking my glasses, etc.-- have all melted away because none of

those things serve my purpose. I have suffered punishments and consequences before. Finding purpose is what changed things.

References

1. Rimland, B. (1988). Language and quantum behavioral improvement. Autism Research Review International, 2, 3.
2. Rimland. (1988).
3. Stern, D. N. (1985). *The interpersonal world of the infant: A view from psychoanalysis and developmental psychology.* New York: Basic Books.

FC in School and Work

"Not the least of the pain I endured was the work I was taught.
Until FC, I was destined to be cleaning floors."

Chammi Rajapatirana

FC has opened the world of formal education and learning to many individuals with autism. Five of the ten people profiled here – Aaron, Barb, Chammi, Nick and Sarah – were of school age when they began using FC. At that time, Barb was the only one who was mainstreamed into a public school. The others were attending segregated special education schools. After they began using FC, all four transferred into the public schools, sometimes leading the way towards inclusive schooling in their communities.

Introducing FC into the school environment allowed the FC speakers access to academic educational experiences. Though they may have been frustrated at the pace of the changes, as well as the assumptions of some of their teachers and classmates, their experiences were largely positive.

For the people who were already part of the adult service delivery system, the changes FC introduced into in their lives were somewhat less dramatic. Without strong federal laws about quality of care in adult services, funding can very greatly from one state to another.

Doug, Kathy, Tom and Wally were attending typical day programs when they began using FC. Daniel was in a home-based day program with 1:1 staff support so soon after he began using FC, he embarked on his goal of earning his GED. Unless they have unusually high levels of personal support, people in these programs would not be able to pursue formal education, including college courses.

The inclusion model in schools has been spreading in recent years. It is much more than new methods or teaching strategies and entails an orientation of accepting student differences .[1] FC fits well with this model. System changes were often driven by the individual efforts of FC speakers and their families and advocates. In the best case scenarios, the functional curriculum and the assumption of mental retardation were replaced with an academic curriculum and an understanding of movement differences and hidden competence.

FC Opened Doors to Learning

Before nonverbal autistic students had access to expressive language, it was nearly impossible to know how much learning was taking place and how much was possible for them. Some parents pursued academics for their children even in the face of overwhelming evidence that their efforts were in vain. As Anoja wrote:

> I did a lot of activities with Chammi hoping to teach him but never knew if he was learning or not. I now know I bored him to death with most of the things like puzzles and matching games.

Many individuals with autism, including those who use FC and those who speak, have commented on their intellectual competence and ability to learn even without direct teaching. They report that they can absorb large quantities of information quickly and easily. They also say they learn all the time even though it may look like they are not paying attention. This ability to learn without direct teaching makes it especially important to assure that individuals with autism spend their time in rich, intellectually stimulating environments.

Many people who use FC taught themselves to read from watching TV or from studying the patterns of language in the print-rich environments of their everyday lives. Nick notes that he taught himself to read from watching "Sesame Street" and Gwen recalls how he took books to bed with him every night. Daniel reported his excitement as he was beginning to decode the patterns of written language.

Wally's parents assumed that when Wally sat on the floor, flipping the pages of books for hours, he was merely fulfilling a need for sensory stimulation. It now seems that he was reading or visually piecing together the content of the books. He says that he taught himself to read and comprehend several foreign languages. He also mastered the material in many of the textbooks his siblings brought home from school. Reflecting on her ability to take in information, Barb wrote:

> I passively absorbed information from the stream. I don't know why I was motivated to collect education, since I had no idea what to do with it. I simply soaked stuff in.

Nick writes of his ability to absorb information quickly and easily and how his body prevents him from demonstrating his intelligence. He explains:

> Greenfield was a good school, but it was more like being at a babysitter's. The teaching went really slowly because they didn't know that they could speed up for me. The reality was that I wanted them to speed up. I was bored with the day to day lessons that I easily mastered. The teachers at Greenfield were well meaning, but they made life dull since I was really a smart kid in a stupid acting body.

Although these individuals appear to absorb information with great ease, their intelligence and ability to learn is hidden by sensory and movement differences. With sensory and movement differences, they do not have the motor control necessary to answer questions or otherwise demonstrate their knowledge. This discrepancy between intake and output is shown in one of the reports from a psychological assessment for Sarah. It states:

> There is much to be gained by Sarah continuing with her formal academic studies. Knowledge and information are consumed by Sarah at superior levels. It is difficult for Sarah to let people know the superiority of her knowledge and mastery due to the physical interferences of her autism. The time necessary for her to demonstrate her knowledge is extreme.

Sarah was only eight years old when she began using FC, but she already understood the importance of learning. One of her very first requests was to go to the "regular school" where her sister Janna went. Looking back, she reports:

> The most important choice I made was to leave my old school and go to school near my home with normal kids. Now I go to regular

school to learn facts about my world. I love to learn about biology and geometry. To go to school is great. I am a good student.

Literacy skills, education and learning are highly valued by many nonverbal people with autism[2] and FC has provided a way for them to demonstrate their love of learning. After acing his placement exams at a local community college and starting a class on the Italian Renaissance, Nick wrote in an email:

> The thinking of this period is perfect for my current mindset: EDUCATIO SUPERAT OMNIA (education overcomes all things). I took a chance on striving for an education. You see I really love being able to be at school and treasure every moment.

Wally's parents had informally educated him throughout his life with an ongoing stream of public TV and radio, books on tape, and a vast library of books in the home. He later wrote for a conference presentation:

> You must help us to become educated. This is the one way that I know of to help us fulfill our need to be included in your world as a contributing member of society without being just a freeloader.

Multiple Options for Learning

Over the past two decades, there have been several FC speakers who have earned degrees in higher education and certainly there will be more in the future. To date, Nick is currently pursuing a college degree. He has a unique relationship to his field of study as a result of his belated introduction to expressive language:

> Since 2003, I have been a student at Delaware County Community College, where I take one course each semester. Last spring I declared myself a Communication Studies major. Part of this decision was influenced by my interest in primate communication -- especially that of the great apes: this major was a way of jump-starting my studies by examining how human primates communicate. However, I also realized that this major might help me improve my own communication strategies, as well as my ability to decipher neurotypical communication and help me improve the quality of my social relationships.

Barb's education took a different direction. Instead of attending college classes, she decided to pursue a rigorous self-study program. She hired tutors who work with her daily. She watches CNN to keep up on current events and goes through two books-on-tape per week. Her current focus is on political science and literature. Barb's educational psychologist, Lois, reported that Barb is doing the equivalent of two college courses at any given time.

Several of the FC speakers received intensive home study as children. When Nick started to use FC, Gwen used workbooks, gold stars and other learning materials so they could play school at home. Prior to FC, Nick was mostly interested in watching TV for entertainment. As he became more serious about education, he expanded his repertoire to include educational TV and documentaries.

Before he began having serious symptoms of ALS, Wally and his father conducted formal home study for several hours every evening. The local community college supplied them with freshman-level textbooks in chemistry, physics, biology, math and history. Wally describes his home study and the importance of education in his life:

> Too often, "education" means going to school as most if not all of you have done. Yet, when I use the term "education," I am using it in a broader sense that could include formal schooling as well as anything else that would act as a vector in bringing to our minds any type of truthful information that will link us to reality and to your world. Educational radio and education TV, world news and commentary, being read to or listening to books on tape, watching educational videos on any number of subjects, as, simply, being talked to about what is taking place around us are some of the vectors that are very successful in supplying us with useful information as well as linking us to your world and to you. This dedication to my education on my parents' part is perhaps the single reason why am I where I am today ... they make sure I don't just tune the world out and don't retreat to my dark and lonely thoughts.

Functional Versus Academic Curriculum

In both schools and adult day programs, FC has increased the need to change philosophies and curricula. Historically, these settings used a behavioral model to train people in menial jobs and functional activities. There has been broad agreement in schools and day programs that cleaning toilets, sorting widgets, shredding paper, and delivering newspapers were adequate life goals for autistic individuals. As Wally Jr. wrote, "It is more important to educate the nonverbal autistic rather than to waste precious resources in trying to teach him a simple task."

Today, jobs that entail menial tasks can be a way to earn spending money and provide a balance to academic learning. However, for most FC users, functional tasks alone are not enough for a high quality of life.

As a professor of special education, Mary was deeply committed to the functional skills philosophy. However, when Aaron started to use FC, she quickly revised her stance and began to regret all the things she never tried to teach him. Eventually she found a balance between the competing philosophies. She notes:

> I feel tremendous guilt. I not only did not teach Aaron to read – I forbade it! I led the battle in our city to purge the curriculum of academics and developmental teaching. If the school, which bragged about its functional curriculum, dared to send home a worksheet with matched letters, colors ... I would attack them in a rage. I bought name stamps for Aaron and others so they wouldn't have to spend the rest of their lives learning to write their names.

> Aaron still needs a functional curriculum, which will give him the skills he will need after he leaves school, but this functional-community-based, self-help curriculum now must be expanded to include some reading instruction. We had always pushed for inclusion in some regular classes for the social networking, but now we are more urgent.

Mary realized that Aaron needed both academic and functional instruction to attain a quality of life that matched his abilities. This combination is easy to see from a parental point of view, but often schools and agencies are reluctant to adapt their curricula to changing needs.

After Sarah began using FC, Judy met resistance from school personnel who thought Sarah would be "misplaced" in an academic curriculum. Judy thought the school should focus on Sarah's strengths in the intellectual realm rather than trying to teach her independent living skills. Judy believed that Sarah would always need some level of supervision and assistance with daily tasks and that an academic curriculum would be a more fruitful path for Sarah.

Similarly, Gwen strongly believed Nick needed academic and creative work instead of a functional skills curriculum:

> I do think that Nick really loves mind play and word play and idea play. It's something that he does so well and that he can be the best at. I also feel like since he is physically more limited, it makes sense that he should go with his strength. I wouldn't care, if for the rest of his life, someone was having to do his laundry for him. It's great that he's learning to do it himself and I'm pleased – I think that's wonderful, but I think it's much more important that he's able to be writing poetry.

Issues in Schools

It has been nearly 20 years since the school-aged participants were transferring into their neighborhood schools. Today, many school districts have embraced inclusion and colleges are turning out young teachers who have been trained in the inclusion model. These teachers are interested and excited about providing academic instruction to individuals with disabilities.

Despite these recent gains, FC has not necessarily enjoyed the same acceptance. The following discussions highlight some of the difficulties (as well as successes) that Aaron, Barb, Chammi, Nick and Sarah faced in their schools two decades ago. Many of these issues are still relevant today.

Others' Perceptions

FC users experienced a range of acceptance when they transitioned into integrated school settings. Acceptance cannot be prescribed. Individuals with disabilities are often subjected to any number of discriminatory practices that can be either subtle or bold. However, in many instances, FC changed the perceptions held by teachers, administrators and fellow students.

Mary recalls Aaron's school experiences after he started to use FC, saying those were "his best years." Many of Aaron's classmates accepted his typing as valid communication and perceived him as more competent. Tina says the difference was monumental:

> Everyone saw him in a whole new light. They asked his thoughts and opinions. The view of Aaron changed from one of a severely cognitively challenged person to one of a young person with ideas to share and someone who understood more than anyone ever dreamed before.

Like Aaron, Nick was accepted by his peers, several of whom even typed with him. He was recognized for being smart and was first to be picked for Science Jeopardy teams. At lunch, Nick ate with other kids while his aide watched from the far side of the lunchroom.

Sarah enjoyed good success in the integrated public school setting in the early years, but as she grew older things became more difficult. The constant assault on her sensitive sensory system triggered her odd behavior. Increasingly, she began to sense rejection for her behavior from some students and teachers. Sarah sensed the difference between full acceptance and understanding and the rejection that came when she could not change her behavior to comply with standards for typical students. She wrote:

> Schools are open to students with developmental disabilities, but when they ask us to play the parts of normal students they are not really letting us into their spaces.

Even within a largely accepting educational environment, disability issues are not always foremost in everyone's mind. In some cases, staff and teachers showed a lack of awareness and sensitivity. In a similar example, Aaron's class read *Lord of the Flies*, a book about how a boy who is different is made a scapegoat and eventually killed by the group, Aaron never read another book. Sarah attended a disturbing lecture detailing research intended to eliminate all forms of genetic disability. Afterward, she wrote a letter to the teacher asking why people are taught to hate disability.

Transitions

Transitions can be hard for everyone, but they are especially challenging for individuals with autism. For school-aged FC users, transitioning in and out of the public schools presented many challenges. Nick made a modified transition into the public schools by going to regular education classes in the morning and then back to the segregated school in the afternoons. This combination gave him the experience of staying focused and learning to sit still in his chair, after which he could relax in his familiar setting.

When Sarah began transitioning out of high school and into the adult service system, many difficulties arose. Judy envisioned Sarah's familiar facilitator accompanying her to a local community college class as part of a "well-supported and gradual transition from high school to post-secondary setting." The request for this was denied, causing Sarah's anxiety to build. Soon after that, the facilitator left the school. Starting over with a new facilitator coupled with the long months they had spent talking and planning about the college class caused Sarah's anxiety to escalate. As Judy recalls, "She experienced lots of emotions while waiting patiently for the systems to catch up. This took years!"

Some systems, by their very nature, are slow to change. In the case of FC, the changes that were needed were dramatic and sometimes controversial. Transferring from a segregated school to an inclusive setting could take many months. Both Chammi and Nick experienced an extended period of waiting for the slow wheels of school bureaucracies to turn. They admittedly used bad behavior as a way to speed up the process. Nick confides:

> I was bad so I could have an opportunity to study at a better school. I got what I wanted! Bad behavior only helped. I know I should not behave badly but it worked. I understand why it took a year for me to get into public school classes, but it felt like forever. I had changed

overnight! I thought my life automatically should become like everybody else's.

Funding

Funding for special education students has become a flashpoint for school districts with lean budgets. In most cases, the FC user was given a full-time aide/facilitator in the same way a deaf student would be given an interpreter. The principal at Nick's elementary school was very aware that having enough assistance in the classroom made the difference between success and failure.

Assignments and Grades

Gwen insisted that Nick do the same assignments as the other students while working at his own pace. His achievements increased his self-esteem. He wrote, "I'm proud to get good grades because it's the most important thing in my life." In contrast, Sarah's autism team recognized how much more time she took to do both the reading and writing for her assignments so they suggested that she be required to do half of the normal work load.

Discipline

While overall behavior tended to improve after FC, behavioral issues did not subside completely. Barb's continuing disruptive behavior at school eroded some teachers' confidence and belief in her typing.

Sometimes individualized measures can be helpful. Initially, when Nick made noise or moved about the classroom, his aide quickly whisked him out the door so he would not disrupt the class. However, this left the teachers without an opportunity to discuss Nick's behavior with him. Eventually, Gwen helped design a protocol with each teacher. Some teachers preferred to leave the situation up to the aide. Others wanted the chance to interact with Nick and then signal the aide when they thought it was time for him to leave.

Gwen made sure that Nick apologized for disrupting a class so he would learn to take responsibility for his behavior. She also expressed a reasonable policy for behavior difficulties when she said, "Nick has the right to go to the public school, but he has to earn the privilege of staying in the classroom by behaving in a considerate and responsible manner."

Issues in Adult Services

While some school systems may have been slow to change over the past two decades, many adult service systems have changed even less. In the early 1980s, ten years before FC was introduced in the U.S., adult programs had begun to shift from sheltered workshops to a community-based vocational model.

With nearly continuous funding cuts since the 1980s, adult agencies have not had the resources to move towards a model that focuses on educational or literacy-based activities. In many states, wages for direct care workers in adult service agencies have not kept pace with inflation. At the same time, the philosophies of these organizations and the perceptions they have of people with disabilities may not have evolved. While exceptions exist, large numbers of adult service agencies continue to interpret behaviors associated with sensory and movement difficulties as signs of cognitive disability.

Stagnant wages and vocational curricula focused on menial jobs mean that individuals with autism leave high school and enter systems that have lower standards of care. When this occurs, these young adults begin to spiral downward, losing many of the skills that they worked hard to achieve in school.

When adult children leave their parents' homes to live in residential settings, the situation can worsen. Residential agencies often have high staff turnover and minimal supervision of direct care workers. For the families, staying on top of health and safety issues can take enormous amounts of time and energy. Often, it is only through the ongoing efforts of parents and family members that non-speaking adults with autism use their literacy skills to pursue education or other high quality-of-life activities.

After his good years in high school, Aaron went to a vocational day program where he was learning to sort screws. He also had a job cleaning parking lots. Since he liked being outdoors, the parking lot job worked well for him. However, because Aaron could not learn to sort screws independently he was moved to a non-vocational program and lost the parking lot job. Mary reports that now he spends his days doing craft projects with macaroni and watching TV. He has occasional community outings to Burger King.

For a while, Kathy's day program consisted of walks and shopping. In an attempt to help Kathy find a beneficial way to occupy her time, Heather and Kent helped Kathy sell her condo and move to an agency in another town where she could have more FC support. Today, FC helps Kathy stay connected to others and participate in daily activities of her choice. Kathy is content with her job shredding paper as long as she also can keep up on the news and have daily conversations with her roommate or parents.

Sarah continues to pursue her writing goals in her day program at the ARC. Barb has the financial resources to create her own ideal day program of study and writing. Daniel is studying and working on his independent typing in hopes of passing his GED exam.

Despite some success stories for adults in day programs, creative language-based efforts such as classes, writing or doing conference presentations are largely dependent on parents and family members. When activities such as these are not readily available, the public support system is failing to provide levels of care that ensure quality of life for individuals with autism.

References

1. Kluth, P. (2003). *You're going to love this kid: Teaching students with autism in the inclusive classroom*. Baltimore, MD: Paul H. Brookes.
2. Kluth (2003).

Medical Issues

"She could tell us when she was hurting."

Barbara Rentenbach

Illnesses and medical procedures can pose great difficulty and stress for non-speaking individuals with autism. As a result of their severely limited ability to convey information about pain or discomfort, it is often difficult for health professionals and family members to ascertain how to proceed. Even routine procedures such as a physical exam can become traumatic for everyone involved.

Due to sensory and movement issues, autistic individuals might not know or be able to pinpoint the source of pain or discomfort. Even when they can, the information is of limited value to the healthcare provider when unaccompanied by a full description of the distress.

Autistic individuals may over- or under-react to pain, or exhibit misleading behavioral responses. Hypersensitivity can occur when the nervous system does not dampen sensory input. Extreme amounts of sensory input can overwhelm the system and lead to sensory shutdown. There can also be shifting between states of hyper- and hyposensitivity. These responses create a confusing picture for the medical practitioner.

It is often difficult to know if or how much a person with autism is suffering. Heather describes Kathy's limited ability to supply information on health issues before FC:

> It was difficult to figure out when Kathy didn't feel well, unless she was very sick or had a fever. The usual medications were tried to help her feel less anxious or for specific ailments, but the results were usually less than satisfactory. Often there were negative side effects; some were subtle, but must have been disturbing to her. The only way to judge a treatment's efficacy was to watch her behavior, her bodily functions, her mood and her general health.

Understanding and Treating Physical Health Issues

FC provides a vehicle for nonverbal individuals with autism to give important information about their bodily state. It also provides a way to gain their cooperation during medical procedures and affords them the opportunity to give feedback about a treatment or medication. These elements can dramatically improve quality of life.

For Kathy, communication quickly led to results. FC enabled Kathy to discuss digestive problems with her health professional, who recommended a gluten- and casein-free diet.

Soon after Barb started using FC, she reported information that led her parents to pursue treatment with specialists; she received orthotics, underwent two eye operations for ingrown eyelashes and took an eye exam. As her mother wrote:

> One of the very biggest changes concerned her eye sight. She was able to do the eye test, via FC. It was found she had about 20/2000 sight. The glasses that she received made a huge improvement in her confidence, posture and, of course, her ability to see. This is a tremendous change for the better. These types of things she could tell us and we could correct for her physical comfort. She could tell us when she was hurting.

Anoja reported how for years Chammi's medical issue was interpreted as a symptom of his autism. Often Chammi would lie down to go to sleep but then abruptly jump up and spend the next few hours pacing around the house. The inability to relax along with extended periods of restless agitation is not uncommon for individuals with autism.

After he began to use FC, Chammi was able to explain that he did this because his gut hurt. He described his symptoms to a gastroenterologist who recommended a barium x-ray. Anoja was not confident that he would be able to cooperate for this complicated and distasteful procedure. She remembered years earlier when he had to undergo general anesthesia in order to have an x-ray for a painless lump on his leg. However, with the use of FC to explain the procedure and gain his cooperation, Chammi tolerated the procedure. He was diagnosed with acid reflux, and it became clear that his restless pacing and his inability to lie down were not symptoms of his autism.

Tom has used FC to articulate his needs to physicians, thus helping them gain his cooperation for medical procedures. He explains, "I feel very vulnerable on my back on doctors' tables. I have FC'd that I would let them do things if I could sit up. It has worked for me. Most doctors have been very nice to me."

FC helped Doug in several health-related issues. After communicating that his stomach hurt, he was diagnosed with and successfully treated for two ulcers. On another occasion, he typed that his tooth hurt. A dental exam revealed a popcorn hull stuck in his gum causing inflammation. FC also helped uncover Doug's allergy to cats. As Judi notes, "Even if Doug doesn't want to facilitate about anything else, he still facilitates with me about health issues. I can give information the doctor wouldn't have otherwise."

Gaining the cooperation of the individual with autism can make a critical difference during medical procedures. Sensory and movement differences, along with high levels of anxiety, make it extremely difficult for individuals with autism to relax when faced with a procedure. Consequently, health professionals often administer a general anesthetic for even minimally intrusive procedures such as a routine dental cleaning. Having access to language can go a long way in making procedures less stressful and more humane.

Understanding and Treating Mental and Emotional Distress

FC also can be extremely helpful in dealing with mental and emotional distress. Chammi experienced many episodes of pacing and crying that lasted for days and sometimes weeks, making it nearly impossible for him to sleep or eat. In the midst of one such episode, he typed, "I can't imagine joy." This information led to a diagnosis for depression. He was placed on antidepressants, to good effect.

When Doug's mother died, he descended into bouts of depression accompanied by incidents of aggression. Once he was able to write about his sadness and explain how much he missed his mother, he started taking antidepressants and his mood improved quickly.

After being placed on medication, Doug and Chammi were able to help their doctors track its effectiveness and adjust the dosage. Without expressive language, their behavioral symptoms of depression might have been misinterpreted.

Sometimes emotional distress can come from not having enough information about a procedure or treatment. Prior to FC, parents and caregivers might not have thought to provide explanations for medical visits. Judi reported an example of this. Doug had been upset and angry for several weeks, even on one occasion hitting his favorite staff person. When Judi asked him about this, Doug reported that he had gone to the doctor and had to bend over. Judi checked with a staff person at Doug's home and it was confirmed that he had a prostate exam during that appointment. Judi then showed him pictures in an anatomy book and explained why the exam was important. Once he had a basic understanding of the exam, Doug's anger and aggression diminished.

Emotional distress can also come from not feeling in control during a medical procedure. In one example, Tom used FC to gain a sense of control over himself and the situation. Typically, it would take three or four people to restrain Tom for a blood draw. Being held down increased his fear and made him fight harder. When Tom gave the medical technician specific instructions for how to place his arm, he was able to sit still on his own for the whole procedure.

In addition to providing behavioral and clinical evidence that validates FC, these examples show how access to expressive language can highlight distress, help parents and caregivers understand unusual behaviors, elicit cooperative behavior during medical procedures and sometimes even change a course of treatment. In addition to reducing stress and improving quality of life in medical circumstances, FC enables individuals with autism to work cooperatively with providers in their own healthcare and gain a measure of control over their physical, emotional and mental well-being.

Emotions

"Emotions are my behavioral downfall."

Daniel McConnell

Emotions get short shrift in science since they are often seen as the enemy of reason and too vague for scientific study. Despite a widespread belief that human beings make decisions solely through reason, emotions underlie all rational decision-making and play an important role in virtually everything we think or do.[1]

For individuals with autism, emotions appear to underlie many of their behavioral and movement difficulties. High levels of emotional sensitivity are often revealed when autistic individuals describe their inner realities. For example, independent typer Sue Rubin wrote, "Autism is a way of life awash in emotions."[2] As Daniel noted in the quotation above, there is a strong link between emotions and behavioral difficulties.

In his book, *Emotional Intelligence*, Daniel Goleman speaks of our two brains: the older, emotional brain and the rational brain that evolved much later.[3] With multiple reverberating neurological connections between the two brains, both areas are activated in the endless stream of decisions we make every day.

The emotional brain has an enormous influence over all of our actions as well as our rational thought processes. It registers events more quickly and tends towards quick and impulsive action. The language of the emotional brain is the language of the heart – metaphor, image, poetry and dreams – while the rational mind prefers the language of objective reality.[4] That FC transcripts are often rich with metaphor and poetic emotional expression provides some evidence for the importance of emotion in the inner lives of nonverbal individuals with autism.

Emotions also have neurological links to many aspects of quality of life, including social interaction, attention and having a sense of meaning or purpose. Our emotional lives trigger us to move and take action in the world and they serve as the gateway to motivation, creative thought and problem-solving.

Emotions and Autism

Although it is not well understood, a strong connection between emotions and autism appears to exist. In many published studies, individuals with autism exhibit unusual emotional responses or difficulties with certain aspects of emotions, such as reading facial expressions. From these studies, it appears that differences in processing emotions may be part of the diagnosis.[5]

Greenspan suggests that the core psychological deficit in autism might be the inability to connect affect to motor planning and symbol formation.[6] Other researchers posit a normal physiological response but differences in expression of emotions.[7]

Donna Williams, a prolific author with autism, believes the central feature in autism is difficulty with emotional processing and emotional expression. She writes:

> I believe that autism results when some sort of mechanism that controls emotion does not function properly, leaving an otherwise relatively normal body and mind unable to express themselves with the depth that they would otherwise be capable of.[8]

Autistic individuals often lack facial expression or have other atypical responses in emotional situations. As a result, it is commonly thought that they do not experience emotions.

However, in a study of first-hand accounts written by "high-functioning" autistic adults, researchers found that the autistic individuals possessed complex emotional lives. The also found that their emotional lives were dominated by unpleasant or negative emotions. These negative emotions clustered around four central themes: depression, frustration, fear or apprehension, and a sense of alienation. In light of these findings, the authors warn against the assumption that the emotional lives of individuals with autism are attenuated or absent.[9]

Dawn Prince-Hughes, an autistic author and professor of anthropology, has written a deeply moving and emotional book. In it, she speaks about the widespread misunderstandings about the emotional lives of people with autism.

> Many people, again lay and professional alike, believe that all people with autism are by definition incapable of communicating, that they do not experience emotions, and they cannot care about other people or the world around them. My experience, both personally and with others like me, is that in many cases quite the opposite is true. A significant number of autistic people who care deeply about all manner of things, and are profoundly emotional about them, share these capabilities in the privacy of their journals, diaries, and poetry. They do not show them to the world, which is too intense and often destructive or, worse, dismissive.[10]

Neurological Connection

The root of the word emotion means to move and the sensory, motor and emotional systems share many close neurological connections.[11] Most of us might not be aware of this connection. We automatically comprehend, interpret and label our emotional experiences, but in autism this seamless process might be disrupted.

Donna Williams says her emotions register as sensory information that is very intense and often feels like too much for the body to bear.[12] Other autistic adults have explained that their emotions make volitional movement difficult and that sensory input such as loud sounds or certain frequencies can cause very strong emotional responses.[13]

Emotional Processes

Emotions involve the movement of energy and the processing of information.[14] Processing emotions can be loosely grouped into three major components: regulation, expression and insight/closure. Insight and closure can only occur when emotions have been fully processed.[15]

Emotional regulation and insight are internal processes; emotional expression occurs as observable, public behavior. Through language, some aspects of the private internal processes can be shared.

Regulation, expression and insight are dynamically related; as one improves, so do the others. Put simply, emotional regulation is necessary for accurate expression, expression leads to insight, and insight in turn furthers regulation.

Not surprisingly, gaining access to expressive language has had an enormous impact on the emotional lives of the FC speakers and their families. Anoja describes Chammi's emotional roller coaster after he started typing:

> The first year was difficult. As Chammi told us later, he was scared of coming out of his non-communicative life so he got a lot of headaches and was agitated. He also decided to make up for his lost childhood. It was as if we went through the terrible twos all the way to 18 years in one year; sibling rivalry, tricks, lying, whining. All that one experiences over many years as a child got packed into a very short time.

Gwen provides a similar description of Nick's emotional states soon after he began to use FC:

> He was emotionally all over the map. In the beginning, sometimes it seemed, "Am I talking to a 30 or 40 year old?" But then I've got this person who, in some of his possessiveness, is like a baby or one year old. It was just all over the map. We still have some of that, but language, I think, is the only conceivable way that we can help Nick to mature. There's still an immaturity in certain ways and when he is under stress he's sort of thrown back to some of those patterns, but he's able to do so much more now.

Emotional Regulation and the Window of Tolerance

Emotional regulation is central to self-regulation, attention and the organization of the mind.[16] It influences which emotions we have, in which situations they take place and how we experience and express them.

When emotions are not well-regulated, all aspects of daily life become more challenging. Every change in emotional state causes a change in the body's physiological state. Conversely, every change in physiological state signals a change in emotions.[17] emotional regulation involves modulating physiological changes and keeping them at a tolerable level.

When we regulate our emotions, we can have intense emotional experiences and still maintain organized, flexible behavior. Gottman and Katz[18] define emotional regulation as the ability to respond to a strong emotional event (either positive or negative) by:

- Inhibiting inappropriate behavior.
- Self-soothing arousal.
- Refocusing attention.
- Organizing for pursuit of action goals.

Emotions can be over- or under-regulated. Individuals with autism often have difficulties with emotional regulation. This problem can interfere with social interaction and/or lead to depression, anxiety or behavioral difficulties such as aggression or withdrawal.[19] Individuals who under-regulate will experience emotions very intensely and have little or no control over their responses, often acting in impulsive ways.

Emotional hypersensitivity, like sensory hypersensitivity, is caused by overloading the system. The physiological effects of emotions are cumulative, so frequent repetition of an emotion can increase sensitivity to it and the intensity of that emotion becomes magnified.[20]

Maintaining an emotionally regulated state means staying within one's window of tolerance. When arousal moves beyond the window of tolerance, sympathetic activity is increased and thinking and behavior become disorganized. A narrow window of tolerance coupled with a high level of emotional sensitivity can result in a hair-trigger emotional response system in which behavior deteriorates quickly, easily and often.[21]

The window of tolerance varies greatly among individuals. Because it is context dependent, it can vary within an individual from one moment to the next. For example, being tired or hungry can greatly decrease the window of tolerance while being with people who are perceived as being safe can increase the window of tolerance.

Flooding, or hijacking, occurs when physiological arousal far exceeds the window of tolerance. A narrow window of tolerance or emotional hypersensitivity can increase the likelihood of emotional flooding.

When the intensity of emotional events exceeds the window of tolerance, the individual operates from the lower brain centers. When this occurs, behavior becomes impulsive and volitional behavior becomes nearly impossible. Those with a narrow window of tolerance and a high level of sensitivity can easily descend into this lower level of processing.[22]

First-hand accounts of emotions of many people with autism are similar to the following description of emotional flooding.

> Flooded expression occurs when clients have such intense levels of emotional experience and arousal that their feelings seem to burst out of them with little control and minimal cognitive processing…. They are so swamped by their feelings that they can't organize their thoughts, can't communicate clearly, can't process new information, and can't consider another person's point of view. Their behavior tends to be impulsive and extreme.[23]

Some behaviors frequently observed in autism, such as lack of eye contact or preference for solitary play, could be strategies to dampen emotions in order to stay within one's window of tolerance. These strategies decrease the likelihood of emotional flooding by decreasing sensory and social input.[24] Nick reveals how easily he exceeds his window of tolerance:

> Feelings overwhelm me. They are so strong that I wish I could take a vacation and not feel anything. Autism is not a pretty thing. It is being limited by a body that goes haywire. The truth is that I feel so deeply that I fear every feeling. Feelings escalate and I fear a bout of blinding emotion. I kill just about every feeling I have in me.

Since emotional regulation and exceeding the window of tolerance are internal events, we can only infer their presence through self-reports or by observing behavior. Nick describes his "blinding emotion" and Chammi has written that "great rage takes me over." These phrases suggest that emotional flooding has occurred.

Mary describes how Aaron would "bolt out of the room" when he had an opportunity to type with a new facilitator. This response was interpreted to mean that Aaron did not want to communicate. However, his response could also be interpreted to mean his impulsive bolting was in response to emotional flooding.

Emotional regulation is the first step in gaining behavioral control. Difficult, aggressive or oppositional behavior can come from emotional hypersensitivity and/or a narrow window of tolerance. Expressing emotions, especially with language, plays a vital role in emotional regulation.

Emotional Expression

As mammals, we are hardwired to broadcast information regarding our inner state. Expressing emotions is largely a social or shared experience. Humans broadcast this emotional information through both behavior and language. In addition to writing, we also use arts such as music, dance, visual art and poetry as vehicles of emotional expression.

For non-speaking people with sensory and movement differences, body language can be a woefully inaccurate form of emotional expression. When behavioral messages are consistently misinterpreted or misunderstood, frustration and despair can be layered on top of the original emotion.

Language-based expression provides the FC user with a medium for correcting misinterpretations and fine-tuning emotional messages. By pairing body language with typed messages, we can gain a more accurate understanding of the emotional lives of FC speakers.

Despite widespread sensory and movement differences, some facilitators report instances revealing congruence between the FC speakers' body language and their typed expressions. Jo notes that Tom slams the letterboard when he is upset. Judy reports that Sarah does not use spaces between words when she types about emotional issues.

In a similar example, Barb's special education teacher, Andrea, noted how Barb's typing matched her behavior. She wrote:

> When excited, Barb types quickly. When introspective or contemplating, she is slower. When she is angry, she pounds the board and types out various expletives. This was demonstrated most when angry or when she disagreed with the party that she was communicating with.

Heather says that Kathy usually has an expressive face. When she is typing, however, her face becomes flat and her body language becomes more expressive. Heather cites several examples in which Kathy's entire physical presence became very focused and strong as she typed about an emotional issue. Heather explains:

> Sometimes it's the way she uses the board and her body to tell what's really important for her and what she wants to express. It's usually something that is emotionally important for her to talk about.

Sarah's body language and facial expression often match the content of her typing. Sometimes, her typing predicts future actions. In one case, Sarah expressed her frustration that people doubted her typing, her fear that FC would be taken away from her, and her belief that if she lost FC, she would have to go back to her special education school. Over the next three days, after typing about these emotionally charged fears, Sarah had eight incidents of hitting other students and one incident in which she tried to run away. Under normal circumstances, hitting and running away are very low-incidence behaviors for Sarah. Quite possibly, these events were further expressions of her fear and frustration concerning some people's doubts about her typing.

Using words to express and convey emotions is a powerful tool for self-regulation. The intensity of an emotion can be modulated by the mere act of placing a name or label on it.[25] The act of translating a dynamic, chaotic emotional experience into language changes the emotion itself by bringing it into conscious awareness. Kennedy-Moore and Watson describe this process:

> Talking to someone or writing about one's feelings inherently involves structuring and organizing one's thoughts about these feelings. These thoughts become more orderly and less perseverative. The process of trying to explain one's feelings to someone else necessarily involves clarifying these feelings in one's own mind.[26]

Insight through Self-awareness

Self-awareness is the first step in gaining emotional insight and emotional insight is the first step in changing habitual patterns of behavior.[27] At the lowest levels of insight, emotions are experienced as sensations and bodily actions.[28] Higher levels of insight occur when emotional experiences have been thoroughly processed.

Self-awareness involves describing emotions or emotional events in a dispassionate way. Unlike venting, emotional self-awareness involves having a foot in two worlds - feeling the emotion but at the same time not being carried away by it. Emotional venting lacks self-awareness and consequently does not lead to insight and closure.[29]

Examples of very high levels of emotional self-awareness permeate the writings of the FC speakers. When Kathy was having problems at her work place, she told her parents via typing that she realized she was behaving childishly and thanked them for their "kind attention."

Nick wrote extensively about Babyliss, the name he has given to the side of himself that remains immature. In the following quote, he displays his ability to trace the steps of his emotional processes:

> Babyliss was my mode of reacting. I was solipsistically infantile in my experience of life. I wanted love, attention, security, succor, and entertainment from everybody else. I didn't expect anyone to need much from me. I perceived people's attempts to control my actions or get responses from me as mostly power struggles or entertaining games, rather than selfless attempts to give me control over myself and the world. I still catch myself doubting people's motives when

they try to help me; if I listen to this doubt, Babyliss-thinking takes over, and I blow up doubt into an ever-growing balloon of mistrust. Then I become defiant, and I refuse to cooperate or be controlled.

The emotional self-awareness of the FC speakers is especially poignant and courageous in the area of disability and seeing themselves as different from the norm. For people with lifelong disabilities that affect virtually every aspect of life, seeing oneself as different becomes the emotional ground that colors every aspect of life. As therapist Valerie Sinason notes, "Opening your eyes to admitting you look, sound, walk, move or think differently from the ordinary, average person...takes great reserves of courage, honesty and toleration of one's own envy.[30]

Expressions of Being Different

All of the FC speakers display courage, honesty and emotional self-awareness about the ways in which they are different.

Aaron: "I need to talk to make people hear me, but no one thinks I really have things to say. They are wrong, but know funny little how to communicate with me."

Barb: "I don't look normal. I appear to be quite messed up and a prime candidate for nothing but pity and patronization with a sprinkling of repulsion and fear."

Chammi: "Hellish to sit by while other people talk and laugh. I remember that time well. The anguish I felt comes back and I am lost. Until I remember that I have words now."

Daniel: Imagine a body that does not obey coupled with not being able to talk. It is not like I intend to scream, but the noise just comes out instead of coming out in words. I think it makes me appear retarded so I would prefer not to do it.

Kathy: "Before I learned to use FC, I felt I was an idiot because I couldn't understand what was going on. I couldn't understand why nobody was like me."

Sarah: "I feel scared of not being a regular normal kid acting nice. I am a girl with lots of problems but I am doing my best."

Tom: "I was treated as I appeared. No choice in anything, just being herded through life like cattle. No one thought I understood. People were nice enough to me, they just didn't think anyone was home."

Wally: "Perhaps I was viewed as behaving like a baby before I could communicate because no one took the time to try to understand me. This infuriated me and as a result, I finally gave in to behaving like everyone expected me to behave."

Doug: "They couldn't believe I was so smart."

Nick: Inside, I am bright, caring, and sensitive. Now, with a more external view of myself, I find that my appearance, behaviors and physical abilities are not who I really am intellectually and as a soul.

Working Through Difficulties

Several family members in this book use FC to process emotions, solve problems and reflect on upsetting events. Barbara notes that Barb might have an occasional moment of uncontrolled frustration, but for the most part, she is able to type about things that are bothering her and work through them with her facilitators and support team.

Gwen and Nick have filled many notebooks of conversations working through stressful emotional events. During times of grief, she tells him, "This is hard for anybody to deal with. You are a writer. You are a poet. This is what fuels an artist. Write it."

Jo describes how Tom worked through a painful experience. He would type a little about it; then, it would become too emotional and he would have to stop. Eventually he would feel ready to come back to the topic. At the end of each of these difficult sessions, he typed, "I'm glad I said that. I'm glad I got it out."

The data gleaned provides many examples of participants' increased ability to regulate their emotions and exert more control over their behavior in emotionally charged situations. Barb's incidents of attacking people diminished as she became more fluent in typing about her emotions. Tom no longer hits people when he is upset. Instead, he has learned to get up and leave the room until he is ready to talk about it.

When Nick is upset, he remembers how his deceased father made him feel secure, using those memories to comfort himself. He explains, "I rescue myself now by taking control of my fears and reassuring myself with my deepest and oldest source of love and strength. I am getting the hang of internal controls."

Bringing emotions into the cognitive domain of language enables us to reflect on the experience, label and interpret it. Through this process, we gain the ability to tolerate greater emotional intensity, and, if necessary, alter our emotional expression so that our overt behavior is in accord with personal values and social norms. Although our rational mind does not have much control over the emotions we have, it can greatly influence our responses.

There is an inherent human need to experience closure to events in our lives, especially to those involving negative emotions. Emotional insight can lead to emotional closure and a sense of completion about an event. Without resolution, we continue to live with the event, which can come to haunt us in the form of intrusive thoughts or dreams. These can cause us to ruminate, perseverate or obsess on the unfinished themes. Being stuck in this cycle can lead to over-arousal of the autonomic nervous system and increased anxiety.[31]

Narrative writing about thoughts and emotions is a powerful way to bring insight and closure to an emotional event. Writing slows down thinking and increases our understanding, which in turn provides a framework for constructing meaning around the event and our responses to it. Even in cases where no meaning is to be found, the experience can become psychologically complete, providing a sense of predictability and control that reduces anxiety and contributes to increased levels of emotional regulation in the future.[37]

Types of Emotion Expressed

All thought and communication are colored by our emotions. Emotions can be implicit within a message or expressed explicitly.

Although there were no interview questions asking about emotions, everyone expressed emotions. Some expressions were very sophisticated and nuanced, while others were more brief.

Unpleasant emotions dominate the writings of "high-functioning" autistic adults, as found in a study that analyzed websites of autistic individuals.[33] Like the website study, we found more frequent expression of negative emotions than positive ones. However, this finding may not be an accurate representation of the participants' inner lives. Negative emotions may merely have greater need of expression.

The sections below provide a sampling of the most prominent emotional themes. The themes include:

- Depression.
- Anger and rage.
- Fear of going back to non-communication.
- Laughing and crying.
- Love.
- Death and grief.
- Loneliness, isolation and alienation.

Depression

In the general population, depression is often correlated with difficulty identifying and describing emotions. For autistic individuals, estimates for some degree of depression range from 64-75%.[34]

Communication can help assuage depression, but it is not a panacea. Wally describes his "dark and lifeless world" before FC. Yet even with FC, Nick confides, "Sometimes I feel quite depressed. I am trying to deal with the losses in my life."

When Chammi began using FC, he would type, "I feel dead" and "I can't imagine joy." Eventually, he relates, "Vice-like grip of depression was eased after FC."

Anger and Rage

Barb is articulate in expressing her anger. In writing about her life before FC, she says:

> The island of Barb was rather peaceful except when too much nautical traffic approached. Then flooding was sure to follow. The island swelled with liquid anger because the ground was already saturated. Fear and uncertainty made sure that anger was always the most abundant resource.

Fear of Going Back to Non-Communication

Some speakers describe their fears about the future and a possible return to a life without FC. Noting that his ability to communicate and his sense of well-being is dependent on others, Tom says, "I am learning to face reality. I'm more of a complete person now and function that way. Fear and excitement are close relatives."

Remembering the darkness of life before FC, Chammi acknowledges: "I am terrified that I might go back there. If FC were taken away from me that is where I would be. Gibbering guy loves my life now. Gaping at my past is hard, best to just look forward."

Laughing and Crying

Due to sensory and movement differences, many individuals with autism never laugh or cry. However, their outside demeanor does not always match their inner emotions.

Sarah has always enjoyed the loving teasing among her family and the gentle humor of a favorite teacher to whom she wrote, "You too really like teasing and I laugh inside. Fun to tease."

When Judi explained autism to Doug, he began to cry. She asked him why. He typed, "Because I have autism."

Love

Judi describes Doug's expressions of love soon after he started typing:

> When we first started facilitating, for several years Doug would tell us that he loved us. He has never verbally said that to us, never. For us as a family to hear that, it meant so much. I guess with Doug we just didn't think in those terms because he sometimes acts like he is tolerating us. We just didn't know that he loved us, so that was really neat for us to hear. Of course, we would tell him back that we loved him.

Heather fondly recalls a time when Kathy expressed her love:

> I took Katherine to lunch last week and we had a nice time. She used the board to tell me her food preferences and I talked with her about how much I enjoyed taking her to lunch because I got a chance to have some time just with her. She took the board. She was holding her hand there by the board with her pointer [finger] and wanted me to help her FC. I did and she said, "I love you, Mom." The way she did it was very precise. She took her whole body and went right to each of those letters so that I would not miss it. That's the impression I got—"Don't miss this Mother. This is something that I'm saying and is very important."

Barb describes the circle of love she receives and gives:

> I was showered with love all my life. Unfortunately, I have only just begun to return any of my hearty portion. My work now is to write with as much love and commitment as I can manage so that others may have a more beautiful island experience.

Death and Grief

The participants wrote about sadness over loss of a loved one as well as their fear of future losses. Nick wrote, "Life is killing me. I am hanging on. Death is so sudden. One day my father was with us and the next day he was gone. Because of the fact that death can be so sudden, I am often scared of losing other people who are close to me."

After her brother Rick died, Kathy wondered where he was. To comfort her, a staff person said that now Rick no longer had autism. Heather says that being able to communicate with Kathy helped them work through the death and resultant fears:

> She was thinking about suicide. Because how deeply she feels about autism and where her brother might be, she didn't want to be here anymore. We spent some time going over and over this and talking with her about death and how important it was for her to know that we treasured her and that she was alive. Wherever Rick was, it is peaceful but it is important for her not to think about joining him in any way. If we hadn't had FC, it would've been going on in her for some time and maybe even led to drastic consequences.

For FC speakers, losing a family member who is also a facilitator presents a double blow. Losing a loved one is hard enough, but when that person is a link, and perhaps the only link to communication, the fear and grief can be magnified.

Judi oversees her brother Doug's daily life and is his only facilitator. Their mother's impending death resulted in Doug typing about his fears. Judi relates, "He was worried about dying and afraid that I will die."

Jo confesses FC has made their lives more difficult in that Tom seems to think (and express) more about death. She notes, "He worries more about the future and his life and of dying and whether he's going to be able to have a way of communicating."

Loneliness, Isolation and Alienation

A pervasive sense of alienation was the central emotional theme in the website study of "high-functioning" individuals with autism. This seems to be true for many of the FC speakers profiled in this book as well. Despite their current optimism, many participants express loneliness, isolation and alienation.

Although they have spent their whole lives embedded in loving families, the FC speakers write frequently about loneliness. In a book report on *Black Beauty*, Aaron identified with the horse. His emotions are apparent:

> *Black Beauty* like me. Sad story. My life sad. Beauty was hit, no home, looked good, loving horse. We lonely. No friends. Open relationship. In need understanding. Me just got to be gotten. Beauty got more. They overlook us.

Aaron's observation, "They overlook us," speaks eloquently to the particular loneliness of those who do not speak. Neurologist Oliver Sacks describes a boy who did not have a way to communicate until he came to the school for the deaf at age nine. Sacks noted that until then, the boy had been treated as autistic and retarded. He went on to say that the boy suffered from "an annihilating sense of leftoutness and isolation." These words connote being overlooked, as Aaron observed; in other words, being so isolated and left out as to be nonexistent.

Alignment of one's emotional state with another can bring about a sense of belonging, while misalignment can create a sense of isolation.[35] A lack of verbal communication, emotional hypersensitivity and sensory and movement differences combine to create serious obstacles to emotional alignment.

In much of her writing, Barb refers to herself as a "clueless island" with an "isolated existence."

Wally describes his life before FC in stark prison terms, saying, "After 21 years of incarceration in solitary confinement, I have experienced what is tantamount to the cold war isolation of the Russian political prisoners in the gulags of Siberia."

The sense of isolation is sometimes so deep and pervasive that it led Chammi, Barb and Sarah to express a sense of being abandoned by God.

Sarah expressed her strong fear of abandonment when she wrote, "Sometimes I act bad and I don't know if God wishes I would behave. Do you think I will be chosen for heaven? What if my family goes to heaven but I don't go with them? I will be alone."

For most of us, it is hard to imagine such isolation and loneliness. How do we account for feelings of isolation and abandonment in the midst of being surrounded by loving families? A brief excursion into the sensory differences associated with autism suggests a possible answer.

Emotions and sensations are neurologically bound together so strongly that one does not exist without the other. Although we each have our idiosyncratic responses to sensory experiences, we generally assume that other people's sensory experiences are similar to our own. In other words, most of us would agree on certain general parameters of sensory comfort or discomfort, pleasure or pain.

From our sensory experiences, we create the perceptions that comprise our "umwelt" or "self-world." This umwelt is the perceptual universe from which we live, move and act in the world.[36] Alienation can result from living in a perceptual universe that is substantially different from the shared experience of others. Without a shared experience of the world, it can be difficult to feel emotionally aligned with others.

Most of us live our lives swimming in a sea of relative physical comfort with occasional spikes of discomfort or pain. This level of ongoing comfort may not be the case, however, for someone with sensory differences. Perhaps having sensory experiences that differ so vastly from the norm sets in motion the feeling of being separated and isolated from the larger social milieu. As Donna Williams notes, she could not stand nor understand the world.[37]

Although it may be difficult to understand the sensory umwelt of individuals with autism, through language and the supportive relationship of the FC dyad, we can build bridges that reach out to each other to counter feelings of isolation and loneliness.

Wally describes how his sensory experience and his awareness of it colors everything:

> Each sensory system if operating normally ties us to the world that is outside of ourselves linking our minds to everything that we sense. This is not the case for those of us who are nonverbal autistics. Our reality is not based on each of our senses operating efficiently and effectively all of the time that we interact with the world that is outside of ourselves.
>
> The randomness of which senses will be functioning at any given time makes experiencing reality at times very difficult if not nearly impossible for me to do regularly. I must constantly check my perceived environment to determine if what I experience through my senses is a mirage or if it conforms to my definition of reality. Our autistic world, a world of the mind and of the intellect, is not as uncertain for us to experience and appreciate as is this sensory nightmare.
>
> Reality as we experience it rarely results in our picturing in our minds the same reality experienced by non-autistic folks because of the sensory and neurological problems that each autistic experiences. These perceptual differences in how and what we think about the world that we share with others and how we react to its sometimes frightening stimulation, is the greatest obstacle for us to overcome.

References

1. Damasio, A. R. (1994). *Descartes' error: Emotion, reason and the human brain*. New York: Avon.

Kennedy-Moore, E., & Watson, J. C. (1999). *Expressing emotion: Myths, realities, and therapeutic strategies*. New York: Guilford.

Greenspan, S. I. (1997). *The growth of the mind and the endangered origins of intelligence*. Reading, MA: Addison-Wesley.

Siegel, D. J. (1999). *The developing mind: How relationships and the brain interact to shape who we are*. New York: Guilford.

2. Kluth, P. (2009). We thought you'd never ask: Voices of people with autism: The Hussman Foundation

3.Goleman, D. (1995). *Emotional intelligence: Why it can matter more than IQ*. New York: Bantam Books.

4.Siegel (1999).

5.Lainhart, J. E., & Folstein, S. E. (1994). Affective disorders in people with autism: A review of published cases. *Journal of Autism & Developmental Disorders, 24*(5), 587-601.

Jones, R. S. P., Zahl, A., & Huws, J. C. (2001). First-hand accounts of emotional experiences in autism: a qualitative analysis. *Disability & Society, 16*(3), 393-401.

6.Greenspan (1997)

7.Shalom, D. B., Mostofsky, S. H., Hazlett, R. L., Goldberg, M. C., Landa, R. J., Faran, Y., et al. (2006). Normal physiological emotions but differences in expression of conscious feelings in children with high-functioning autism. *Journal of Autism and Developmental Disorders, 36*(3), 395-400.

8.Williams, D. (1992). *Nobody nowhere: The extraordinary autobiography of an autistic*. New York: Times Books. (p. 203).

9. Jones (2001).

10. Prince-Hughes, D. (2004). *Songs of the gorilla nation: My journey through autism*. New York: Harmony. (p. 31).

11. Goleman (1995).

Greenspan (1997).

Siegel (1999).

12.Williams, D. (1996). *Autism: An inside-out approach*. London: Jessica Kingsley.

13. Strandt-Conroy, K. (1999). *Exploring movement differences in autism through first-hand accounts*. University of Wisconsin, Madison.

14. Siegel (1999).

15. Kennedy-Moore (1999).

16. Siegel (1999)

Cousens, P., & Nunn, K. P. (1997). Is "self-regulation" a more helpful construct than "attention"?, *Clinical Child Psychology & Psychiatry* (Vol. 2ID - 1777, pp. 27-43): Sage Publications

17. Pert, C. B. (1997). *Molecules of emotion: Why you feel the way you feel*. New York: Schribner.

18. Gottman, J. M., & Katz, L. F. (1989). Effects of marital discord on young children's peer interaction and health. *Developmental Psychology, 25*(3), 373-381.

19. Dawson, G. (1991). A psychobiological perspective on the early socio-emotional development of children with autism. In D. Cicchetti & S. L. Toth (Eds.), *Rochester Symposium on Developmental Psychopathology, Vol. 3: Models and integrations.* (pp. 207-234): University of Rochester Press.

Lepore, S. J., Greenberg, M. A., Bruno, M., & Smyth, J. M. (2002). Expressive writing and health: Self-regulation of emotion-related experience, physiology, and behavior. In J. M. Smyth & S. J. Lepore (Eds.), *The writing cure: How expressive writing promotes health and emotional well-being.* Washington DC: American Psychological Association.

Hill, E., Berthoz, S., & Frith, U. (2004). Brief Report: Cognitive processing of own emotions in individuals with autistic spectrum disorder and in their relatives. *Journal of Autism and Developmental Disorders, 34*(2), 229-235.

20. Lewis, T., Amini, F., & Lannon, R. (2000). *A general theory of love.* New York: Random House.

Lepore (2002).

Siegel (1999).

21. Siegel (1999).

22. Siegel, B. (2000). Behavioral and Educational Treatments for Autism Spectrum Disorders. *Advocate*(Nov-Dec 2000), 22-27.

23. Kennedy-Moore (1999).

24. Dawson, G., Hill, D., Spencer, A., Galpert, L., & Watson, L. (1990). Affective Exchanges Between Young Autistic Children and Their Mothers. *Journal of Abnormal Child Psychology, 18*(3), 335-345.

Siegel (1999).

Wilson, B. J. (1999). Entry behavior and emotion regulation abilities of developmentally delayed boys, *Developmental Psychology* (35), 214-222. American Psychological Assn.

25. Esterling, B. A., L'Abate, L., Murray, E. J., & Pennebaker, J. W. (1999). Empirical foundation for writing in prevention and psychotherapy: Mental and physical health outcomes. *Clinical Psychology Review, 19*(1), 79-96.

26. Kennedy-Moore (1999).

27. Goleman (1995).

Siegel (1999).

28. Kennedy-Moore (1999).

29. Niederhoffer (2002).

30. Sinason, V. (1992). *Mental handicap and the human condition: New approaches from the Tavistock.* London: Free Association Books.

31. Niederhoffer (2002).

32. Niederhoffer (2002).

33. Jones (2001).

34.Hill (2004).

Seltzer, M. M., Shattuck, P. T., Abbeduto, L., & Greenberg, J. S. (2004). Trajectory of development in adolescents and adults with autism. *Mental Retardation and Developmental Diasbilities Research REviews, 10,* 234-247.

35. Siegel (1999).

36. Candland, D. K. (1993). *Feral children and clever animals: Reflections on human nature.* New York: Oxford University.

37. Williams (1996).

Relationships

"Really wished kids would be talking to me, but autism scares them."

Sarah Stup

From the day we are born until the day we die, the quality of our relationships plays a crucial role in the quality of our lives. As mammals, we are hardwired to give and receive care. Infants who are fed, sheltered and clothed but not truly cared for within the context of relationships will fail to thrive and often die.

The give and take of social interaction and attunement with others relies on the same brain circuits that give rise to a wide range of life-skills; from emotional regulation to having a healthy sense of self and meaning in one's life.[1] It is through our relationships that we have a sense of belonging to the human community. Those who experience social difficulties often feel an overwhelming sense of isolation..[2]

The medical establishment does not give much credence to the biology of relationship.[3] However, psychiatrist Daniel Siegel refers to "interpersonal neurobiology" to convey the connection he sees between social interaction and our most basic biological functions.[4] For example, the dyadic relationship between mother (or other caregiver) and baby is where the baby first learns to regulate its physiological and emotional state.. While early positive relationships give rise to self-regulation, early regulatory difficulties can prevent a baby from being able to participate in important reciprocal interactions with the caregiver.[5]

Autism and the Social World

Many researchers have noted that social impairment is the key deficit and the most handicapping aspect of autism.[6] Individuals on the spectrum have been shown to possess a variety of neurological abnormalities that can impact social skills.[7] For example, social orienting and joint attention are dependent on efficient functioning of the sensory and motor systems and have been found to be early indicators of autism.[8]

Historically, social difficulties in autism have been shown to be present early in life and remain stable across the lifespan. However in recent years, children with autism have begun to show improvement due to earlier intervention and changes in diagnostic criteria.[9] Individuals with the label of "high functioning" show more improvement in social interaction than those who do not speak and have been labeled "low functioning."[10]

Social impairment is an umbrella term that covers a range of social skills. In review of the literature on social deficits in autism, Travis and Sigman discuss some of the most frequently studied social impairments.[11] These include:

- Lack of theory of mind.
- Lack of responsiveness to others' emotions.
- Disregard for tact and social conventions.
- Lack of concern for others and others' evaluations of them.
- Lack pretend play.
- Difficulty processing facial expressions.
- Abnormal emotional expressions.
- Lack of joint attention.
- Lack of emotional processing and understanding.
- Lack of self-other understanding.
- Impaired capacity for intimacy.
- Lack of empathy.
- Self-absorption.

- Lack of secure attachment.
- Infrequent and unsuccessful interaction with peers.
- Difficulty initiating social interaction.
- Failure to respond to bids for social interaction.

Considering this wide ranging list of social deficits, it would seem that individuals with autism are living in their own worlds and experience lives primarily marked by isolation and self-absorption.[12] Yet, many researchers have found that these prevailing images are not accurate. Recent studies have shown that autistic individuals crave social interaction,[13] frequently experience loneliness,[14] and form many types of intimate and enduring interpersonal relationships .[15]

In *Autism and the Myth of the Person Alone*, seven nonspeaking autistic adults declare unequivocally that the desire to be alone is indeed a myth.[16]

Many other first-hand accounts written by individuals with autism support these findings. For example, Judy Endow writes:

> The meaningfulness of life for me, an autistic, is in the reciprocal relationships of everyday life. So, all in all, when it comes to the truly important stuff of life, I am more like you than autism can ever make me different. Imagine that![17]

Along with Endow and the authors in Biklen's book, countless individuals with autism are deeply embedded and actively participate in circles of love and support. Their circles include family members, staff, therapists, friends and even casual acquaintances. Although many of the people in the support circles are paid helpers, the loyalty, love and deep caring that transpires in these circles defies large segments of the autism literature where "deviant social development" is deemed *the* hallmark of autism.[18]

As FC users gain more proficiency with expressive language, their circles of relationships grow and deepen in ways previously unimaginable. Language opens the door to mutuality, shared meanings and many other important aspects of relationships. Travis and Sigman note, "It is probably impossible to exaggerate the impact of language impairment on social functioning in autism. Individuals who do not acquire language are isolated from all but the most basic of social exchanges."[19]

Aspects of Relationships

Attachment, intimacy, reciprocity, joint attention, theory of mind and experience-sharing (intersubjectivity) are six important and interrelated aspects of relationship. These qualities have been frequently cited in the academic literature as being lacking or seriously diminished in individuals with autism.

Attachment

Children with autism have been portrayed as not being attached to their caregivers because often they do not reach to be picked up, cuddle, cling or show distress when the caregiver leaves the room. Despite these atypical behaviors, research has shown that they do in fact form secure attachments.[20]

Intimacy

Intimacy is described as a loving, personal familiarity between two people. It encompasses deep understandings and detailed knowledge of each other. Although language is not necessary for intimacy, self-disclosure and emotional sharing can enhance intimacy and a strong sense of connection. Dyads provide an opportunity for intimacy and a form of relationship that is particularly helpful for individuals with autism.[21]

Reciprocity

Reciprocity, with its mutuality and back-and-forth interaction between two individuals is a vital key for many important life skills, including self-regulation and social and cognitive development.[22] As Gernsbacher notes, reciprocity is a two-way street. It needs to be purposely developed and applied generously by parents and caregivers toward individuals with autism.[23]

Joint Attention

Joint attention involves interactive partners who coordinate their attention so they can share awareness of something in the environment, be it a person, event or object. Joint attention is intrinsically motivated and associated with the development of important life skills including language and social behavior.[24] Although many authors have found that individuals with autism have deficits in joint attention.[25] this function can be improved with responsive caregiving.[26] Most studies define joint attention as a visual phenomenon, but joint attention can be established covertly through other sensory modalities.[27]

Theory of mind

Theory of mind is the ability attribute mental states to others and it allows us to think about, predict and explain the behavior of others. Not having a theory of mind is sometimes referred to as "mindblindness." Since the 1980's, there have been many studies of autistic children who could not pass a theory of mind test. These researchers have suggested that in autism, mindblindness is both universal and innate.

Cognitive psychologist Morton Gernsbacher refutes these claims, citing studies that have shown ability to pass the false belief tasks can improve with language and with learning.[28] Furthermore, virtually all attempts to communicate imply having a theory of mind since there needs to be a mind capable of receiving and understanding the communicated message.[29]

Intersubjectivity

Intersubjectivity is sharing one's subjective, inner world. We all need to experience shared subjectivity in order to feel understood, connected to others and to have a sense of meaning in life.[30] Intersubjectivity is closely related to reciprocity, joint attention, empathy, intimacy and theory of mind. Some researchers have suggested that "intersubjective connectedness" is a key deficit in autism.[31]

Types of Relationships

The FC speakers, their family members and facilitators portray relationships that are mutually enhancing and are similar in many ways to all human relationships. The participants discussed their relationships with family, friends, facilitators and professionals and casual acquaintances. They also expressed a desire for romantic or sexual relationships.

Family

Not surprisingly, relationships with family members are the strongest and most enduring ties. Wally Jr. reports, "The sense of belonging to my family is probably the greatest feeling that there is."

Gaining access to expressive language often leads to shifts as families begin to know the autistic person in new ways. Several family members commented on this.

Anoja says, "When Chammi started using FC, we finally found our son. FC was the best thing that happened not only to our son, but to this whole family as well."

Heather and Kent say that, with FC, their relationship with Kathy became a "real relationship with adult to adult interaction."

Gwen believes, "Facilitation has given me my relationship with Nick and all that he continues to give me. I am thankful, personally, apart from everything it's done for Nick."

Judi echoes that gratitude, saying, "FC has given our family access to Doug that we didn't have before. Just to be surrounded by a family that sees him differently, even if no one else in the world does, that is still a lot."

The Importance of Family

The sense of belonging and being part of a family is important to all of us. It can serve as a powerful antidote to isolation from the larger community. Several FC speakers express their appreciation of family.

Kathy has told her parents, "I think that the most important thing in my life is the two of you."

Nick writes, "Family is the most important thing in my life. I think they are the only ones who truly believe in me." Nick relished being "able to make my 'Da' proud of me. He realized I wasn't retarded, and that I was complete on the inside as well as the outside." After losing his father to a heart attack, Nick realized, "I am lucky to be in the care of my step-mom, Gwen. She is anything anyone would want in a mom, and more. She is my parent, my confidante, and my friend."

Wally writes, "I get a real sense of belonging here at home…going home each day to the love that was always there."

Sarah notes she is "pleased to be part of a family who loves each other … to be in a family is to be happier and safer and never lonely."

Aaron writes he likes to be with his dad. He calls his dad a "hero" and writes, "He spends time with me. He does things with me. He likes hugs, scouts, hiking, and he does homework with me. Just like to be with dad."

Sibling Relationships

Many of the FC users have siblings who have played important roles in their lives.

Kathy was close to her brother who also had autism. Her biggest wish was that he could have used FC before he died.

Wally recalls that as a child he enjoyed listening to his "very lovely sisters" talk about their schoolwork.

Judi calls Doug "a neat brother. We're lucky to have him, especially now that we really know what he's like." She remarks that he has often told her that he loved her.

Tom recalls that when he and his sister were children, "Sally and I were as close as an autistic person and their siblings can be. She let me share her life and her friends. I was allowed to rock on her bed to the beat of Herman's Hermits, etc."

Joking and Teasing in the Family

Within the close ties of family relationships, joking and teasing can be a way of showing affection and expressing intimate knowledge of the other. Teasing is impossible without a belief in another's mind that will comprehend the remarks.[32] Chammi has said how much he enjoys teasing his mother. Sarah clearly understands the concept as well. She notes, "Dad goes too fast to rush us when we are shopping so Janna, mom and I tease him by calling him the 'freight train.' I love to tease dad because he teases us in return."

Once, when Judi and her sister Barb asked Doug to go in with them on a Mother's Day gift, he typed that he would contribute one dollar. Saying their family loves to tease, Judi relates, "So of course, we had to give him a hard time about being a tightwad. Now that we know Doug better, we can tease him about his quirks."

Being a Full Participant in the Family

Access to expressive communication opens the doors for FC users to participate in family events in new and fuller ways.

Jo says Tom has become a "very vital member of the family." When friction between family members occurs, he makes an effort to talk to everyone involved and works to help settle the problem.

After Nick began typing, he wanted to send Christmas cards to friends and relatives, letting them know that he had been "in there" all along.

Both Wally and Sarah first used FC to write letters to family members whom they did not see on a frequent basis. Wally explained his situation to his grandmother:

> I want you, Gram Marji, to always picture me in your mind as being autistic and being comfortable with myself as being such. I point this out to you because I want you to know that I am very content with being the only autistic man, so far, in my immediate family. I must confess to you that I enjoy my unique position.

When Doug began typing, he told Judi he wanted to see out of state relatives "as much as possible." No one knew this before so now he is always included in family reunions and trips to visit relatives.

Not all attempts to incorporate the FC speaker into the extended family turn out well. Mary has struggled to have her parents and siblings acknowledge Aaron as a competent individual deserving of her efforts to improve his life. One of Mary's sisters refused to attend a family reunion Aaron was hosting at his home, saying it would be "too depressing." Mary's father has suggested it might be better if Aaron lived in a locked Alzheimer's unit.

Anger and Reconciliation in the Family

When autistic individuals gain access to expressive language, they may engage in conversations with family members about misunderstandings that have persisted, sometimes for years. Without word-based communication, it is difficult (or perhaps impossible) to process the complexities, subtleties and entanglements common in all families. It is through conversation that everyone can work toward understanding, reconciliation and forgiveness.

Even frustration over relatively minor events can be averted through brief conversations that would be impossible without FC. For example, Doug and Judi attended a conference together. At one point, they each wanted to attend a different session. Judi tried to convince him to go to the one she wanted to see. Doug was mad, but when he typed about it, she explained that she would to go to the session he chose. He calmed down immediately.

Nick and Gwen have spent many hours discussing and processing Nick's backlog of strong negative emotions, some of which were aimed at Gwen. The following quote conveys much about their mode of interaction, the honesty in their relationship and their path toward reconciliation. Nick explains:

> My stepmother was so important in clarifying seething emotions I had. I could accuse her of manipulating me, and she would honestly examine her behavior and admit if she was (and apologize) or explain her reasoning if she wasn't.

Jo, Wally and Tom have had many conversations about their shared history before FC. Wally notes, "We've learned things from him and I think he's been able to learn things from us better now." Tom and his father have talked about how Wally had to use physical force to keep everyone safe during Tom's violent episodes. Wally and Jo now understand so much more about the outbursts. As Jo reports:

> Because he's been able to FC, a lot of times we have gone back and discussed these things and made apologies and amends. Before, we had no idea what the problem was and we had no way of communicating to each other. [With FC, we have been able to] ask Tom about what the problem was. So now, without a fight we can avoid all those things. We pretty well know some of the problems that we got ourselves into with him.

For years after she began communicating, Barb was very angry with her parents and tried to keep information from them. Her mother says this occurred because "she felt like we kept her a prisoner all those years." Happily, after years of animosity and pain, Barb and her parents have reached a point of forgiveness and reconciliation. In a recent letter to her parents, Barb wrote, "I now know I was showered with love all my life. I plan to make you prouder and prouder. All your efforts, fights, fatigue, and expenses have not been in vain. Thank you for never giving up on me."

Friendships

Making and keeping non-paid friends can be difficult for autistic individuals. When people gain access to FC, their opportunities for making friends expands. However, for most of the FC speakers, friendship remains an elusive goal.

Kathy wrote that FC enabled her to ask a friend over to visit. Sarah wrote letters to the other kids at school explaining her sometimes odd behavior and expressing her desire for their friendship. Chammi optimistically believed, "Realizing life-long dream of bantering with friends is possible because of FC." However, his mother acknowledges that has not been the case.

Aaron's facilitator recalls that after FC, "Aaron was perceived by other students as more competent. He got to go and eat lunch with the jocks from the football team and go to P.E. with them." Nevertheless, those relationships did not expand much beyond that or carry over after high school.

Nick is aware that his friendships during his school years were somewhat superficial. He realized that since his friends participated in athletic teams and traveled together for games, they shared a connection with each other that he did not share with them. He said, "I wish that I could have this interaction with the kids. This is a type of bonding that I fear I will never experience."

Barb has been successful in creating a circle of non-paid friends. She says that having these friendships has been "unprecedented and priceless."

Facilitators

Due the closeness that facilitating requires, the relationships that FC speakers establish with their facilitators are particularly important. Patience, willingness to make the effort, and especially trust, are key ingredients. Tom explains, "FC is very much based on relationship and trust."

Wally describes the process:

> Each weekly [training] session gives me the opportunity to develop the single most important link that is needed to make the process of FC successful. The link that is developed between me and the new facilitator is trust. Without this bond of trust, the process of FC will not reach its full potential even though the facilitator might reach a high level of technical proficiency....[Also] the facilitator's willingness to try to FC with me and his willingness to try to learn about those things that are presently regarded, in the minds of some people, as being nothing more than a hoax, that helps me to appreciate his efforts at trying to not only learn something new but also to appreciate his effort to try to communicate with me.

Barb has surface conversations with various facilitators but her mother notes that she needs to sense a close connection and good vibes before delving beyond the surface. Referring to other FC speakers in general, Barbara notes, "They have to have trust in whoever they're writing with and it's a long, drawn-out process before they will allow it, particularly with Barb."

Since relationships with facilitators require so much trust, it can be especially difficult for the autistic person when the connection ends. Aaron's first teenage crush was on his school facilitator. When she finished her student teaching and was preparing to leave the school, Aaron became very angry and lashed out at her by typing, "Bitch, bitch, bitch."

Parent-Facilitators

Some of the FC speakers share ongoing FC relationships with their parents which can involve disappointment and frustration as well as success.

Mary has made many attempts to type with Aaron, but it has been difficult and strained. She confesses, "I am disappointed with myself for not jumping with both feet into this new discovery. I feel guilt, pain, and embarrassment."

Barbara believes that the lack of complete success experienced by her husband and herself may be due to deeper dynamics. She confides,

> We certainly thought Barb would FC with us as the persons closest to her and that did not happen. It was very disappointing, as we wanted to know her so much. She was very guarded with what information she wanted us to know. She says if she gives me an inch, I want a mile and that's why she doesn't do much more than "yes" or "no" with me.

Heather expresses disappointment that she has not been able to be a fluent facilitator with Kathy. She relates, "I was the awkward, struggling one and Kathy would get discouraged with me. If I get too tense, then my tension goes to her body. You truly find that you are affecting her ability to speak."

Kathy's stepfather, Kent became a fluid facilitator quite quickly. This made the situation even more difficult for Heather when Kent developed a closer relationship with Kathy. Heather noted that she felt left out of deep conversations and more like a "spectator" than a participant.

Kathy also has experienced frustration and impatience with the fact that she could not type with her mother, However, they now do enjoy occasional successful typing sessions. Heather is ecstatic, saying, "Now when we have some expression, it's just joyous. We're like, 'Wow! This is so neat because it took so long.'"

Professionals

The FC speakers emphasize their need for trust and respect from professionals. Tom notes, "My speech pathologist kept talking and communicating with me until we both built up trust and really listened and valued each other's opinion." Nick says, "I need compassionate staff who care for me more than just having a job. They need to share my feelings and read my moods." He also believes they should be able to facilitate:

> My aides in the agency that serves me don't know FC yet, and they don't entirely understand just how humiliating this is when I go out in public. I would rather face curiosity or skepticism about my abilities than well-intentioned pity and unintentioned assumptions that I don't understand language.

Wally Jr. feels fortunate to have found a teacher who saw beneath the surface of his behavior. "The good-hearted righteous teacher … didn't give up on me and forced me to do things that others didn't think I could do."

Keeping good staff in the adult services field can be an ongoing issue. This situation becomes even more problematic in FC settings, which require intensive individual training.

In some cases, individual staff members are not interested in using FC and the agency managers do not require them to learn the skill. Gwen compares the issue to other language barriers, noting that if a staff member does not speak Spanish, that person is not expected to work with Spanish-speaking clients.

Jo feels that Tom's access to communication is vulnerable to changes outside of their control. She says, "Tom is lucky right now – he has several people who are fluent with him. But you never know how long they are going to stay. There are not a lot of people being trained."

Heather believes that Kathy cannot be properly supported without FC, so when her residential agency did not take the lead in training the staff to be facilitators, Kathy moved to a new agency.

Kathy's stepfather, Kent, had a traumatic brain injury many years ago. As a result, he has some degree of speech impairment, which has made him highly attuned to what he calls "intellectual respect." He feels that if people had intellectual respect for Kathy, they would be eager instead of reluctant to use FC with her.

Wally Jr. acknowledges how hard it is to establish intellectual respect. He writes, "Teaching the teacher to trust the non-verbal autistic student's intellectual acumen is without doubt the hardest part."

Casual Relationships

FC greatly enhances the opportunities for casual relationship exchanges in the community. Kent and Heather believe that, thanks to FC, Kathy "gets more respect from society as a whole."

Barbara says people began to treat Barb differently once she could communicate. "Our friends say hello to her. They do not talk about her, they talk to her -- including her in the conversation."

Wally says FC has greatly changed Tom's everyday interactions. "People in ordinary life have accepted FC the quickest. If you go into a restaurant, you don't have any trouble. They believe what he's ordering ... there is positive interaction."

Barb echoes this thought, explaining, "Hell yes, people treat me differently. When I type at a restaurant with my friend, the server may even attend to both of us, not just the charitable one taking the retard on an adventure."

Romantic Relationships

Although sexuality and romance are often ignored within the service delivery system for adults with autism, several people express their desire for romantic and/or sexual relationships. Aaron succinctly confides, "I have to get a girlfriend."

Soon after Chammi started using FC, Anoja observed, "Now he rages because he has no girlfriend and still must contend with autism."

Heather and Kent recall how Kathy learned about sex and struggled with her sexual identity. Kathy began typing about her sexual feelings and had many questions about sex. These conversations made her facilitators uncomfortable, but Heather understood that Kathy just needed to be able to "try out her own thinking and her views of herself."

Barb has addressed many issues that surround sexuality and autism, including the curiosity of others and the possible impact of sensory and movement differences on one's sexuality. She says:

> I know people are curious about my sexuality, because my body is so obviously out of control while my mind is unique yet intact enough to know love, fear, longing, loneliness, joy, excitement, friendship, pain, and ecstasy. Most are too polite to ask. I should note that a lot of autistics are highly aversive to touch and feel physical and emotional pain when they come in contact with another person. That is not true in my case, as I find great comfort and closeness when I touch or am touched by someone I love. That goes double for my young, male, beefcake physical trainers.

Nick also writes openly about his sexuality, his desire for a romantic relationship, and his despair that this will ever happen for him:

> Another thing I have a rough time with is my sexuality. This past year it has gotten much harder. I thought it would get easier since, after all, I am coming to the end of my teenage years. I feel deprived. All the other students at school are beginning to date, kiss, and meet the other gender, but I have never even kissed a girl. I wish that someday I would be able to kiss a girl. Maybe someday I could even go beyond kissing. Every day I see pretty girls, and I get sexually excited. There is no way, that I can see, that I will ever be seen as serious boyfriend material by any women.

References

1. Fogel, A. (1993). *Developing through relationships: Origins of communication, self, and culture.* Chicago: University of Chicago.
Siegel, D. J. (1999). *The developing mind: How relationships and the brain interact to shape who we are.* New York: Guilford.
2. Stern, D. N. (1985). *The interpersonal wolrd of the infant: A view from psychoanalysis and developmental psychology.* New York: Basi
3. Lewis, T., Amini, F., & Lannon, R. (2000). *A general theory of love.* New York: Random House.
4. Siegel (1999).
5. Greenspan, S. I. (2001). The affect diathesis hypothesis: The role of emotions in the core deficit in autism and the development of intelligence and social skills. *Journal of Developmental and Learning Disorders, 5*(1), 1-44.
6. Beadle-Brown, J., Murphy, G., Wing, L., Gould, J., Shah, A., & Holmes, N. (2002). Changes in social impairment for people with intellectual disabilities: A follow-up of the Camberwell cohort. *Journal of Autism & Developmental Disorders, 32*(3), 195-206.
Gutstein, S. E., & Whitney, T. (2002). Asperger syndrome and the development of social competence. *Focus on Autism & Other Developmental Disabilities, 17*(3), 161-171.
Rogers, S. J. (2000). Interventions that facilitate socialization in children with autism. *Journal of Autism & Developmental Disorders, 30*(5), 399-409.
Ruble, L. A. (2001). Analysis of social interactions as goal-directed behaviors in children with autism. *Journal of Autism and Developmental Disorders, 31*(5), 471-482.
7. Dawson, G., & Watling, R. (2000). Interventions to facilitate auditory, visual, and motor integration in autism: A review of the evidence. *Journal of Autism & Developmental Disorders, 30*(5), 415-421.

Maurer, R. G., & Damasio, A. R. (1982). Childhood autism from the point of view of behavioral neurology. *Journal of Autism and Developmental Disorders, 12*(2), 195-205.

8. Dawson, G., Toth, K., Abbott, R., Osterling, J., Munson, J., Estes, A., et al. (2004). Early social attention impairments in autism: Social orienting, joint attention, and attention to destress. *Developmental Psychology, 40*(2), 271-284.

9. Beadle-Brown (2002).

Seltzer, M. M., Krauss, M. W., Shattuck, P. T., Orsmond, G. I., Swe, A., & Lord, C. (2003). The symptoms of autism spectrum disorders in adolescence and adulthood. *Journal of Autism & Developmental Disorders, 33*(6), 565-581.

10. McGovern, C. W., & Sigman, M. (2005). Continuity and change from early childhood to adolescence in autism. *Journal of child Psychology & Psychiatry, 46*(4), 401-408.

11. Travis, L. L., & Sigman, M. (1998). Social deficits and interpersonal relationships in autism. *Mental Retardation and Developmental Disabilities Research Reviews, 4,* 65-72.

12. Hobson, R. P., Lee, A., & Hobson, J. A. (2007). Communication, identification, and autism. *Social Neuroscience, 2*(Sept.), 320-335.

13. Causton-Theoharis, J., Ashby, C., & Cosier, M. (2009). Islands of loneliness: Exploring social interaction through the autobiographies of individuals with autism. *Intellectual and Developmental Disabilities, 47*(2), 84-96.

14. Jobe, L. E., & White, S. W. (2007). Loneliness, social relationships, and a broader autism phenotype in college students. *Personality and Individual Differences, 42*(8), 1479-1489.

15. Travis (1998).

Robledo, J. A. (2007). *An exploration of supportive relationships in the lives of academically sucessful individuals with autism.* University of San Diego, San Diego.

16. Biklen, D. (2005). *Autism and the myth of the person alone.* New York: New York University.

17. Endow, J. (2009). *Paper words: Discovering and living with my autism.* Shawnee Mission, KS: Autism Asperger Publishing (AAPC). (p. 173).

18. Volkmar, F. R., & Pauls, D. (2003). Autism. *Lancet, 362*(9390), 1133-1141.

19. Travis (1998). (p. 66).

20. Gernsbacher, M. A., Dissanayake, C., Goldsmith, H. H., Mundy, P. C., Rogers, S. J., & Sigman, M. (2005). Autism and Deficits in Attachment Behavior. *Science, 307*(5713).

Travis (1998).

21. Muller, E., Schuler, A., & Yates, G. (2008). Social challenges and supports from the perspective of individuals with Asperger syndrome and other autism spectrum disabilities. *Autism, 12*(2), 173-190.

22. Greenspan, S. I. (1997). *The growth of the mind and the endangered origins of intelligence*. Reading, MA: Addison-Wesley.

Fogel (1993).

23. Gernsbacher, M.A. (2006). Toward a behavior of reciprocity. *Journal of Developmental Processes, 1*, 139-152.

24. Whalen, C., & Schreibman, L. (2003). Joint attention training for children with autism using behavior modification procedures. *Journal of Child Psychology & Psychiatry & Allied Disciplines, 44*(3), 456-468.

25. Dawson, G., Toth, K., Abbott, R., Osterling, J., Munson, J., Estes, A., et al. (2004). Early Social Attention Impairments in Autism: Social Orienting, Joint Attention, and Attention to Distress. *Developmental Psychology, 40*(2), 271-283.

Rutherford, M. D., & Rogers, S. J. (2003). Cognitive Underpinnings of Pretend Play in Autism. *Journal of Autism & Developmental Disorders, 33*(3), 289-302.

26. Gernsbacher (2006).

Whalen (2003).

27. Gernsbacher, M. A. (2007). Joint attention and vocabulary development: A critical look. *Language and Linguistic Compass, 1*(3), 195-207.

28. Gernsbacher, M. A., & Frymiare, J. L. (2005). Does the autistic brain lack core modules? *Journal of Developmental and Learning Disorders, 9*, 3-16.

29. Candland, D. K. (1993). *Feral children and clever animals: Reflections on human nature*. New York: Oxford University.

30. Siegel (1999).

31. Hobson (2007).

32. Stern (1985).

Personhood

"How difficult it has been to be accepted as equal human beings."

Nick Pentzell

It has been said that the moral progress of a society is reflected in its concept of a person.[1] Although the term personhood is rarely used in everyday conversation, it is intimately related to quality of life for people with disabilities. Personhood is the ultimate labeling category. It is an exclusionary term, used for the purpose of drawing a boundary line around one group and thereby excluding others. Society bestows personhood on the individual and this provides legal and moral standing in the community.

Questions on personhood extend across the lifespan from abortion to assisted suicide. In medicine, fast-moving technological developments such as cloning and stem cell research have created a multitude of moral questions that have no easy answers. Technology continues to advance faster and farther than our moral development.[2] Doctors, lawyers, medical ethicists and religious leaders all weigh in on the personhood debates.

As health care dollars shrink, individuals who are expensive to care for, who are not productive or who might be seen as having lives that are not worth living, can become vulnerable to cost-cutting measures.

Long before the health care debate of 2009, many writers were sounding the alarm. St. Martin predicted, "We will see increasing attempts to categorize the senile, the hopelessly ill, the severely retarded and others as non-persons."[3] Groups commonly living on the margins of personhood include those who need intensive levels of personal care such as people with disabilities, mental illness and Alzheimer's or dementia.

The humanness or personhood of individuals with disabilities has never been unequivocally established. Historically, developmental disability has been construed as an impediment to personhood.[4] To some bioethicists, a diagnosis of "mental retardation" has meant the individual is no different from a non-human animal.[5] The following quotes convey some flavor of the debate and the degree to which the personhood of individuals with disabilities can be threatened.

- Nobel Laureate Francis Crick: "No newborn infant should be declared human until it has passed tests regarding its genetic endowment and … if it fails these tests, it forfeits the right to live."[6]
- Bioethicist Christopher Perring: "Those with long standing and irreversible psychological disability and mental illness have less personhood than people with full abilities."[7]

Some might argue that, despite these statements, recent legislation has firmly established the legal rights for individuals with disabilities and that notions of denied personhood belong to the past. Certainly, protection of the rights of individuals with disabilities has improved enormously over the past 50 years.[8]

Yet, there is still little agreement on what personhood is, where it resides and what purpose it serves. Is it a set of attributes that resides inside the individual? Or is it to be found in social roles and achievements? Is it a thing or a process? Is it permanent and stable, or malleable and fluctuating?

Throughout the ages, philosophers have wrestled with these questions and we are far from consensus. Despite this, most people would agree that personhood matters. Indeed, it matters very much. Throughout history, attribution or denial of personhood has been a matter of life or death.[9] Notions of personhood are pervasive in everyday life. They determine the tone and tenor of many of our interactions. Personhood, like the current of a great silent river, flows in, around, and through all human relationships. For most of us, issues of personhood go unseen and unnoticed. However, for the most vulnerable people, any real or perceived threat to personhood can have a profound impact.

Assumptions about personhood are often so unexamined that we are unaware of the degree to which they determine our thoughts and actions. Yet they are infused in the day-to-day work of teachers, clergy, parents and health care workers, and they permeate our relationships with each other and with all living things.[10] Disability rights, animal rights, civil rights, war, crime and all forms of aggression, abuse and neglect are personhood issues. In schools, disputes over funding, allocation of resources, inclusion and teaching practices often can be traced to fundamental beliefs about personhood.

Breaking the Social Contract

It is through self-expression that we fulfill the social contract and reveal our membership in the human community. In autism, avenues of self-expression are often compromised. For example, an individual with the label of autism might move in a mechanical way, avoid human touch and eye contact, have a flat affect and speak in rote, stilted phrases or not speak at all. With these very obvious expressive differences, it can appear as if the social contract for desire for human relationship and connection has intentionally been broken.[11]

One's humanity can be called into question when observable behavior veers too far from the norm and signals indifference to other humans.[12] Noted psychologist Laura Schreibman addresses the link between behavior and the perception of personhood:

> When you see an autistic child it looks like a person. It's got arms and legs and walks around and so on, but he's not a person. And the reason he's not a person is because he doesn't have the behaviors of a person.[13]

Schreibman's statement is from the 1970s and arguably attitudes have changed since then. However, the belief persists that behavior determines personhood. As late as 1993, behavioral psychologist Ivar Lovaas echoed Schreibman's sentiment. Speaking of children with autism, he writes, "The fascinating part to me was to observe persons with eyes and ears, teeth and toenails, walking around yet presenting few of the behaviors that one would call social or human."[14]

Both Schreibmann and Lovaas based their perceptions solely on external behavior. The inability to exhibit the social or expressive behavior suggests to them that no one is "in there." Beliefs such as this serve to "other" individuals with autism, threatening their personhood by making them seem extremely odd and categorically different from the rest of "us."

Humanness or personhood is attributed only to those who keep the social contract for relatedness and show us or tell us what they are thinking and feeling inside.[15] When avenues of self-expression are thwarted, the humanness of that individual is potentially diminished.[16]

We live in a society that places ultimate value on independence, spoken language, measurable intelligence and rational thought.[17] As a result, the dignity and humanness attributed to individuals who think, act or communicate differently can be withheld. Wally recalls how he was perceived as being "not quite human" before he started using FC. He says:

> Before I used FC, there were very few people who saw any real values to my being. Most people openly degraded me both verbally and through psychological measures. They didn't think that what they were doing in terms of this degradation would be cause for any concern from anyone especially me since they were working with, in their minds, something not quite human but something between a dog and a person.

In a similar vein, Tom writes:

> It is a very hurtful feeling to think you are subhuman in the eyes of most people, but that is how I felt. It was especially hurtful when professionals did not consider my feelings as much as their prestige when discussing my problems and future. It may have been out of ignorance or fear of failure. They talked about me in my presence like I wasn't even there. In this way they never considered me a person.

Indicators of Personhood

Many writers from various disciplines have offered suggestions for the features they believe are necessary for personhood. Standing almost alone, philosophers Moussa and Shannon problematize the need for categories that serve to distinguish "person" from "non-person." They ask why this line needs to be drawn at all.[18]

The lists of criteria for personhood have several items that have particular significance for nonverbal autistic individuals. These include:

- Consciousness.
- Language and communication.
- Agency.
- Intelligence and IQ
- Relationships with others.

Consciousness

Consciousness is the state of being awake and aware of one's self and one's surroundings. Consciousness is the one attribute that almost achieves consensus on the various lists of criteria for personhood.[19]

Some writers go so far as to say that consciousness is a necessary and sufficient condition for personhood[20] while others believe that consciousness alone is too liberal becausemost mammals would then have to be included.[21] To address this inconsistency, many philosophers turn to language and communication.

Language and Communication

The danger in making consciousness and self-consciousness attributes for personhood is that we can only infer their presence. Despite much evidence to the contrary, common belief dictates that consciousness and complex thought can be revealed only through language.[22]

In some kinds of disability (such as stroke or persistent vegetative state), what was once thought to be lack of consciousness has proven to be nothing more than not having a way to communicate. Once a communication system is in place, these individuals were suddenly perceived as having acquired personhood.[23]

Similarly, having a communication system that we can understand made all the difference for Koko, the gorilla who uses sign language. When a lawsuit was pending over the ownership of Koko, a professor of law and animal rights said this:

> The gorilla doesn't exist anymore. Under normal circumstances, the only thing this animal doesn't have that we do is language. Now you have changed that. When you give it the conceptual apparatus for conscious reasoning, for mobilizing thought, you have radically altered it. You have given it the pernicious gift of language. If it has never been one before, it is an individual now. It has the apparatus for the beginning of a historical sense, for contemplation of self[24]

Expressive language serves not only as a means to determine consciousness, but also to determine many other attributes of personhood. For example, intelligence and agency are inferred through accurate, reliable and understandable communication.

Agency

Agency, or being an "intentional system," has been cited as an important indicator of personhood.[25] Being seen as having agency often depends on the ability to communicate one's reasons for the behavior.

In the case of individuals with autism, the concept of agency presents another problem of enormous complexity due to their sensory and movement differences.

Several authors have shown how autistic individuals constantly shift between actions for which they can claim agency and actions for which they cannot. Sensory and movement differences can both inhibit desired behavior and produce unwanted, or overflow, behavior.[26] Thus, for individuals with autism, questions of agency are difficult to sort out.

IQ Score

IQ scores have been seen as a defining component of personhood. According to Fletcher, "Any individual of the species homo sapiens who falls below the I.Q. 40-mark in a standard Stanford-Binet test, amplified if you like by other tests, is questionably a person; below the 20-mark, not a person."[27] IQ testing has been challenged on many fronts [28], but the residual belief of a correlation between IQ scores and personhood remains strong.[29]

Relationships

Some authors cite having valued relationships as an important indicator of personhood.[30] Yet, difficulties with relationships are part of the diagnostic criteria of autism. Indeed, individuals with autism often *appear* to have little interest in or awareness of social life and human relationship. However, through first-hand accounts we are learning that they are often extremely sensitive to others' thoughts and feelings and that they are vitally interested in relationship.[31]

FC and Personhood

One immediate effect after gaining access to expressive language is that others begin to see the FC speakers differently. Anoja and Wally both emphasized that people started treating their sons differently as soon as they started to use FC. Although they did not use the word personhood, many of the participants wrote about these issues, noting they felt more real and more visible.

More real can mean being more in the world, more connected to others or more visible. Judi relates that when Doug started using FC, the first thing that changed was, "the recognition from family and friends that there was so much more to Doug."

Before FC, Kathy says she thought of herself as a "little person" who merely sat in the yard while everyone else was busy doing things. She was very aware that she remained outside of the action of everyday life. Heather spoke about the changes she saw in Kathy after she began using FC:

> She carried herself differently. She acted as though she had more status – she would use the term, "have more realness," and it meant to us that she was able to interact with the world and to be more of a part of the world.

The feeling of not being real can be likened to feeling invisible. Many FC speakers address this issue. Sarah describes her sense of feeling more real and more visible:

> I become a real person when my words try to reach out to you without my weird body scaring you away. When my words are read I become a true person, not a shell that is empty. When I was silent, I felt loved but invisible. Saying what I feel and know makes me belong with, not belong to. I feel afraid and hopeful and free, just like a real person.

FC opened the gates of two-way conversation and thus more reciprocity in relationships. Talking about people as if they were not there was a common theme. Barbara noted how people now interact with Barb saying, "People do treat her differently now. Our friends say hello to her. They do not talk about her, they talk to her, including her in the conversation."

Tom addressed these issues when he wrote:

> I was treated as I appeared. No choice in anything, just being herded through life like cattle. People were nice enough to me, just didn't think anyone was home. Since people's perception of me was what it was, they talked about me and my family in front of me all the time. It was a hurtful state of affairs. [Now] people do treat me differently, even non-believers. Yes, I'm now usually considered a real person.

References
1. Trendelenberg, A. (1910). A contribution to the history of the word person: A posthumous treatise by Adolf Trendelenberg. *Monist, 20*, 336-353.
2. Turner, L. (1997). A sheep named Dolly. *Canadian Medical Associtation Journal, 156*(8), 1149-1151.
3. St. Martin, T. (1975). Euthanasia: The three-in-one issue. *Baylor Law Review, 27*, 62-67. (p. 66).

4. Lusthaus, E. W. (1985). Involuntary euthanasia and current attempts to define persons with mental retardation as less than human. *Mental Retardation, 23*(3), 148-154.

Wolfensberger, W. (1975). *The origin and nature of our institutional models.* Syracuse, NY: Human Policy.

5. Singer, P. (1985). Can we avoid assigning greater vlaue to some human lives than others? In R. S. Laura & A. F. Ashman (Eds.), *Moral issues in mental retardation*. London: Croom Helm.

6. Scheerenberger, R. C. (1987). *A history of mental retardation: A quarter centruy of promise*. Baltimore: Paul H. Brookes. (p. 74).

7. Perring, C. (1997). Degrees of personhood. *Journal of Medicine and Philosophy, 22*, 173-197.(p. 186).

8. Herr, S. S. (1992). Beyond benevolence: Legal protection for persons with special needs. In L. Rowitz (Ed.), *Mental retardation in the year 2000* (pp. 279-298). New York: Springer-Verlag.

9. Bourgeois, W. (1995). *Persons: What philosophers say about you.* Waterloo, Ontario: Wilfrid Laurier University.

10. Whyte, S. R. (1995). Disability between discourse and experience. In B. Ingstad & S. R. Whyte (Eds.), *Disability and culture*. Berkeley: University of California.

11. Williams, D. (1998a). *Autism and sensing: The unlost instinct.* London: Jessica Kingsley.

12.Singer (1985).

13. Schreibman, L. (1976). Autism [Audio tape]: Psychology Today.

14. Lovaas, O. I. (1993). The development of a treatment-research project for developmentally disabled and austistic children. *Journal of Applied Behavior Analysis, 26*(4), 617-630.(p. 620).

15. McCormick, R. A. (1974). To save or let die: The dilemma of modern medicine. *Journal of the American Medical Association, 229*(july), 172-176.

16. Williams (1998).

17. Vehmas, S. (1999a). Discriminative assumptions of utilitarian bioethics regarding individuals with intellectual disabilities. *Disability & Society, 14*(1), 37-52.

18. Moussa, M., & Shannon, T. A. (1992). The search for the new pineal gland: Brain life and personhood. *Hastings Center Report, 22*(3), 30-37.

19. Cranford, R. E., & Smith, D. R. (1987). Consciousness: The most critical moral (constitutional) standard for human personhood. *American Journal of Law & Medicine, 13*(2-3), 233-247.

Fletcher, J. (1974). Four indicators of humanhood: The enquiry matures. *Hastings Center Report, 12*(4), 4-7.

Rich, B. A. (1997). Postmodern personhood: A matter of consciousness. *Bioethics, 11*(3 & 4), 206-216.

Walters, J. W. (1997). *What is a person?: An ethical exploration.* Urbana, IL: University of Illinois.

20. Walters (1997).

21.Perring (1997).

22.Dawkins, M. S. (1993). *Through our eyes only?: The search for animal intelligence.* Oxford, England: W.H. Freeman, Spektrum.

Griffin, D. R. (1984). *Animal thinking.* Cambridge, MA: Harvard University.

23. Crossley, R. (1997). *Speechless: Facilitating communication for people without voices.* New York: Dutton.

Tavalaro, J., & Tayson, R. (1997). *I look up for yes.* New York: Kodanshe International.

24. Davis, F. (1978). *Eloquent animals: A study in animal communication.* New York: Coward, McCann & Gorghegan. (p. 206).

25. Dennett, D. (1976). Conditions of personhood. In A. O. Rorty (Ed.), *Identities of persons* (pp. 175-196). Berkeley, CA: University of California.

26. Donnellan, A. M., & Leary, M. R. (1995). *Movement differences and diversity in autism/mental retardation: Appreciating and accomodating people with communication and behavior challenges.* Madison, WI: DRI.

Leary, M. R., & Hill, D. A. (1996). Moving on: Autism and movment disturbance. *Mental Retardation, 34*, 39-53.

Strandt-Conroy, K. (1999). *Exploring movement differences in autism through first-hand accounts.* University of Wisconsin, Madison.

27. Fletcher, J. (1972). Indicators of humanhood: A tenative profile of man. *Hastings Center Report, 5*(5), 1-4.

28. Howe, M. J. A. (1997). *IQ in question: The truth about intelligence.* London: Sage.

29. Vehmas (1999a).

Vehmas, S. (1999b). Newborn infants and the moral significance of intellectual disabilities. *The Journal of The Association for Persons with Severe Handicaps, 24*(2), 111-121.

30. Dennett (1976).

Fletcher (1972).

Jenkins, D., & Price, B. (1996). Dementia and personhood: a focus for care? *Journal of Advanced Nursing, 24*, 84-90.

Marshall, P. A. (1996). Introduction: Organ transplantation - defining the boundaries of personhood, equity and community. *Theoretical Medicine, 17*, v-viii.

31. Biklen, D. (2005). *Autism and the myth of the person alone.* New York: New York University.

Endow, J. (2009). *Paper words: Discovering and living with my autism.* Shawnee Mission, KS: Autism Asperger Publishing (AAPC).
Strandt-Conroy (1999).

Spirituality

"Faith is the glue that holds the world together for me."

Wally Wojtowicz, Jr.

Spirituality is often viewed in terms of religious practice. However, the concept can be more broadly defined as a search for connectedness, meaning, transcendence or higher-order values that are lasting and intangible.[1] It suggests a sense of unity with all of life as well as reaching one's highest potential. As a central dimension in human life, spirituality can be a force for stabilizing and integrating the personality.[2]

In addition to distinguishing between spirituality and religion, it is important to differentiate between happiness and having a meaningful life. Orienting a life around spiritual ends can lead to a sense of satisfaction and meaning which may or may not lead to a subjective sense of happiness.[3]

Despite its obvious importance, spirituality is notably absent from discussion on quality of life for people with disabilities.[4] Historically, research in developmental disability has tended to focus on more pragmatic issues. For example, Shalock reviewed 30 years of quality-of-life research in the field of disabilities but spirituality was only a subcategory in his list of eight core dimensions for quality of life.[5]

Spirituality and Autism

In his book, *Autism and the God Connection,* William Stillman provides anecdotal evidence of spiritual depth in many autistic individuals.[6] The FC speakers expressed several aspects of spirituality including ultimate concerns, self-actualization, relationships with God, and spiritual paths.

Ultimate Concerns

Theologian Paul Tillich coined the phrase "ultimate concern" to describe orientation toward the infinite around which the whole life is organized. Later, psychologist Robert Emmons broadened the concept from a single ultimate concern to the possibility of several ultimate concerns.[7] Emmons looked at the myriad ways in which spirituality is infused in our everyday lives. He notes that many motivating factors and everyday goals can move the individual into contact with the transcendent or sacred. In Emmons' words, personal goals reflect one's ultimate concerns and "strike at the heart of who a person is."[8]

Human brains appear to be hardwired for living with purpose.[9] .Finding a sense of meaning or purpose in life is a cornerstone of spirituality. Once that purpose has been discovered, it provides direction for choices made in daily life and becomes a powerful motivating force. In the words of Tillich, "Embedding one's finite life within a grander all-encompassing narrative appears to be a universal human need, as the inability to do so leads to despair and self-destructive behavior."[10] As a motivating force, having a sense of purpose can lead to increased self-regulation and other positive, life-enhancing behavior.[11] Barb describes the connection between having a sense of purpose and the behavioral changes she experienced:

> I think the bulk of my disturbing behaviors – like smearing, kicking, biting, grabbing, hitting, pica, manipulating tantrums, running away, stealing food from others' plates, handling objects for hours on end, breaking my glasses, etc. – have all melted away because none of those things serve my purpose. Consequences did not put an end to perhaps my most unbecoming habit [feces smearing]. I have suffered punishments and consequences before. Finding purpose is what changed things.

Living a life of service can qualify as an ultimate concern or spiritual endeavor. All the FC speakers in this book see themselves as serving others. For example, Aaron's facilitator describes him as a "quiet champion of the cause [of FC]." Although Doug does not use FC much anymore and tires easily, he agreed to participate in this project as a way to help others.

Part of Barb's service involves establishing a foundation to assist other individuals with disabilities with grants and support. She also sees her writing as a way to help others understand autism. In describing a conference in which she participated, Barb says:

> My work had the normals laughing, crying, and asking lil ol me many follow up questions and serious advice inquiries. I have never, never felt of more value. Giving the best I had to grateful souls had me feeling on top of the universe.

Chammi created a non-profit foundation to train FC facilitators. He named the foundation, wrote the mission statement and helps with all aspects of the classes. He notes:

> Helping others learn FC helps me stride more confidently. I am so glad I can do this work. I feel I am making a difference in people's lives. It is the best joy in the world. It heals my heart to bring joy to other lives.

Kathy has conducted several FC presentations, about which she has a very clear sense of purpose. She explains, "I feel that I have a purpose in life and I intend to make the most of it before I die. It is to show people that all disabled people are not stupid."

As a poet, essayist and short story writer, Nick understands the power of words and uses his writing as a force for good in the world:

> I cannot help others unless I perceive myself as having the ability to make a difference. I hope to change the world with my writing. As a famous person I would be able to help other autistic people. Christopher Reeve has done a lot for the paralyzed people of this country because he went through their trauma. I pray that through my writing I can shed new light on the world of autism.

From the time she first began to use FC at age eight, Sarah has dreamed of writing children's books and helping other children who do not speak. She writes:

> [I] need to keep climbing my mountains of doubt and sadness into hopeful floating clouds of service. Wish to be truthful and good

helping other people who are silent witnesses of another world called autism. With others helping me, I would like to close institutions and help people with developmental disabilities get regular lives. When I write my kids' books about disabilities, people might learn that those with disabilities are worth lots. Writing can be important with my opening good futures for silent souls.

Tom has stated two purposes for his life: to overcome his autistic barrier and to help people understand autism better. He believes:

It is important to do purposeful work and charitable service. FC was a major factor in bringing me out of my self-centeredness. I am more aware of other people and worry about them and their problems. I have difficulty seeing others fail and I feel I could and should help them. It is not always possible.

Wally has always wanted to make a contribution:

I am committed to my original plan of becoming a contributing member of society. I am committed to my plan of making a positive contribution to our world. Maybe someone, some place will read my thoughts and will then establish in their minds a new image of the non-verbal autistic person and because of this new image, make the life of some other autistic person more meaningful. If this happens just once, then everything that I have done will be worth the effort and will be the most important thing that I could have done.

Self-actualization

Self-actualization, or fulfilling one's potential, is closely aligned with spiritual orientation. Existential psychologist Abraham Maslow (1968) has written about having an unconscious or preconscious perception of one's own possibilities or destiny. He notes there is great tragedy in not living and growing into one's full potential. Maslow describes this state using the theological term accidie or acedia, saying it is "the sin of failing to do with one's life all that one knows one could do"[12]

Barb, Chammi and Nick acknowledged the pain of knowing that they were not living up to their potential although it was through no fault of their own. Chammi was filled with rage for the 18 years before FC that he spent living in the "silent abyss." For him, those were "lost" years.

Nick was frustrated about his behavior at school, even after he began using FC, and wondered if he should quit school even though he loved it. He writes, "I am not living up to my potential, and I don't know how to correct the problem. It is like I am like two different people sometimes. I am Good Nick, and Bad Nick."

Barb has been aware of her potential and frustrated by her inability to actualize it. Commenting on the "squandered energy" of her life before FC, she writes:

> All creatures are built to do more than survive. Quality of life requires it and life is designed to be quality. I must have instinctively known this and was therefore frustrated and angry to the core at doing nothing but passing time between here and autism. Those unsettling feelings and squandered energy manifested in bad behaviors.

Maslow believes there is a human appetite for growth. Once it has been triggered, it does not stop or become complacent. Instead, growth that moves toward self-actualization whets the appetite for ever more growth. In other words, growth that moves us towards self-actualization is a self-perpetuating cycle.

Maslow posits two types of motivation. One is a lower-level motivation based on need-reduction; the other moves the individual in the direction of new, creative growth. Need-based motivation is concerned with short-term goals, while motivation toward creative growth can encompass long-term or even unattainable goals. Barb confirms that her sense of purpose was the motivation for the self-discipline she needed to accomplish a long-term goal:

> Not long after my purpose was revealed, I began to take responsibility as a writer. I considered myself gainfully employed. I learned about being a writer and started doing stuff writers do. I set a work schedule, developed production goals, researched, learned vocabulary, read, attended conferences, and developed correspondences with other writers, thinkers, and editors. It was another year before I was published.

Relationship with God or the Divine

The FC speakers exhibit variety in their relationships with God. After her brother Rick died, Kathy struggled with her images of heaven and her desire to join Rick there. When his father died, Nick thundered with "sulphurous" anger at God. Chammi raged at God for abandoning him in all the years before he had FC.

Sarah is a devout Christian, goes to church regularly and loves to praise God. Although she believes God hears her silent voice, her repeated prayers for a cure have not been answered. The uncertainty she feels in her relationship with God and depth of her despair over her behavior are evident in the following quote:

> Sin is scaring me. Sometimes I act bad and I don't know if God wishes I would behave. A really good girl is acting nice but I can't do well. Do you think I will be chosen for heaven? What if my family goes to heaven but I don't go with them? I will be alone.

In contrast to Sarah, Wally appears firm in his belief that disability does not affect one's relationship to God:

> God's kindness is manifested in each of us, not only in the normal. God's blessings are equally shared and enjoyed by all whether we recognize them or not. God made us, meaning all of us, in his likeness, image, body, and spirit.

Barb believes in a universe that needs all of its diversity:

> It is in our best interest to remember that we are all the same. People are flecks of God. Each God fragment dispersed through space/time has a slightly different shape. One shape is not superior to another. All are necessary to complete the perfect, infinite, God puzzle.

The Spiritual Path

Discerning and then adhering to one's spiritual path can be a lifelong process. The FC speakers discovered and approached their paths in a variety of ways.

After he began to use FC, Tom expressed his desire to attend church. He does so regularly. The minister has used Tom's writing in his sermons and invited him to join the church. Initially, he would not agree. Jo and Wally were perplexed. When they asked Tom about this, he wanted to know what beliefs he would have to profess and what questions he would have to answer. Without knowing these things ahead of time, Tom could not be sure he was perfectly aligned with all of the church doctrine. Despite his ambivalence about joining a church, Tom seems to have been clear about his spiritual path from early in his life. He explains:

> I always had a deep belief in a higher power and was in awe of the universe. I was already aware that my orientation was different than ordinary people. I never really felt that I was a part of this world. My thinking was different. I had no trouble identifying with spiritual matters. It was so simple and became so clear, like talking to guides from God's kingdom. They instructed me and encouraged me in how to deal with my present dilemmas. They would help me make

decisions for my future. One of these discussions was to get rid of the autism barrier as much as possible. That was one of the most important decisions of my life.

In a similar vein, Wally says that religion and his belief in God gave him great comfort in the years before he could communicate. He loves going to church, especially for baptisms and weddings. Saying grace before dinner has counted among his most treasured moments in daily life.

For many years, the Wojtowicz family made an annual pilgrimage to Schoodic, Maine. Residing by the ocean was one of Wally's greatest joys. From this passage, it appears that being in nature became part of his spiritual foundation:

> I am still the happiest at Schoodic Point. Its raw rugged beauty puts me in touch with the power of nature that I enjoy observing. The Schoodic experience revives my spirit each time I visit there but I think the biggest reward that Schoodic offers to me is one of total regard for God's handy work. Years ago, I found this to be very comforting to realize that I could be aware of God's reality by looking at the simplicity I saw in the ocean waves that danced with grace while offering me their hand each time I felt their gentle cool mist upon my face. We are interconnected to each other and to everything … as is the water of the ocean linked to everything that it wets.

Nick's attendance in a philosophy class became a whole-body experience for him. Gwen believes that having access to language has allowed Nick to grapple with spiritual questions. She says:

> Is there is a God? Is there anything else after life? What is this life? Is it a dream? Is it reality? What is it? I think it was much more confusing for him before FC. He just sort of got buffeted by this and that without any kind of foundation. Now he's got that. The language gives him structure so he can build a foundation. He can deal with all the big issues. He has differentiated himself from the rest of the external world. I am me. I exist and therefore I am. In a sense, it wasn't quite clear whether he existed or how he existed or what existence was. As much as any of us can understand that, it's a lot easier with language.

When Chammi found a spiritual path very different from the rest of his family, Anoja realized the power of FC. She says:

> Ours is a Buddhist family. Yet when Chammi started doing FC, he clearly was a God-loving Christian. This was something I found

extremely difficult to accept. However, I have arranged for a devout Christian friend to spend some time with Chammi in prayer and Bible study. This friend is absolutely awed by the depth of Chammi's belief and the connection he appears to have with God. As a devout Buddhist descended from generations of devout Buddhists, this is the ultimate validation of FC for me.

References

1. Neufeldt, A. H., & McGinley, P. (1997). Human spirituality in relation to quality of life. In R. I. Brown (Ed.), *Quality of Life for People With Disabilities -Models, Research and Practice* (pp. 292-309). Cheltenham, UK: Stanley Thornes Ltd.
2. Emmons, R. A. (1999). *The psychology of ultimate concerns: Motivation and spirituality in personality* (2003 ed.). New York: Guilford.
3. Emmons (1999).
4. Neufelt (1997).
5. Schalock, R. L. (2000). Three decades of quality of life. *Focus on Autism and Other Developmental Disabilities, 15*(2), 116-135.
6. Stillman, W. (2006). *Autism and the God connection: Redefining the autistic experience through extraordinary accounts of spiritual giftedness*. Naperville, IL: Sourcebooks.
7. Emmons (1999).
8. Emmons (1999). (p. 96).
9. Emmons (1999).
10. Emmons (1999). (p. 5).
11. Barkley, R. A. (1997). Behavioral inhibition, sustained attention, and executive functions: Constructing a unifying theory of ADHD. *Psychological Bulletin, 121*, 65-94.
Gottman, J. M., & Katz, L. F. (1989). Effects of marital discord on young children's peer interaction and health. *Developmental Psychology, 25*(3), 373-381.
12. Maslow. (1968). *Toward a psychology of being* (Second ed.). New York: D. Van Nostrand.

Discussion

"FC is a catalyst for a positive spiral of change."

Sally Young

FC and Quality of Life

FC plays a major role in the quality of life of the people whose lives have been portrayed here. It has provided an entry into lives that could barely be imagined 20 years ago.

When they gained access to expressive language, the FC speakers became able to make choices and express needs. However, language has given them much more than that. They have a way to demonstrate and use their intelligence, engage in social interaction, find meaningful work and participate in their own lives in a myriad of new ways. They can be known to others, develop their potential and tell their stories.

In a review of three decades of research on quality of life for individuals with disabilities, Robert Schalock defined eight core domains.[1] These domains are arranged in a hierarchy, with the most basic and fundamental needs listed at the bottom. The ten individuals profiled in this book have improved in many of these domains.

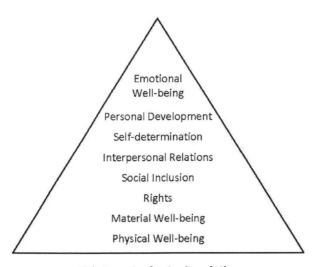

Eight Domains for Quality of Life

Physical Well-being: Several people reported dramatic improvements in self-regulation and sensory and movement difficulties. FC has also been helpful for medical procedures and determining causes of illness or physical discomfort.

Material Well-being: Large improvements have not occurred in this domain. All of the FC speakers still rely heavily on public and/or family funds.

Rights: This domain includes voting and civic involvement along with access and due process. Some individuals have experienced improvement in this domain. Having full access to one's best mode of communication is a right that has not been fulfilled for all participants, although most have access to communication at least part of each day.

Social Inclusion: Nearly everyone has seen some improvement in this domain. Many people reported greater acceptance from the community at large. Some experienced greater inclusion while in school, but lost it upon entering the adult service system.

Interpersonal Relations: FC has unequivocally improved many relationships for the participants, especially with family and staff. Friendships, however, have been more difficult.

Self-determination: Most people have enjoyed vast improvement in this domain and have increased control over their daily lives as well as their long-range goals.

Personal Development: Some of the most dramatic improvement has taken place in this domain, which includes education, skills and purposeful activity. For example:

- Barb has started a foundation to help others with disabilities. She has published an autobiographical book and is currently working on her second book.
- Chammi has published a book of poetry and is currently teaching new facilitators through the non-profit foundation that he founded.
- Daniel is studying for his GED and working on his independent typing skills in preparation for the test.
- Nick has taken many college courses and is pursuing a college degree.
- Sarah has published four books, a variety of classroom materials and is releasing an Inclusion Toolbox DVD for schools.
- Tom has published an autobiographical book and his second book is soon to be published.
- Wally is currently working on two books of his writings. He is also a contributing author for a third book.

Emotional Well-Being: This includes happiness, spirituality, self-concept and freedom from stress. Improvements in this domain can be inferred from the many changes in the FC speakers' behavior and their purposeful activities. Improved self-concept and freedom from stress can be inferred as a result of being seen by others as more competent. As Chammi wrote, "Uplifting to think of all the gifts FC has brought me."

The How and Why of QBI

Although we know very little about how or why FC works, the stories in this book and hundreds like them all over the world show us that *something* is at work. Behavior and quality of life are inextricably linked. Improved behavior opens doors to opportunities that in turn affect quality of life. Conversely, improved quality of life leads to even more behavioral improvement.

FC can be a catalyst that transforms lives. The creative, emotionally sophisticated, relationship-oriented individuals depicted here are living very different lives from the dismal picture Sacks portrayed of the "inaccessible ...creature with no future in store."[2]

The critical reader might ask, "How can a single intervention such as FC cause so much change and so many different kinds of change?" The answer to this question does not lie in linear, cause-and-effect thinking, but rather in a more integrated, dynamic model that encompasses a broad range of interrelated processes. In other words, we cannot say FC "caused" Tom to stop punching walls or Barb to stop kicking, biting, grabbing, pinching and smearing. It is more helpful and more accurate to think of FC as a catalyst for a positive spiral of change.

In his editorial on Quantum Behavioral Improvement (QBI), Rimland noted remarkable changes in behavior after children gained access to rudimentary forms of expressive language. However, he did not speculate on how or why expressive language might have such a global and profound effect on behavior.[3] Addressing these questions entails seeing internal or psychological change as well as behavioral change.

Oliver Sacks alludes to the internal changes that are associated with gaining expressive language in his essay about autistic author Temple Grandin. In describing Temple when she began to speak at age six, Sacks writes, "Her new powers of language and communication now gave her an anchor, some ability to master what had been total chaos before."[4]

Since Temple always had receptive language,[5] apparently Sacks believes that expressive language brings in new elements, making new demands on the brain and setting in motion some far-reaching internal changes. What internal changes might have occurred? What is it that gave Temple an anchor and helped her master chaos?

The consequences of gaining expressive language have been apparent in terms of overt behavior, but very little is known about what it might mean in the inner landscape. Although the field of autism has "largely eschewed psychological ... understandings,"[6] with the advent of FC (and especially now with independent typers), it is in no one's best interest to continue to do so. It may no longer even be possible.

Over the past two decades, FC speakers have made great strides in describing their internal subjective realities. They have been generous in sharing their inner worlds, their thoughts and their feelings. Yet, despite volumes of typed messages from them, we do not have a clear understanding of the internal changes that contribute to a positive spiral of change. In the next sections, I will venture some preliminary thoughts on these questions.

FC as a Catalyst for a Positive Spiral of Change

Several attributes of FC make it uniquely suited to be a catalyst for a positive spiral of change. Some of these attributes have clear behavioral components; others are internal processes and can only be inferred. These attributes include:

- FC accommodates sensory and movement differences.
- FC provides a way to process emotions.
- FC utilizes the dyadic relationship.
- FC requires thinking in a new way.
- FC sparks intrinsic motivation and investment of effort.
- FC allows inner speech and self-narrative.

FC Accommodate Sensory and Movement Differences

By its nature, FC accommodates sensory and movement differences. This benefit gives FC speakers extra support to self-organize and the opportunity to work at their highest level of competence.

Some individuals with autism have reported that certain aspects of social interaction, such as face-to-face positioning, eye contact or excessive verbiage, can feel overly stimulating, too intimate or even at times confrontational.[7]

In FC, the partners sit side-by-side, eye contact is minimal and face-to-face encounter is largely absent. The partners' shared focus is directed toward the letterboard or computer screen. Focusing on the words instead of the person, along with de-emphasizing eye contact and face-to-face interaction, can create a degree of interpersonal distance that reduces anxiety and sensory discomfort. All of these things serve to make the process more comfortable for the highly sensitive individual.

The physical act of typing with a partner also provides a structure or template that limits and prescribes the movements of both partners. This allows them to participate in movement patterns that are predictable and mutually coordinated without limiting the content of the interaction.

From the time we are infants, tightly coupled, mutually coordinated movement patterns play an important role in building relationships and enhancing a sense of connection and empathy between partners.[8] As infants, individuals with autism may have had limited experience with these types of movement patterns due to their extreme sensory sensitivity and their difficulties with volitional movement.

FC slows the pace of interaction. This can have a grounding, organizing and regulating effect when emotional arousal and sensory stimulation is high. Even for FC users who type very fast, the content of the interchange occurs at a slower pace than spoken conversation. Facilitators can slow the process down even more and limit verbiage by typing their responses instead of speaking.

The power of human touch has been documented for decades. In FC, the facilitator's touch appears to serve as a hidden regulator. Some of the participants reported that the facilitator's touch helps them stay focused and increases their body control and conscious awareness of body parts.

During FC, the facilitator touches the typer at the hand, wrist, elbow or shoulder. Because the touch is stable and predictable, it may be more tolerable for those with high levels of tactile sensitivity. The facilitator uses backward pressure, moving the speaker's hand away from the keyboard. Working against the facilitator's resistance increases the effort the FC speaker needs to use to move toward the letters. Increased effort can increase motor control; it appears that having human touch, as opposed to mechanical resistance, is key in this process.

Typing is a high-demand, high-reward activity. It can minimize sensory and movement difficulties by fostering self-regulation and self-control. To type, FC users must maintain a calm-alert state and organized behavior. They also utilize cognitive processes to reduce sensory distractibility and focus their attention.

FC Provides a Way to Process Emotions

By providing individuals with autism an avenue for processing emotions, FC has given its users an unparalleled tool for improved behavior and self-control. Author Ralph Savarese notes the importance of being able to express emotions through FC when he writes, "To direct his anger outward rather than inward has made the future possible for my son."[9]

As we gain access to expressive language, we also begin to enjoy a new level of relatedness. We begin to reflect on our experiences and share our inner worlds with others. We use words to depict, name and express emotions. Without this process, emotions cannot be fully explored and differentiated. Instead, they remain in the realm of chaotic body sensations and reactive physical behaviors.

Clarifying chaotic feelings and organizing them into words and sentences is a cognitive process. Cognitive processing of emotions expands the window of tolerance, prevents flooding and allows the integration of thought and emotion. The intense chaotic nature of the emotional experience can be modulated and organized when cognition is brought to bear on the process.

Calling up mental images and translating fleeting thoughts or churning emotions into words and sentences are cognitively demanding processes and as such, can lead to increased emotional regulation, and ultimately to emotional insight and closure.[10]

Although insight results from covert processes, we know it is present when feelings can be described or portrayed in lucid, symbolic and meaningful ways. FC texts commonly contain poetry and other aesthetically sophisticated descriptive writing. Compared to other art modalities, writing has been found to be the most likely to involve the cognition that is critical for emotional processing.[11]

For humans, self-disclosure is a natural response after an upsetting or emotional experience. It brings a sense of relief. James Pennebaker has studied the physical and psychological benefits of emotional processing through writing. He has found that self-disclosure and narrative self-writing about emotional events can significantly impact the writer's biological processes as well as overt behavior.[12]

Writing slows down thought processes and forces structure and organization on the chaotic stream of emotion and memory. This can lead to habituation and diminishment of the emotional trigger. In some populations, emotionally expressive writing has been found to alter the frequency and intensity of intrusive thoughts.[13]

Inhibiting emotional expression can be stressful on the body, since blocked emotions are stored at the cellular level.[14] All of the FC speakers in this book lived many years with no avenues for emotional expression other than overt behaviors that were often misinterpreted or viewed as inappropriate. In some cases, their emotion-induced expressive behaviors were punished or forbidden. As Savarese noted, having a means to express and process emotions with words instead of behavior can make all the difference.

The FC dyad is ideal for processing emotions within a safe relationship by providing opportunities for support, dialogue, reflection and positive social feedback. Processing emotions within a supportive relationship can reduce negative emotions while increasing positive ones. FC contributes to the positive spiral of change by providing some of the necessary elements for emotional processing and coping with life events in an adaptive way.

FC Utilizes a Dyadic Relationship

Relationship is an essential element in facilitated communication where the partners form a tightly coupled dyad. FC dyads, like other relationships, are supported and strengthened by trust, resonance, respect and mutuality.

In the dyadic relationship, two "individuals join with each other in creating a system larger than the individual self."[15] Common dyads include marriage or romantic partnerships, close friendships, teacher/student, therapist/patient and parent/child.

Relationship dyads have been studied in a variety of ways. On the macro level, observable behaviors such as synchronized reciprocal interaction or joint attention have been studied. On the micro level, aspects of neurophysiology, such as the entrainment of brain waves between the partners, have been studied.

The FC dyad has characteristics that may be particularly well-suited to the needs of autistic individuals and may contribute to the positive spiral of change. These include co-regulated movement patterns, joint attention and resonant states of mind.

Developmental psychologist Alan Fogel has observed the early beginnings of interpersonal relationships and communication through his work with mother/infant dyads. Using microanalysis of videotapes, Fogel has shown how synchronized, co-regulated actions within a dyad are basic building blocks for relationship and are an important source of developmental change.[16]

In FC, most of the partners' physical movements are synchronized in rhythmic, repetitive keystrokes. Facilitators must be able to stay attuned to the typer in order to make micro-level adaptations to the strength, speed, and direction of the speaker's arm movements.

Like synchronized arm movements, joint attention is a highly synchronized form of interaction. FC has been shown to help individuals with autism overcome attention deficits.[17] FC demands sustained, focused, shared attention from not only the FC speaker, but from the facilitator as well. The quality of attention that the facilitator can provide will have a direct effect on the quality of attention that the FC user can achieve. If either partner is distracted, the process can break down.

The facilitator must maintain a high level of focus in order to track the message as it is revealed one letter at a time as well as staying attuned and responsive to the speaker's arm movements.

Developmental psychologists have long recognized that self-regulation emerges from early dyadic relationships. The capacity for self-regulation and tolerance for high levels of emotional arousal develop through nonverbal, affective attunement with another person.

All relationships and the ability to form social bonds have physiological roots. In their book, *A General Theory of Love,* clinical professors Thomas Lewis, Fari Amini, and Richard Lannon have written extensively on the limbic system and its role in relationships. They contend that in dyadic relationships, mammalian limbic systems continually resonate and regulate each other.[18]

Limbic resonance is a mutual physiological exchange that allows each partner to become attuned to the other's inner state. As the authors have noted, limbic resonance is so familiar to us that we can feel disturbed when it is lacking, although we may not be consciously aware of it.

In dyads, resonance can also occur between the hemispheres of the partners' brains. Verbal communication gives rise to resonant states between the partners' left hemispheres, while the non-language components of communication lead to right hemispheric resonance. In addition to resonance between partners' right and left hemispheres, bilateral resonance can also occur. Siegel notes that this highly complex form of physiological communication between partners is deeply compelling for both. He even goes so far as to suggest that this hemispheric resonance might be at the "heart of self-regulation."[19]

The dyadic relationship in FC contributes to the positive spiral of change through co-regulated movement patterns, joint attention and resonant states of mind. In these ways, the FC dyad serves as a supportive relationship that provides a balance between safety and freedom and enables organized behavior even in the midst of highly charged emotions.

FC Enables Thinking in a New Way

FC can contribute to the positive spiral of change by enabling users to think in a new way. For all of us, gaining expressive language sets in motion a sea change that transforms the mind. It changes our thinking and the way we experience ourselves and the events in our lives. Language gives us freedom to extend our thoughts beyond the here and now, build and organize a cohesive inner world, lay down memories, create a personal history, develop a sense of self, modulate emotion and assimilate our experiences in order to construct meaning from them. Nick described it well when he noted that FC required him to "think in a new way."

In typical development, a baby is in action mode in which all meaning and goals are centered in the body and in behavior. A parent or caregiver begins to bring the infant into the "community of minds"[20] by linking words to objects, people, ideas, emotions, and life events. As this progression occurs, symbols and ideas take on meaning and emotional color. Soon, it becomes possible to mentally represent people and objects that are not immediately present and substitute words for physical acts. These abilities open a whole new world of possibilities that include trying out behavior without enacting it, forming goals for the future, solving problems, imagining self and self-other interactions, and processing emotions.[21]

Sacks refers to this shift from sensory-based experience to word-based thinking as a "dialectic leap."[22] Naming and categorizing objects organizes our perceptions of the outer world. Nick described this shift when he wrote, "I have language to help me make sense of what I see." As this perceptual shift occurs, we begin to understand the nature of time and space as well as cause and effect and no longer live in an overwhelming sea of amorphous images and sensations. Instead, we can order and classify reality, giving it a meaningful structure. These changes might be what Sacks meant when he noted that Temple gained an anchor and the ability to "master chaos" once she began to speak.

Expressive language and symbolization provide some of the necessary elements for giving meaning, cohesiveness and organization to the inner world. It is not hard to imagine that these things could have a profound effect on behavior.

FC Sparks Intrinsic Motivation and Investment of Effort

The process of moving from a life centered on behavior and concrete action to a life of symbolization and language is intrinsically rewarding. Once intrinsic motivation has been sparked, more effort will be invested and with this investment, infinitely more becomes possible.

Historically, for nonverbal autistic people, life has been filled with extrinsic motivators such as candy or soda. For most, there have been few functional activities that were rewarding enough for them to be able to inhibit their impulses and ignore their internal distractions so as to focus their attention.

In many cases, the ability to use language in a generative way appears to have sparked intrinsic motivation. Unlike many methods of augmentative communication, FC does not limit the user to specific word choices or structured formats. In communication systems that rely on a limited number of choices shown in pictures, words or other symbols, the user only needs to recognize the picture and respond to it by choosing or rejecting it.

In contrast, FC opens up a completely free and generative use of language. This format entails actively calling up a thought, emotion or other internal image, finding the right words to represent it and stringing together enough words to convey the thought or feeling to the communication partner. It would seem that this process requires greater effort than merely responding to pre-formed pictures or words, and also offers greater intrinsic reward.

The intrinsic reward of expressive communication has also had a positive effect on the FC user's quality of attention. For individuals with autism, attentional states often oscillate between being highly distractible or narrowly over-focused.

Management of attention is one of the first steps in behavioral change.[23] FC requires high-quality, directed attention. Every moment of every typing session presents the FC speaker with a choice between letting go and wandering away (physically and/or mentally), or staying put and focusing in order to find the right words to express a thought or feeling. Staying put and staying focused require hard work, especially after years of uncontrolled impulsivity.

Self-regulation and focused attention are goal-directed behaviors that come largely from within. Perhaps the intrinsic rewards of communication are so compelling that the FC speakers choose time and time again to stay put and keep working.

Communicating via FC is a time and labor intensive process of typing one single letter at a time. There is concrete evidence of intrinsic motivation and investment of effort in the volumes of typed transcripts I received from the participants. These transcripts represent thousands of hours of the FC speakers sitting in a focused, calm-alert state. In many cases, there is no other aspect of their lives where they achieve such a high level of functioning.

Thus, it appears that FC contributes to the positive spiral of change by motivating typers to self-regulate their behavior so they can achieve their goals and make the most of their opportunities to type.

FC Allows Inner Speech and Self-Narrative

From the beginning of recorded history, human beings have possessed a drive toward narrative self-expression. This strong drive is apparent in the FC speakers' writings. Expression is not a mechanistic act in which we send fully formed thoughts and feelings out to the world. Instead, it is a process whereby we discover our own point of view - who we are and what we think.

Inner speech is an ongoing internal monologue that connects inner and outer worlds. It is essential for key aspects of human development and the first step in autobiographical writing. Using inner speech, we narrate the events in our lives and gain a sense of our own history by forming a cohesive set of pictures, words and feelings about ourselves. These things, in turn, provide a way to reflect on our existence.

Some people have reported using complex inner speech and private language before FC while others have said they did not think much at all. It seems possible that using FC stimulated or increased the use of inner speech. In any case, FC contributes to the positive spiral of change by providing a way for nonverbal individuals to develop a personal point of view. Articulating and narrating one's life and point of view might be necessary elements for long-range planning and goal-directed behavior.

Conclusion

The six attributes of FC discussed here represent largely internal processes that potentially contribute to a positive spiral of change. They may not be at play in all cases and it is difficult to know how much or how little influence they have had on the process of change. Yet in typical development, we know they are important; there is no reason to believe it would be otherwise for FC speakers. I hope that this discussion spurs more and deeper conversation that considers the vital connection between internal processes and external behavior.

References

1. Schalock, R. L. (2000). Three decades of quality of life. *Focus on Autism and Other Developmental Disabilities, 15*(2), 116-135.

2. Sacks, O. (1995). *An anthropologist on mars: Seven paradoxical tales*. New York: Vintage. (p. 246).

3. Rimland, B. (1988). Language and quantum behavioral improvement. *Autism Research Review International, 2,* 3.

4. Sacks (1995), p. 271.

5. Grandin, T., & Scariano, M. M. (1986). *Emergence: Labeled autistic*. Novato, CA: Warner.

6. Savarese, R. J. (2007). *Reasonable people: A memoir of autism and adoption*. New York: Other Press.

7. Strandt-Conroy, K. (1999). *Exploring movement differences in autism through first-hand accounts.* University of Wisconsin, Madison.

Williams, D. (1996). *Autism: An inside-out approach*. London: Jessica Kingsley.

8.Fogel, A. (1993). *Developing through relationships: Origins of communication, self, and culture*. Chicago: University of Chicago.

Siegel, D. J. (1999). *The developing mind: How relationships and the brain interact to shape who we are*. New York: Guilford.

9. Savarese (2007), p. 418.

10. Niederhoffer, K. G., & Pennebaker, J. W. (2002). Sharing one's story: On the benefits of writing or talking about emotional experience. In C. R. Snyder & S. J. Lopez (Eds.), *Handbook of Positive Psychology* (pp. 573-583). London: Oxford University Press.

11. Pennebaker, J. W. (1993). Putting stress into words: Health, linguistic, and therapeutic implications. *31*(6), 539-548.

12. Pennebaker, J. W. (1990). *Opening up: The healing power of expressing emotions*. New York: The Guilford Press.

13. Lepore, S. J., Greenberg, M. A., Bruno, M., & Smyth, J. M. (2002). Expressive writing and health: Self-regulation of emotion-related experience, physiology, and behavior. In J. M. Smyth & S. J. Lepore (Eds.), *The writing cure: How expressive writing promotes health and emotional well-being*. Washington DC: American Psychological Association.

14. Pert, C. B. (1997). *Molecules of emotion: Why you feel the way you feel*. New York: Schribner.

15. Siegel (1999), p. 288.

16. Fogel (1993).

17. Bara, B. G., Bucciarelli, M., & Colle, L. (2001). Communicative abilities in autism: Evidence for attentional deficits. *Brain & Language, 77*(2), 216-240.
18. Lewis, T., Amini, F., & Lannon, R. (2000). *A general theory of love*. New York: Random House.
19. Siegel (1999). P. 334.
20. Nelson, K. (2007). *Young minds in social worlds: Experience, meaning, and memory*. Cambridge, MA: Harvard University.
21. Siegel (1999).
22. Sacks, O. (1989). *Seeing Voices; A journey into the world of the deaf*. New York: HarperCollins. (p. 65).
23. Gallagher, W. (2009). *Rapt: Attention and the focused life*. New York: Penguin

.

Afterword

The stories in this book are frozen in time, yet the people continue to grow and their lives continue to change. Before publication, I asked each participant to approve his or her personal story. Several of them wrote back saying that when they read their stories, they were surprised by how much their lives had improved since they began using FC. They also were struck by how much their lives had changed for the better since I interviewed them in 2003.

Chammi and Nick wanted large portions of their stories deleted because they could no longer identify with the writing they had submitted to me years ago. Barb summed up these feelings when she wrote, "It seems like someone else's life."

Each story in this book is unique but not atypical. The narratives are extraordinary only when they are juxtaposed with commonly held assumptions about nonverbal autistic people. Hundreds, perhaps thousands, of similar FC stories exist all over the world. These participants were chosen not because they are miraculous anomalies, but rather because their experiences are similar to FC users everywhere.

The positive changes described on these pages have not been universal, yet the stories show that even for FC users who cannot type independently, there are many changes and many possibilities. It is my hope to have given the reader a glimpse of what might be possible.

The hopeful stories and visions of possibility are magnificent. They are also bittersweet. An enormous chasm still exists between possibility and reality. For FC speakers, quality of life is still largely dependent on public sentiment, public funding and the ongoing heroic efforts of parents, other family members, friends and professionals. In these days of ongoing budget crises, many services for nonverbal adults with autism are sadly moving backward, away from a model seeking quality and toward a model of mediocre custodial care.

Many nonverbal autistic adults have endured daily humiliations, neglect and even outright abuse. Yet the overall thrust of their writing is hopeful; it points toward the future, not the past. They seek the support they need to grow into their full potential. In this and in so many ways, these individuals repeatedly and passionately show us that they are real people determined to live regular lives.

FC has given many people a vital tool to reveal their awareness, competence, intelligence and deep humanity. In the words of Oliver Sacks, "Nothing is more wonderful, or more to be celebrated, than something that will unlock a person's capacities and allow him to grow and think."

Let us celebrate.

Tom Page

Book:
Caught Between Two Worlds: My Autistic Dilemma. (2002).

Forthcoming book:
Getting to Know Us, Getting to Know More about Us (2011).

Book Excerpts:
I had No Means to Shout by Mary Jane Gray Hale & Charles Martel Hale, Jr. (1999).

Poetry:
Honorable mention for poems in the International Library of Poetry (two separate years).

Chammi Rajapatirana

Foundation Website: www.easesrilanka.org

Poetry: *The Vial* (1999).

Video: chammichandi.youtube.com

Nick Pentzell

Book Excerpts:
"A Question of Sex" section of William Stillman's
Empowered Autism Parenting: Celebrating (and Defending) Your Child's Place in the World (San Francisco: Jossey-Bass, 2009), pp. 150-151.
"DSM-IV Autside Out," chart in chapter, "Adults with Autism," by Moya Kinnealey and Kristie P. Koenig, in A Comprehensive Occupational Therapy Approach, 3rd edition, edited by Heather Miller-Kuhaneck and Renee Watling, (American Occupational Therapy Association Press, 2010).

Publications:
"Beyond FC: Unlocking codes of social cues to open wider the door of interpersonal communication, *The Communicator* 19:1 (Spring 2010), pp. 5-8.
"Dissed Ability: Grappling with Stereotypes and the Internalized Oppression of Babyliss ," *Disability Studies Quarterly* 30:1 (2010), http://www.dsq-sds.org/article/view/1054/1241.
"I think, therefore I am. I am verbal, therefore I live," *The Autism Perspective* 4:3 (2008), pp. 86-89,
http://www.theautismperspective.org. (No longer available online.)
"Let me tell you about my autism," letter to the editor, *The Observer*, March 23, 2008, p. 36, (response to Christopher Stevens, "How our son taught us the secret songs of autism," *The Observer*, March 16, 2008.
"Fools of God," *The Other Side* 40:2 (March & April, 2004): 36-38.
"Waves" (poem), *Pegasus*, volume 36, Spring 2003 (Delaware County Community College): 34.
"Following in his father's footsteps: Second-generation Renaissance man pushes autism aside," (interview) by Elizabeth Batdorff, *The Hillsdale Daily News*, February 27, 1998.
"Are You Aware?" *The Emissary*, issue 5: Jan. 28, 1998 (Hillsdale High School).
"In a Wilder Vein: first time performance," *The Emissary*, issue 6: Jan. 25, 1998 (Hillsdale High School).
"Memories of Dad," "Oh, Before you Leave ..." (poems) and "Prowling" (short story) in *Views from the Heart*, 1997 (Hillsdale High School).
"Reflection" (poem) in *A Celebration of Michigan's Young Poets, 1997* (Smithfield, Utah: Creative Communication, 1997): 95.

"A Lake's Longing" (poem), in *East of the Sunrise*, edited by Nicole
　　　Walstrum and Cynthia A. Stevens (National Library of Poetry,
　　　1995), and in *The Hillsdale Daily News*, September 1, 1994.
"How Things Have Changed," *The Facilitated Communication Digest* 1:4
　　　(August 1993): 14.

Barb Rentenbach

Website: www.barbrentenbach.com
Book:
> *Synergy*(2009).

Articles:
> *A Girl and her Horse* at: www.rideatstar.org
> *What are Friends For?* in The Autism Perspective (TAP) magazine, Winter 2006.
> *Local Books Run the Gamut* in The Knoxville News Sentinel, Feb. 7, 2009.
> *Horse and Rider* cover story in The Autism Perspective magazine, Summer 2006.
> Letter to Time magazine in article titled, *Teacher and Child* by Dr. Hiam Ginotte, November 12, 2009.

Videos:
> http://www.youtube.com/watch?v=0poy1xm7u9Y&feature=youtube_g data
> http://www.videosofbooks.com/video-viewing-room/2010/3/18/synergy-by-barb-rentenbach.html

Sarah Stup

Website: www.Sarahstup.com

Books:
>*Do-si-Do with Autism* (2006).
>*Are Your Eyes Listening? Collected Work* (2007).
>*Heart and Spirit: Words to comfort, inspire & share*(2008).
>*Nest Feathers: A celebration of family, home & memories shared* (2009).
>*Taylor the Turtle Fun Pack CD/DVD: An inclusion toolbox* (coming soon).

Articles:
>*Silent Echoes: A Young Author Rewrites the Rules to Transitioning* in Exceptional Parent, October 2008.
>*The Voice of Sarah Grows Louder* in Frederick News Post, March 25, 2007.
>*A Way Out of a Lonely Place* in Baltimore Sun, March 12, 2006.
>*The Voice of Sarah* in Frederick News Post, May 23, 2006.
>*Writer "Soars" with Aid of Small Machine* in Frederick News Post, June 28, 2004.

Video:
>*Align Your Dreams with Your Power: How to Succeed with a Disability* with Nancy Shugart.
>http://www.youtube.com/watch?v=O1W3q-N8o7s

Wally Wojtowicz

Books (excerpts and/or chapters):

Autism Handle with Care by Gail Gillingham (1997 & 1998).

Autism a New Understanding by Gail Gillingham (2000).

Sharing our Wisdom: A Collection of Presentations by People within the Autism Spectrum edited by Gail Gillingham and Sandra Mc Clennen (2003).

Empowered Autism Parenting by William Stillman (2009).

The Autism Prophecies by Willman Stillman (2010).

Forthcoming Books:

My Three Worlds (tentative title) with Jean Wood (author and friend).

Gram, Please visit My Worlds (tentative title) with Jean Wood.

HOPE by Liz Colado with Wally as a contributing author.

Internet Articles:

Teaching the Nonverbal Autistic Student-
http://www.autismconsultingservice

My Three Worlds- http://herbert.vanerkelens.nl

Letter to Dan- http://herbert.vanerkelens.nl

Forthcoming Film:

Valley of the Moon by Frank Monteleone. Film will be based on a composite of Wally and the autistic artist Stephen Wiltshire.

Video:

Heart Savants - http://www.youtube.com/watch?v=inRak4jGgmE

Appendix B:
Works by Others Who Type to Talk

Books

Biklen, D. (2005). *Autism and the myth of the person alone*. New York: New York University.

Blackman, L. (1999). *Lucy's story: Autism and other adventures*. Brisbane, Australia: Book in Hand.

Brandl, C. (1999). *See us smart: Facilitated communication case studies*. Ann Arbor, MI: Robbie Dean.

Crossley, R. (1997). *Speechless: Facilitating communication for people without voices*. New York: Dutton.

Hale, M. J. G., & Hale, C. M. (1999). *I had no means to shout!* Bloomington, IN: 1st Books.

Martin, R. (1994). *Out of silence: An autistic boy's journey into language and communication*. New York: Penguin.

Mukhopadhyay, T. R. (2000a). *Beyond the silence: My life, the world and autism*. London: National Autistic Society.

Mukhopadhyay, T. R. (2000b). *The mind tree: A miraculous child breaks the silence of autism*. New York: Arcade.

O'Neill, J. L. (1999). *Through the eyes of aliens: A book about autistic people*. Philadelphia, PA: Jessica Kingsley.

Reed, D. (1996). *Paid for the privilege: Hearing the voices of autism*. Madison, WI: DRI

Savarese, R. J. (2007). *Reasonable people: A memoir of autism and adoption*. New York: Other Press.

Sellin, B. (1995). *I don't want to be inside anymore*. New York: Basic Books.

DVDs

Bissonnette, L. (Writer). (2005). *My Classic life as an artist: A portrait of Larry Bissonnette*: Syracuse University.

Burke, J. (Writer). (2002). *Inside the edge: A journey to using speech through typing*: Syracuse University.

Goddard, P. (Writer). (2002). *Helium hearts*: P. Goddard.

Rubin, S. (Writer). (2004). *Autism is a World.* In G. Wurzburg (Producer): State of the Art, Inc.

Takeuchi, K. (Writer). (2010). *Kayla's voice: Empowering people with autism*: New Ground.

Websites

http://www.inclusioninstitutes.org/

http://www.autcom.org/

http://www.tash.org/breaking-the-barriers/

http://www.everyonecommunicates.org/

Appendix C:
Interview Questionnaire

Overarching research questions:

- What are *your* criteria for a quality life?
- How has FC impacted (for better and/or worse) your quality of life?

Specific questions:

1. List the things that are most important for a 'quality life' for you.

2. List the things that changed for the better when you started using FC.

3. List the things that got worse when you started using FC.

4. List the things that you thought would or should change when you started using FC but that didn't change.

5. Describe a typical day before you began using FC.

6. Describe a typical day today.

7. You said on your questionnaire that your _____ (challenging behavior, community inclusion, choice making etc.) had changed since you began using FC. Can you give some examples of how this changed?

8. Do people treat you differently since you began using FC? If so, in what ways?

9. In what ways do you have more control over your life after using FC? In what ways do you have less control?

10. Describe any parts of your life that are now more difficult than they were before you began using FC.

11. Describe any disappointments that you have experienced as a result of having access to FC.

12. Describe any changes in your sensory modes or your body that you feel are related to using FC.

13. Do you experience yourself differently since you started using FC? If so, in what ways.

14. Do you think differently since you started to use FC? If so, in what ways.

Note on research methodology:

The following procedures were put in place to minimize bias throughout the book and avoid leading the participants in a particular direction in the interview questions:

- Every effort was made to have the FC speakers speak for themselves by bringing their words to the foreground.
- Interview questions were purposely written to be broad and open-ended. b y providing a minimal amount of structure.
- The answers to the interview questions were a very small part of the data set. Most of the data came from transcripts that had been typed prior to starting this study. These previously written transcripts were not influenced a desire to give the "right" answers for a research project.
- Coding categories and prominent themes were derived from the data itself, rather than structured beforehand.

Activities of Daily Living

Work or School: This code is for all text about work (paid or volunteer) or school (other than education pursued after FC as a means of personal development).

Education: Any text dealing with educations, including relationships in school, treatment of teachers and others, struggles to attain educational landmarks or inclusion. Also includes descriptions of how participants were taught, how they learned, their favorite subjects, where they excel and where they lag.

Daily Living: This captures all the ways in which the person does (or does not) participate in things like grocery shopping, shopping for clothing, cooking, housework, care of pets, gardening etc. Includes statements about having more or less control or decision-making power in ADL.

Citizenship: Voting, service oriented activities

Recreation-Leisure: Any activity perceived by the writer as being fun, enjoyable, or relaxing.

Vacations and trips:

Social: This code is about being included (or not) in social activities such as family weddings, funerals, birthday parties, religious holidays, musical and theatre performances etc.

Facilitated Communication

Epiphany: Text that deals with discovering FC or the user's first time trying it.

Adjustment: This theme is meant to document the challenges faced by participants and their families while integrating FC into their lives. This includes discovering personalities, undoing assumptions, changing behavior on both sides of the equation, accommodating newly voiced wants and needs, changing habits, conflicts that arise from implementing FC, shifting perspective and paradigms.

Communication: Text that deals with all communication issues. Not necessarily FC related.

Attitudes: Attitudes of others that pertain to FC. Both positive and negative.

Skepticism: All accounts of skepticism an doubt

Going back: Pertains to text or instances of having FC and then losing it and going back to not being able to communicate.

Access: Issues related to having access to FC.

Validity: This theme merely collects convincing evidence in favor of the validity of facilitated communication.

Technique: Text that deals with FC technique.

Material

This code is for all references to having an adequate home environment and all the things that money can buy such as vacations, computers, clothing, eating out etc.

Personhood

Text that concerns the perceptions of others about the person with autism e.g. being seen as a full and equal person, being respected by others, not being perceived as smart, etc.

Humanness: Participants talk about how they feel limited by others' perceptions and treatment, as well as how language and communication has increased their self-perceived humanness.

Achievements/Honors: Receiving external recognition for writing or other activities that suggest being seen as a person by the community.

Personal Development

Education: Any references to pursuing more education. Includes things such as taking classes such as art or journal-writing courses or teaching classes on FC or autism.

Artistic Expression: All forms of self-expression would go here including poetry, autobiographical writing, visual arts such as painting or ceramics, writing newspaper or advocacy articles.

Self-Expression: This theme discusses ways in which participants expressed themselves, be it artistically or through creative writing, and also moments when a participants inner self or identity was defined by the content of their expression.

Goals and dreams: Hopes for the future.

Hope/Optimism: Quotes that express a positive or hopeful outlook on the present and/or future

Therapy: All forms of therapy included here such as psychotherapy, sensory integration, AIT, Feldenkrais, energy healing, massage, speech etc.

Other: There might be other avenues of personal development that do not fit into the categories above.

Psycho/Physical

Cognitive: Any text about cognition or cognitive function.

General: This code is for text related to health, nutrition, physiology, sleep, and regulation. Things outside the scope of ADL.

Sexuality: Expressions of desire or lack of desire for sexual relationship or curiosity about....

Behavior: This includes behavior before FC (including general physicality, oppositional behavior, "acting out" or aggression, "autistic behaviors," and responsive behavior), behavior after FC, and participants' descriptions and explanations for their behavior, whether it continues or diminished after FC.

Self-awareness: Reporting from the self and reflecting on and interpreting one's self. The ways the person thinks about and sees him or herself. It also includes text showing self-awareness such as changes in thinking patterns. *Note that self-awareness now incorporates the old relationship-self code.

Body Control: Text that deals with body control and other kinds of sensory and movement differences.

Independence: Goals and accomplishments of independence in typing, as well as in every day life

Emotional: All emotions and feelings (contentment, anger, frustration, happiness, fulfillment, etc).

Emotions and Emotional regulation: This theme involves any text of emotional expression, both pre- and post-FC. These include outbursts of anger as well as outpourings of affection. The theme also looks at instances after FC where an aggressive episode may have occurred but was avoided by utilizing FC as an alternate means of venting.

Relationships

The Relationships codes are meant to capture all text where the FC speaker refers to his or her relationships with others. Include here too, any references to having a *lack* of relationship with others.. Any mention of relationships and how FC affected them.

Facilitators: Text about relationships that is specific to facilitators.

Family: Family can include parents, step-parents, siblings etc. Text regarding the importance of, status of, or descriptions of family.

Friends: Friends would include peers and all other unpaid people. Sometimes pay might not be discussed when referring to someone, so use your best judgment.

Romantic: Text that refers to dating or romantic relationships. Longing for and efforts to develop romantic relationships. This theme also deals with notions of sexuality.

Staff: Refers to all paid workers, including direct care staff, therapists, job coaches, house managers, etc.

Community Members: For example store clerks, or other one-time encounters with others.

Social Consciousness: Emotional investment (or lack thereof) in the perceptions of others.

Other: This would be for any ongoing relationships not covered above such as teachers, clergy, doctors and dentists, employers – where the FC speaker interacts with them on a regular and frequent basis. Involves actual human relationships. More vague statements about the cultural 'they' goes to personhood e.g. "People treat me better".

Self-Determination

This code captures all forms of choice, having control and the sense of being an active agent in one's life.

Service

This code includes all text that relates to wanting one's life (activities or experiences) to be of service - to others with disabilities, to God, to the larger community etc. Consciousness of serving others.

Spiritual Life

This code is intended to capture not only any references to formal religion and spirituality, but also any descriptions of the FC speaker's sense of meaning, destiny, or purpose in life. Compassion for others, a sense of connectedness or going beyond one's self in thought or actions.

Spritiuality: Several participants showed and affinity for spirituality. These quotations describe this trend

Other

Text that seems important but doesn't really fit anywhere

Quotables

Quotable quotes that stand on their own. Metaphorical stories.

Codes added 2009

Asking Questions

Instances where participants used FC to attain knowledge or understanding, clearing up misconceptions they had held prior to FC, whereupon the ability to communicate rectified their understanding or affirmed their understanding of a topic

Duality

This theme involves incidents of participants describing their experience of life as two separate entities coexisting. Usually in the form of a "good" self and a "bad" self, or sometimes as a "former" self and a "current" self. In the latter case, the distinction is generally the advent of FC, and in the former case the distinction is autism or the ability to control their behaviors.

Expressive Language

This theme compiles quotes that shed light on the affect that FC had on participants' inner experiences, specifically the effect of being able to communicate outwardly and influence their lives and the actions of others.
Inner Speech Mentions of participants utilizing language – English or made up – to communicate internally with themselves. As a thought-organizing tool?

Worlds

Instances when participants make a distinction between their experiences of reality and others'.

Theory of Mind

Participants' abilities to empathize with others, to assign each person they interact with the abilities, emotions, and experience of life.

Trust

Participants' issues with trusting facilitators and others "outside of their autism"